A MAN OF THE THIRTIES

A MAN OF THE THIRTIES

A. L. Rowse

WEIDENFELD AND NICOLSON
LONDON

Weidenfeld and Nicolson
91 Clapham High St   London sw4

ISBN 0 297 776665

Set, printed and bound in Great Britain by
Fakenham Press Limited,
Fakenham, Norfolk

J'ai passé à côté de la vie,
et j'ai pris l'histoire pour la vie.

Contents

Prologue:
Autumn in Cornwall,
1976

Once again I am ensconced in my upstairs study at Trenarren, which I retire to when I want to be alone with my thoughts. The day has been cold, an easterly beating up white horses in the bay.

> Now the wild white horses play,
> Champ and chafe and toss in the spray...

The sea looks leaden and sullen, except where it is ripped white; even the greenery in the garden looks nipped, glum and wintry.

What varied scenes have been framed by this window! Never shall I forget the most beautiful and sinister of them all: that summer Sunday morning when the bay was milk-white and unnaturally still, a mill-pond waiting. Somewhere beyond, I remember an ominous red spot with a touch of unreal blue. By the time evening came there was a raging storm. I was to go over to supper with Raleigh Trevelyan at St Cadix, his romantic hollow beside a creek of the Fowey. Passing St Veep church in the storm of rain, I opened the car-window to hear the church-bells: they blew into the car in a gust of wind and water. That afternoon there went down, out in our bay, a little overcrowded pleasure craft returning from Looe to St Mawes, with everybody on board – thirty-nine souls. It was right out from my window, by then blotted out by the elements.

This summer has produced something quite peculiar: I never remember a drought in Cornwall before – usually too wet, the valley so damp that snails would get into the village post-box and eat the stamps. Never have we waited anxiously for rain day after day, getting up each morning to look out on the garden, anxiety mounting; every evening, in spite of regulations, going round watering, to save the flowers and flowering shrubs. I felt even more concerned for the famous gardens of Cornwall, my neighbours at Trewithen and Caerhays, Trelissick, Penheale. The lawns everywhere were a brown desert, not a blade of grass – like summer in California. It made for a queer autumn: no richness of foliage such as I remember as a boy in the Victorian park at Tregrehan, the Pre-Raphaelite colouring.* On the other hand, we had nothing like so many leaves to pick up – usually we have a thick hemisphere sifted at the bottom of the lawn from the beeches along the upper terrace. However, there was plenty to do. We had a bumper crop of apples down in the orchard, and I was determined to save all we could for this winter of discontent ...

I deeply repent every moment I spent as a Labour candidate, when a young man, propaganding to make things better. One of my old school-friends, whom I have always kept up with, said this autumn, shortly, that 'it had all been a mistake'.

He was largely right, though I don't like to think that it was *all* a mistake. I learned something about the ways of politics and politicians – useful to the historian, as Gibbon said that his service in the Hampshire militia had been to the historian of the Roman Empire. It was interesting to come to know as well as I did Clem Attlee, Herbert Morrison, Ernest Bevin, who themselves subsequently entered into history and took part in historic events. I became acquainted with a crowd of lesser people on the scene, G. D. H. Cole, R. H. Tawney, Harold Laski, Hugh Dalton, Leonard Woolf, Kingsley Martin, Dick Crossman, Douglas Jay, a large number of the intellectuals on the Left. As a matter of fact, I played my part among the Oxford intellectuals of the thirties – though I have kept quiet about that side of my life, having better things to do. Douglas Cole designated me as his heir to the group he used to run, but by that time the war was upon us, I was ill, and anyway had had enough.

I was taken aback by a remark of V. S. Pritchett's *à propos* of *A Cornish Childhood*: he generously called it a masterpiece, but added that I had been on the margin of events of the thirties, in which the Left intellectuals were so much to the fore. This

* See my *A Cornish Childhood*.

bespeaks the perspective of the Left intellectuals: it was *they* who were on the margin. They were not in practical politics, neither did they have much understanding of them; though they were much to the fore where publicity was concerned – Auden, Spender, MacNeice and the rest of them – marching off to Spain, to write their books and poems about it. And what good did it do? Connolly and Auden were completely disillusioned, but they garnered their literary harvest.

All that time, I was an active Labour Party candidate, working up a constituency, attending Party conferences, giving WEA lectures, contributing regularly to the *New Clarion*, as well as writing about politics (the previous volume has shown how much Eliot pressed me to write about politics for *The Criterion*, as did Woolf for *The Political Quarterly*, while Keynes encouraged me to review politics books for his *Economic Journal*). Besides all this I was regularly in touch with Labour Party leaders, not going off at a tangent with the ILP or into the Communist Party.

In spite of being an intellectual, I was a dependable Labour Party man, a political candidate, who had not lost touch with my working-class roots or lost working-class common-sense. It is significant that I never heard Ernest Bevin speak, an indubitably great man, but I was intellectually convinced by what he said. The *New Statesman* crowd hated his guts. There is a story of Kingsley Martin, coming up to hail Bevin at the Party's celebration of its victory in 1945, and Ernest saying, ''Ullo, oogly, and 'ow long before you'll be stabbin' us in the back?' It was precisely three weeks.

By that time I was well out of it. It was these people, the irresponsible intellectuals – whom Bevin detested and Attlee despised – who were on the margin. In the 1930s I was very much, for an Oxford intellectual, in the centre (left-centre) of Labour activities. However, Auden, Spender, Connolly and the others managed to put themselves across as occupying the thirties, good journalists as they were, with their sense of publicity. I was quite as much involved as they were, and far more practically. By the end I was so sickened by the way things went that I could not bear to write about it, but I did put together a selection from the mass of political writing I had done in the thirties, which Macmillan's entitled *The End of an*

Epoch. It was meant simply for the historical record: an epitaph.

Of one thing I am certain: not one of the Left intellectuals could republish what they wrote in the thirties without revealing what idiotic judgments they made about events. Kingsley Martin advocated the dismemberment of Czechoslovakia in 1938, for the benefit of Hitler. G. D. H. Cole, having thrown over the practical state socialism of the Fabians for the will-o'-the wisp of guild socialism, came back to state socialism in 1929, having meanwhile – as Beatrice Webb said to me – taken away all their younger generation and led them up the garden. Dick Crossman, residually German as he was (he had a German grandmother), really thought that Hitler would introduce socialism in Germany. I remember walking him around the quad at All Souls, shouting at the blond brute: couldn't he see that Hitler meant not socialism, but fascism? Dick would defend Hitler with, 'At least you must admit that he is *sincere!*'

Were all the energy and time I put into those Labour activities in the thirties, then, wholly wasted? Did I learn nothing? Well, I made contact with all sorts of people over the country, journeying here and there to give WEA lectures in the Potteries, or in Kent. I remember any number of working-class teas, and squalid meeting places; I even got as far as Wigan. But I didn't need the gratuitous information of Orwell's *Road to Wigan Pier*; I did not need to go slumming, like Orwell and other middle-class Etonians: I already knew the working class from inside. Nor did I suffer from illusions about them, any more than D. H. Lawrence did – my reaction roughly agrees with his.

It is true that the working class should have had a better deal. When I was a boy in the village at Tregonissey some of the villagers hadn't enough to eat, while the Edwardian upper classes stuffed themselves with all the good things going. That needed putting right. People like Clem Attlee, Morrison and Bevin, like MacDonald, Snowden, and Henderson before them, had all done good service in improving the lot of the people at large.

If one was young and intelligent, in the thirties, one could not but be concerned about the way things were going. The election of 1931, which was a shattering experience for the

Labour Movement, was my first experience as a Labour candidate for Parliament. After that everything went wrong. Only fifty-five Labour MPs got back to that unspeakable assembly, with some 550, mostly Tories, overwhelming it. They could have done anything they pleased; Labour couldn't stop them. There was a complete line-up of all the upper and middle classes, with half the bemused working class voting for them, against the Labour Movement. The country has paid for that over and over, and is still paying for it.

That vast majority could have organised security in Europe and kept a ring around Germany, so that when the abscess burst it would have broken internally, instead of ruining us and Europe. Instead of that, they played Hitler's game – thinking that he was playing theirs and would save Europe from Communism. Nobody was a more effective opponent of Communism, at home and abroad, than Bevin was. But Russia was not then the danger; Hitler's Germany was. The Tories connived at sacrificing their country's interests for their class interests. Those who led the country in the thirties were totally unworthy of their ancestors of the Elizabethan age, the eighteenth century, or even the Victorian age, who made Britain what she was.

A friend of mine, brought up in the Montagu Norman family, told me how completely pro-German the atmosphere was; the talk was always anti-French. The City of London was pro-German all through that decade of appeasement. (De Gaulle made them pay for that.) Instead of organising a Grand Alliance for the day when the Germans would try it all over again – and what a marvellous job Hitler did in organising them for it! – keeping the ring round, standing firm with our friends, bringing Russia in if necessary to balance, as Churchill and the Foreign Office knew was necessary, the Tories throughout the thirties played Hitler's game, and Mussolini's, and Franco's.

Down here in Cornwall where I was a Labour candidate throughout the whole period, the Chamberlainite Lord Lieutenant actually had Ribbentrop down to tout him round the country houses. At the country house next door to me the old Colonel who had married the heiress for her inheritance was besotted with Nazi youth and Hitler's Germany, and regularly wrote letters to our *Western Morning News* backing Hitler. Every time he did, a dozen or fifteen copies of the paper would be sent off to his Nazi friends.

When Bishop Frere retired from Truro – a scholar and a saint, moreover a great gentleman – a round-robin was sent up to the Prime Minister of the 'National' Government telling him not to send down 'an Anglo-Catholic Socialist again.' Frere was an Anglo-Catholic, but not a political man at all. They sent down a perfectly safe man, no Anglo-Catholic and certainly no Socialist: Joe Hunkin, an ex-Nonconformist who never rose above the sights of his original Nonconformity. I once asked him – since he detested the Anglo-Catholics, who were the most devoted element among his clergy – why he hadn't remained a Wesleyan. He didn't 'want' that, he replied – what a give-away word to use. I naturally concluded that it was because, as a Nonconformist, he wouldn't have been a bishop, and that was what he really 'wanted'. However, he was well in with the people who had won out in 1931, and made him our bishop down in Cornwall. When Hitler's pocket battleship paid a visit to Falmouth, under the aegis of these people, Bishop Hunkin went along with them to offer up prayers on board. What was the pocket-battleship for, but to sink British sailors?

I was utterly sickened at these goings on in the thirties. I knew Germany, intimately through my friendship with Adam von Trott, and knew what to fear. The fears were all too well founded, though plenty of people on our own side wouldn't see them. With all the anxiety, the exacerbation and overwork (for I was keeping my research and writing and teaching at Oxford going too) my old enemy, the ulcer, got worse and worse; and in the end, it blocked up the food-passage into my stomach with growth of scar-tissue. Even when I had a couple of touch-and-go operations in 1938, I still didn't give up. It was only during the war, when I had another serious haemorrhage, that the doctors *made* me give up: they warned me that I could never lead a normal life, and that if anything went wrong, after my gastro-enterostomy, they could do nothing for me.

This settled the matter, and made for a happier life: I gave up being a Labour candidate after a decade of it. The doctors were only just in time. For when the 1945 election came all my years of work in the Penryn and Falmouth constituency bore fruit: it turned out my old opponent, a Chamberlainite Tory, and returned a Labour man. Having withdrawn, I withdrew totally, and was able to devote all my energy to my writing, instead of for ever trying to make bricks without straw, as I used to put it to myself.

Writing was my real vocation and, thank heaven, during all this time I had never let go of it. Wise old Craster at All Souls, observing the struggle within me, was always convinced that writing would win. And I realise now, as I half did then, that the life of a professional politician would have killed me. I had to accept what the doctors said and make my physical condition the condition of my life and work.

Oddly enough, though, I hadn't been a bad candidate. In the *débâcle* of 1931 I kept the Labour vote steady at 10,000; we dropped only 1000 from our top vote in 1929. In the election of 1935 I moved up to second place with 13,000, the Tory ahead with 15,000; I got the Liberal to the bottom of the poll. By 1945 Penryn and Falmouth was a Labour seat; but, though I repined a bit, what an almighty deliverance that I had been made to drop it!

So, had it all been a mistake, as my old friend, a faithful supporter, said?

Not altogether. I learned how to speak, the hard way – though how I hated the weary round of speaking at street-corners against the traffic, the indifference to appeasement, and the people's lack of awareness of the constantly increasing danger. I was more patient with their idiocy then than now – though no less maddened by it. In taking leave, I said that henceforth I should feel free to say exactly what I thought – to the dismay of my kindly old school-friend. I certainly had staunch friends, with whom I had learned to cooperate. With no resources we founded a little Labour paper, *The Cornish Labour News*, for which I wrote regularly. Would I had kept a complete file: it would make an interesting bibliographical item. So I had good friends, even some capacity for leadership.

When I threw it all over, I had many bad moments the first few years – all that work, and energy, and time wasted! Once when I happened to be down on the quay at Mevagissey,

7

where I had often spoken on summer evenings during vacations when I might have been enjoying myself abroad, one of the fishermen looked up from his boat and said, 'You don't come down to see us much now.' It went to my heart. Some of those fellows around my home did not forget me; I felt sad at deserting them.

All the same, the misery of that decade, what I had to put up with in the way of ill-feeling, personal insults, whispers about my family – when I was largely right about Baldwin, Chamberlain and those old men ruining their country – the endless frustration at the hands of people pretty inferior intellectually, damaged my relationship to my native Cornwall: for many years afterwards I would not make any further contribution, or even speak in the county. They had had their chance; they could now stick with their third-raters. (D. H. Lawrence would never go back to Eastwood again.)

I did not wholly cut myself off; I merely cut public contacts, and ceased to know people, except those few old friends who had been faithful. I always kept my home in Cornwall and supported my parents. I went on subscribing to the Labour Party financially, so I remained a sleeping member right up till Suez,* though I had long ago ceased to subscribe intellectually. By then the battle for decent treatment of the working class had been won – it was for them now to make a success of what was their show.

The emotional reason for my political involvement was, paradoxically, pride. Celts are, fundamentally, proud. A working-class lad, I would not have it said that, just because I had gone to Oxford and got to All Souls in its old grand days, I had become a Tory out of snobbery. There was more inverted snobbery, an obvious form pride takes, in my attitude: I made a point of emphasising my working-class background. My manners and tastes were élitist, as many Celts' are. Quiller-Couch, who had done a man's work for educational progress in Cornwall, one day said to me: 'The thing is to be politically liberal, and socially conservative.' He had been quite radical in his younger days – and had had it said that his education had been paid for by the Fortescues. In the

---

* Hartley Shawcross and I were the two members of the Labour Party who left it over Suez.

same way it was put about in 1931 that my education had been paid for by my political opponents – after I had worked my guts out to get all those scholarships to pay for myself! This is what people are.

Q.'s view exactly expressed my own. Cultivated man as he was, I was even more of an aesthete, even more devoted to objects of beauty and taste; and in those days the *train-de-vie* at All Souls was that of old-fashioned country-house life. That chimed in with my nature. I can honestly say that, with my tastes, I hated being born in a working-class home. Wasn't that perfectly natural for someone with a complex ambivalent nature and artistic sensibilities? I loved music and literature and things of beauty. There wasn't a book in our house (I have rather over-compensated for that today, with ten or fifteen thousand.) All my mother's people had been brought up on the estate at Tregrehan, that William-and-Mary house with the portico and the sunken Italian garden described in *A Cornish Childhood*. Why wasn't *I* born there? – I should have been better suited to it than the nitwits that were, or many of the other asses who didn't appreciate the historic houses and possessions they had inherited. I was country-born – another rift between me and the Left intellectuals, with their background of suburbia and the *déréglé* life they lived.

The village life at Tregonissey had its authentic folklore character, and I put up with it well enough as a boy. But I grew ashamed of a home that had no conveniences, not even water inside the house, just a tap for everything at the door. When I first went to Oxford, we moved to a small council house, which for the first time in our lives had at least a bath. To come home to that from life at All Souls was bad enough; but to be cheek-by-jowl with council-house neighbours, their kids screaming at all hours in the avenue outside, when I wanted quiet and solitude in which to work, drove one frantic. (There is an early poem about that.) Besides I was ill, and grew far too ill to move, even when I could have afforded it; and a council house was appropriate for the simple stance of a Labour candidate.

As soon as I was over my operations and a bit stronger – after a long recuperation – I bought a charming villa away to itself, among fields off the road to Porthpean, with trees and a

9

blissful view of the bay. I furnished it myself, to suit my own taste, with lovely things I had collected in Oxford and bought that summer at country-house sales for a song: antiques, rugs, modern paintings I had collected including Piper, Céria, Lowry, Coldstream, Christopher Wood. When my mother entered this pretty house, her first words were, 'This ed'n like my 'ouse at all.' And ungratefully, she never did like it: it was away from the fatuities she liked to view from the front room of the council house.

When she died, I was at length free. At that moment, Trenarren at last fell vacant, the place of my dreams ever since I was a schoolboy. My poor father, knowing about my fixation, one day looked in at the gate, and said to my mother: 'I dare say he'll come to live here one day; but I shan't live to see it.' He was a good, simple man, and he always had a touching confidence in me. I don't know about her: in the end she even grew envious of her son who was so like her. She was like a character out of a D. H. Lawrence novel, or a Madam Golovlyov, a tremendously strong, psychotic personality – wilfully illiterate, for all her contempt for ordinary human beings – eating up all the weaker characters that came within a mile of her. I was the only one who could stand up to her – though her victim too.

Anyway, I was now free to come to the place of my dream, though it was never – just like a dream – to be mine. But against all the early frustrations and setbacks, I have lived now far longer here than in any other home of my own. Save for one great private grief, I have found much happiness here. I have been happy in myself ever since giving up politics and killing myself to no point.

Such are the thoughts that haunt me as I look out from my window upon the exquisite scene, the magic valley at Trenarren – like the human race, under a cloud.

1
Oxford Term

I broke off a previous volume* at the beginning of my emotional attachment to Adam von Trott – at the height of a mutual attachment. All my past life is present with me now, which might be taken to bear out Croce's view of the contemporaneity of history. But I am not a Crocean, and it reflects something else: the existence of that inner life, which is my real life, not that of external contacts, where even the external contacts are used to feed the inner life, which is continuous and gives almost total recall. The Diary exists as evidence of the continuous inner life.

Perhaps this secret fixation was one reason why I didn't put myself forward when my acquaintance of the thirties were pushing themselves and each other forward. I think now that a lot of what they published was immature. (Are *The Dog beneath the Skin* and *The Ascent of F6* really any good as drama? I doubt it. They are too adolescent, and haven't lasted, as *Murder in the Cathedral* has done.) The Diary witnesses to what my real interests of mind were: literary and intellectual pursuits, poetry and pictures; the way things looked, the things one heard. There was little about politics in it. I shall have to look elsewhere for that – rather like historical research. However, the conscientious historian has kept the materials; and when I have done with them, America shall have them.

On top of the Diary there are scores of little pocket-books, in which I endeavoured to catch life on the wing, the *Buch des Lebens* I called them. A main motive for keeping them was simply that, with such continual returns of illness, I was afraid I might die before I had accomplished anything.

When I have fears that I may cease to be...

* *A Cornishman Abroad.*

I would quote to myself, or 'Time's wingèd chariot hurrying near.' In the end, with scores of these, they afford a more *continuous* insight into the life of a mind than anything I can think of – at least on so extended a scale. They will pile up into an immense archive, like Boswell's or Horace Walpole's: I can see a Rowse industry, like theirs in and around Yale, in the 21st century. Yes, I hope America may have them.

In the spring of 1929 I was in Dublin in pursuit of Swift:

My days here are so busy. I have written twice to Adam, this morning's a reasonable reply to his, in which it seemed at last that his side of the infatuation had caved in. An extraordinary degree of sympathy, even of telepathy, binds us together even at this distance of space and time. He intuits exactly what is in my mind: I have never met anything like it. Just when I was thinking that life was becoming quite tolerable without him, our love passing into the second phase of his parting telegram, 'Desire and Memory' – his letter came this morning expressing the same thought. A landscape, he said, from which the storm had passed. It is best this way; yet, now that it has come, I like it less than the storm which preceded. Still, what more could one expect?

Anyway, there was always the *Buch des Lebens*, if not life itself, to resort to for consolation.

26 April 1929. In Oxford again – divine place, but a prison. I cherish the chains that bind me. The night I came back there were the bells for welcome coming down the High: that lovely peal from All Saints, the church with Dean Aldrich's spire at the corner of the Turl. All its enchantments put forward to lure one into submission. Even the memory of Ireland made hardly any resistance – when previously, coming back from Paris or Germany or Cornwall, I have known their spell go on and on in mind when my body is here. Coming back from Dublin, there was no struggle, no lag-behind, at all.

Is it that this place is overcoming me, getting such a grip on me after all? There are areas of my mind where neither its enchantments, nor anything else of it, have ever penetrated. Still, I don't think I am submitting: I would go away from it all tomorrow, if the chance I look for offered.

Here was the dilemma. Richard Pares told me that when I was elected to All Souls, the doubt expressed was whether I would stay. It seems ironical now, for in the event I stayed there most of my working life. I didn't mean to; I meant politics plus literature, or literature plus politics, certainly not the life of a teaching don or a professor. Richard, who was a conventional bourgeois beneath the undergraduate playboy exterior – intimate friend of Evelyn Waugh and the rest – confessed that his 'hackles were wrung' when he learned what I thought of being a professor. That is what he settled for. *Ich nicht*: either a writer or a politician, preferably both.

Yet this last hour I have been doing nothing but watch the garden. The trees are so decorative in their light clothing of green shoots, a thrush singing from a corner to the emptiness. Nothing has stirred, nobody come into it; an occasional bird threads the branches with black or grey. Then the light changes, a moment ago a sudden raising of all the colours, as if the garden were a stage-set and all the lights were going on. So it is a scene: the background of that part of my life that is a waking dream: that part which sits by, and watches the hours, days, years pass: a plot of ground whereon my consciousness of time is projected. Perhaps the reason for my submission to the dream this time is the dream of love. When I came back to the room the first thing I thought of was that Adam had been here those few long hours, there was such a strong impression of his presence still.

The 'dream' really meant the passive life, which I equated with Oxford. As undergraduates studying Aristotle we learned that the active life was morally superior to that of passive contemplation. I was already quite strong on contemplation, and I thought that I needed to fill myself out on the side of practical action, where I was wanting. Paradoxically, the communal atmosphere of All Souls encouraged this, for all the talk was of public affairs, and the people I admired in college were its public figures. This meant politics.

I don't know what might have happened if I had received more encouragement; for, contrary to what it might seem, I was easily discouraged by other people, and accepted their nudges, outwardly at least. It is true that Eliot was a constant encourager, but he was always pressing me to write about politics; so was Leonard Woolf, I was writing prosepieces along with poems, and short stories. One short story I sent to Desmond MacCarthy, who kept it a long time before saying that he was 'fascinated' by it, but couldn't make out whether he had missed the point or whether that wasn't the point – so he sent it back. He was not so discouraging to Cyril Connolly or David Cecil, who ultimately married his daughter. And what did Desmond MacCarthy achieve with his life? For all the *réclame* he had then – thought to be the best conversationist in London, etc. – few remember him now. All that he achieved was literary journalism. When I eventually met him, under Ottoline Morrell's aegis at Garsington, instead of listening to his literary chat, I treated him instead to a Marxist tirade. I never saw him again.

So term and teaching settled on my head – quite a number of pupils, read me essays like one the beginning of which I noted for its fatuity: 'The service Henry VII rendered to the Tudor dynasty it would be hard to exaggerate: without him Henry VIII and Elizabeth would have been impossible.' After I had taken a tutorial on the 'Foundations of the Tudor Monarchy' a hundred and one times, I began to feel, when I heard the heavy footsteps of my pupils thudding up my stairs, like a tired tart waiting for her clients, and thought it time to make a change. It was then that I moved to London – but that was still a year or two ahead.

In my first week back Maurice Bowra came on two after-noons for a talk. There have been so many tributes from my generation to Maurice – from Connolly, John Betjeman, John Sparrow and even Hugh Gaitskell – and what they owed to him in developing their minds and tastes that it is odd that he had no such effect on me. David Cecil had immeasurably more. Maurice and I cannot have been on the same wavelength, and I cannot think what impelled him to come and seek me out so much. Years later I had a good straight relationship of mutual respect with him; but in these early days I was never influenced by him, was not a member of his salon, and would have been put off by all that eating and drinking, and roaring cameraderie. I had something of a circle of my own, and rather discouraged Maurice.

A note in the *Buch des Lebens* reveals the kind of thing we talked about: about the place poetry of Rilke, for example. I considered that:

the actual place is not the essential part of the experience in these poems: as 'subjects' they merely differentiate one poem from another. What is common to them all is the usual content of Rilke's poetry: the record of impressions of the external world, the impact of these upon his extreme sensibility. These poems are therefore not different in kind from others: the fact that one is about 'Kindheit' and another about 'l'Ange du Méridien' at Chartres does not make their essence any different, though it may limit their appeal.

Rilke meant much to me: one sees his influence, as also that of Virginia Woolf, in the continued attempt to catch sense-impressions on the wing and express them in words. I seem to have been for ever unsatisfied, or perhaps insatiable.

On a lower plane I remember well, though he would not, that it was I who introduced Geoffrey Grigson to the poetry of Rilke, of which he was to make more later. I was more taken with another Cornish associate whom I met this term, Charles Henderson, who was to become one of my dearest friends. I was surprised when this red-faced giant of 6 feet 7 inches, dining in Hall one Sunday night, turned out to be he. I thought that I had caught sight of him as a pale-faced attendant one day at a seminar of Sir Charles Firth. That turned out to have been Hamilton Jenkin, who was embarked on his book, *The Cornish Miner* – and Charles and Jenkin were mutually exclusive. I had not these difficulties with either, for I was their junior and no competitor in the field of Cornish history. In the event, things turned out very differently.

Charles was an extraordinary phenomenon, apart from his height. He had had a very one-sided development, passionately interested in antiquarianism from the time he was a boy. The result was that he had a unique familiarity with medieval Cornwall, documents, deeds, terriers, registers, what not. He knew Cornwall as no one has ever known it, every parish and church, its farms, bridges, fields and people, from tramping over the land with his long stride, over hedges and ditches – nothing daunted him in his pursuit of the Cornish past. It all lay there like an open book to him.

He had the advantage – though only one-quarter Cornish, as I used to tease him – of being connected, through his mother, with a number of the county families, and so most doors, not all (one rather mean exception was Tregothnan of the Boscawens), were open to him. Charles lived in an eighteenth-century country house, Penmount, a draughty spot off the road to Newquay looking down on our little cathedral city. (The place, of which I have such endearing memories, is now a crematorium.) Few of these country-houses were open to me – but then I wasn't interested; Cornish history was not my subject, history in general, literature and politics were. So Charles and I, instead of being rivals, complemented each other and became close friends. Again he was the active partner, who went all out to make my acquaintance – I was really rather passive about knowing people and did not make the running.

Charles had sat for the Fellowship at All Souls, but had not made it any more than David Cecil had – or Belloc, John Buchan, Aldous Huxley, historians like Tout, Powicke, Bruce McFarlane, Trevor-Roper, and many others who would have made a College as distinguished and even more various than All Souls in its best days. Charles had then gone down to a part-time lectureship in Cornish history, at the University of Exeter, and made an impression all over Cornwall by his lectures and his enthusiasm.

This wasn't my line. My mentor had all along been Q., my field, literature. But Charles took me under his wing in Cornwall, had me to stay often at Penmount, took me around the county I had not had the wherewithal to explore, opened my eyes to things, and shared his enthusiasm with me. When he died so young, at thirty-three, I was heart-broken – it worked out strangely that I should become his inheritor. He was essentially a medievalist, not attracted to the Tudor period. It fell to me to write *Tudor Cornwall*, and to dedicate it to his memory – since I was determined to do everything I could to keep it green.

When he came back to Oxford as history tutor at Corpus, he was like a fish out of water; a very large fish in that small pond. Here I was able though three years his junior, to take him under my wing; suggested historical reading for his teaching, and got him to read contemporary literature; Virginia Woolf, D. H. Lawrence, Eliot, Strachey. Dear Charles was like a large faithful dog, who came round every afternoon to All Souls until I, impatient and with so many things on hand, told him that there wasn't anybody I wanted to see every afternoon of my life. He was of an angelic disposition, and never minded this; we became inseparable, until I went to London; he then married and died on his honeymoon. For years I was desolated. It was a tragedy for Cornwall too, though Cornish people – who rightly worshipped his memory, as I still do – didn't realise that before his death he was changing and developing, broadening his interests outside of Cornwall.

Charles had spotted the promise of a young Pauline at Corpus, Isaiah Berlin. Isaiah, who could have been described as a *jolie laide* if he had been a girl, presented Charles with a facer – what did he think of his appearance? Charles was rather embarrassed by this, and passed the same question on to me: what did I think of *his* face? When I looked into it I noticed something revealing: the two sides of his parentage. On one side was the *mécontent*, dissatisfied look of his father; on the other, the good-humoured, euphoric look of his mother. A bit of a strain existed between Charles and his father the Major, a disappointed man who had made nothing much of his life; whereas the mother was a fine woman, staunch and kind, noble and true. On the Cornish side she was related to the Williams clan, famous gardeners, who had made such a fortune out of the Industrial Revolution in Cornwall, then married into the county families and acquired half a dozen of its finest estates. On the other side she was a Carus-Wilson, and told me that the proprietor of Charlotte Brontë's school was nothing like so bad as he was painted.

I made Charles free of my own friends, lonely as he was on his return; and Charles hospitably invited them to stay at Penmount. Bruce McFarlane was another medievalist, so occasionally there was a brush between them. Bruce had a malicious streak which could be amusing; he also had a disagreeable love of pin-pricking. Once they were in a Cornish church when Charles was querying the date of the font with the local parson, who put him down with, 'But Mr. Henderson thinks otherwise', not knowing who he was. Bruce remained maliciously mum, greatly enjoying the *contretemps*. Charles was quite cross when they got outside – 'to think that I shall never be able to go into that church, or meet that parson again.' It would not have amused me to play such tricks, but Bruce was *méchant*, and in relation to me later quite psychotic –

he was jealous of my friends, and still more of my books, since he had a curious inability to write his own.

Geoffrey Hudson, of an equable disposition, raised no such awkwardness. His trouble was absentmindedness. When he came to stay with Charles – there wasn't room to put up my friends in our cramped council house – they went church-crawling as usual. It was winter and cold. They set out by bus; when they came to have their picnic, Geoffrey had left his sandwiches in the bus. How much I enjoyed those winter picnics! I can see us all now on the top of Trencrom, in view of both seas, Bristol and English Channels, the wind in our hair, faces plunged into 'splits', homemade blackberry jelly, Cornish cream streaking the corners of our mouths. Alas, the picnics of nearly half a century ago!

At All Souls I had quite enough of a social life of my own – more in fact than I liked. In those days people could afford to entertain, and I was constantly being asked out. No wonder I didn't attend Maurice's parties – it would have aroused my inhibitions; going out to lunch or dine with interesting people was another matter.

11 May: These are divine days, summer at its loveliest: every walk out is a revelation. Today, coming back from North Oxford, I took the path across the Parks where the flowering trees are: one so beautiful, I stood back to take in all its points, slimness unlike a plum, so thick with blossom one could hardly see any leaves. I stood under it and let the tree spread its crinoline over me, looking up rather self-consciously at the patch-work of black trunk and branches in perspective, starred with blossom. In my walk around Magdalen I stayed to admire a fruit tree in bloom, just where Bruce and I find little service-apples strewn in autumn: a copper-gold tree behind it, fresh green on the other side of the path.

At night David and I were shut in Wadham garden, so we went round to the little cloister, to see the cherry with its pink boughs in the angle of grey stone. A grave slab nearby has the date 1676 on it. David chose that place to say, what I had never heard from him before, that he thought he ought to leave Oxford if he were to be really good as a writer. It is just what I feel and nothing would keep me back if I had his independent means. Yet, whenever he came back to Oxford, he felt that there was nothing in the world like it, even after coming back from Venice. In Wadham garden, on a summer night, he would feel a fool ever to have left it. He went on about politics, wondering why it was that I was attracted by it: he thought I should so much dislike the life of practical compromise. Not for the first time I saw that David doesn't think me suited for politics: he sees so much the literary and intellectual side – the other he doesn't see much of. [How right he was! 1977] The last few days I have been hammering at a poem, and I am elated tonight for it is just finished.

I had to go to another of Rudler's lunch-parties, first to meet a French poet, Paul Valéry, who spoke on the tip of his lips so that he was unintelligible. Today there was Fernand Gregh. An awful to-do about getting there: I'd forgotten all about it, and at ten-to-two was quietly enjoying my coffee, chatting with Penderel Moon's father and Oman, when a telephone message arrived and I went careering in a taxi up to North Oxford, tying my shoes and putting myself to rights as I went. Arrived – people not very far advanced, my salmon mayonnaise awaiting me, and a seat between two ladies: one with Italian eyes, Mme Fernand Gregh, the other French-Jewish, Madame Halévy. Both took pains to calm down my agitation.

Madame Halévy was particularly charming, and informative about John Dillon. The last time she saw him he had said, in despair after a lifetime in the Irish cause: 'Now I think we were happier under the English than as we are.' Conversation with Madame Gregh was more difficult, much casting up of eyes to the ceiling, to which I responded with equal expressiveness and incomprehension. She was voluble about André Maurois, and talked about the *Discours* [sic] *du Colonel Bramble*; I haven't read it, or I might have replied with *Les Silences* [sic] *du Docteur O'Grady*. We all got up at once and went chattering like jays into the over-crowded drawing room (Lady Firth describes Madame Rudler as a 'honey-pot' woman: all the men buzz round her). The party crowded into the bay looking into the garden, leaving Madame Rudler's little dog alone on its bum in the middle of the room, solemnly masturbating. I longed to say among all these French folk, 'Le plus que je vois ce chien, le plus je respecte les hommes.'

Maytime in Oxford, the peak of the year in all its pride and flourish! – the May of 1929, when there was still hope, and especially for those of us who cared intensely for the way things were going for the country, and for Europe, the hopes that we attached to the Labour Movement. We were a small minority then, but it contained some of the most intelligent among our generation. I was nothing if not serious-minded – I drove myself relentlessly forward into political activity that was not really natural to me; in many ways I hated it. Later,

with the disaster of 1931 to the Labour Movement in Britain –
fons et origo malorum – then the disaster of 1933 to German and
Europe, the succession of Nazi and Fascist victories over
Abyssinia, the Rhineland, Austria, the Spanish Civil War,
Munich, Czechoslovakia, all with the supineness or connivance of the British upper classes through the living hypocrisy
of their 'National' Government – well, one couldn't but be
driven frantic with anguish and despair. It is increasingly
evident in the political pieces I wrote at the time, as well as the
poems which I did not publish until 1941.

> A day will come when there shall descend on them
> From the skies they do not observe, some stratagem
>
> Of fate to search and sear their flesh with fire,
> Seal the eyes that are stupid with desire:
>
> Liquid gas will rain down from the air,
> Will suddenly arrive upon them there
>
> And lick their bodies up and burn their bones,
> No-one at hand to hear their mutual groans:
>
> For these are they who, warned of what's to come,
> Walk blindly on to their appointed doom.

(The perceptive critic will note the concatenation of sexual
resentment with the apocalyptic, the hatred of the *profanum
vulgus* on both scores: not a good recipe for a duodenal ulcer.)
   This poem was written in 1937, and I am anticipating –
really to make clear what the situation was in the thirties, to the
succeeding generations. One of these younger men, Michael
Howard, who fought in the Second World War, comments
upon our generation, as described by Anthony Powell:

was any group of such exceptionally able, highly educated young
men ever quite so indifferent to the affairs of the outside world? Here
yet again we have the Eton of Harold Acton and Brian Howard and
Cyril Connolly. Here yet again we have the Oxford of Cyril Connolly and Brian Howard and Harold Acton, of Sligger Urquhart and
Maurice Bowra and Evelyn Waugh. How intelligent, cultivated,
amusing, colourful, altogether fortunate in their generation were
those Waughs, those Actons, those Clarks, those Quennells, those
Bowras, those Betjemen! What a scintillating era do they chronicle in
the memoirs they have compulsively written about themselves and
about each other!

He sums them up under the heading 'the Spoiled Generation'. This just comment from our junior helps to make me clear to myself. This was my generation – yet I did not *belong*. I knew practically every one of them so much to the fore, but only on the margin. The truth was that I disapproved of them as wasters or drunks. Later on, when their talents flowered and they mostly fulfilled their gifts, I thought what a prig I had been. Richard Pares, who had been one of them but reformed early, realised that I disapproved of them, and of Sligger Urquhart and his *jeunesse dorée*. It also accounts for my rejection of Maurice Bowra's obvious friendliness. Later on, Maurice became a serious character, and nothing could exceed his services to the university. At this earlier date, Maurice dropped his attentions when I was innocent enough to warn one of his *protégés* against an unsuitable pursuit he was engaged in. Maurice thought at the time that I was a 'persecutor' of homos – quite wrongly: I was afraid for the young man, who in fact was quite capable of looking after himself. (Isaiah described him as 'very sure-footed'.)

So naturally I do not appear in their records: I did not 'belong'. They didn't know that I was keeping a more careful 'chronicle' of them, a marginal eye on their activities. This chronicle supplies a correction to Michael Howard's conclusion: here was someone very far from 'indifferent to the affairs of the outside world'. Nor was I the only one. Richard Pares was concerned; Maurice himself, as the situation worsened, became concerned and had a good record about appeasement, and in helping refugees from Nazi Germany. Fanatic as I was, I managed to recruit a number of my friends to the Labour Party – Richard and Bruce, Geoffrey Hudson and A. H. M. Jones, Douglas and Peggy Jay (whom I recommended to Herbert Morrison at the London County Council, where she did years of service and good work).

Hugh Gaitskell, surprisingly enough, was one of the Bowra circle who emerged a professional politician. I hardly knew him; I knew rather better his friends Evan Durbin (whom I didn't fall for: too much of the Nonconformist for me, with that bright moon-faced cheeriness), and Frank Pakenham, (whom I thought of as erratic, falling into the arms of

Catholicism). Father D'Arcy was most attentive in his religious pursuit of me and Douglas Jay: in vain.

My Diary bears witness to all this activity. Here I was speaking on successive nights for the Labour Party in the City, once in the East Labour Hall, for all its discouraging squalor. Then I dashed home to Cornwall to hold a Workers' Educational Association course at my old school. The new Headmaster, a liberal-minded type, was enthusiastic about my ability to hold an audience. He did not repeat the experiment; when I became a Labour candidate, he was too conscious of the presence of my Tory opponent's family among his governors to risk anything of the sort again. I rewarded this rather weak type – who made a fortune by his investments in the china-clay industry when shares were low in the Depression – with some contempt. So much for liberal-mindedness – I much preferred the honest Toryism of his predecessor, my old Headmaster, with whom I remained friends all his life.

His successor, a Cambridge man, was progressive enough to know better; a supporter of the League of Nations and collective security, he was afraid to declare himself because of his Governors, a lot of small-minded locals. I did not expect him to come out publicly for me, but I despised him for his lack of backbone. Such was the atmosphere of the thirties. The Tories had everything their own way. They were so bent on taking the wrong line about Hitler and Mussolini that, when Harold Nicolson, who was anti-appeasement, was visiting Cornwall, a local Tory MP, possessor of a famous garden, refused to let Harold in to see it! They were *determined* that people should kowtow to their disastrous line. In South Dorset the Tories threatened to put up a candidate against Cranborne, later Lord Salisbury, although he was right. It may be imagined what I had to put up with from these people at home. I wanted to educate my own people in the sense of their own interest – and to open the eyes of the blind towards the dangers of appeasing Germans, after what we had endured from them in 1914–1918. I learned my lesson: you never can open people's eyes until it is too late, and I am no longer interested in the education of the ineducable.

I continued to speak at the University Labour Club, of which I retained the first Minute Book, as its last custodian – an interesting historic document now with all those names of people who became subsequently well known. I kept up with old school friends, and new recruits – what Richard called my 'Cornish clientèle'. Jimmy Crowther kept an eye on my Leftist development – not sufficiently Left to please him, whose contacts were Communist. I had more sense than to jump on to that tumbril, on the way to the guillotine – unlike Christopher Hill, who enjoyed such veneration from the faithful, in spite of such appalling misjudgment. In the thirties Stalin exterminated nine out of eleven members of Lenin's Politburo; he got Russia's ablest soldier, Marshal Tukachevsky, condemned to death by military tribunal – and then expertly murdered the members of the tribunal, obliterating the evidence. A wit summed up the process: 'Every Russian soldier carries a Field-Marshal's tombstone in his knapsack.' But, in fact, weren't the intellectuals who went Communist in the thirties simply bloody fools? Though much influenced by Marxism intellectually – in due course I became quite well read in the works – I remained a good Labour man. The Labour Movement was the only practical instrument of social progress, the only possible fulcrum that could give any effective leverage. I kept arguing this with Keynes: if you want to have any effect you must put yourself into relation with a mass-movement that could render you effective. This was my gospel which I argued ad nauseam. Why couldn't Keynes see that?

Others, who were in the Labour Party, didn't see this Marxist point either: Stafford Cripps and Mosley, those improbable Wykehamists, for example. My line about Cripps, whom I knew, was that, having joined the Party, he should accept its implications and carry them out (as Dalton, for all his Cambridge background did) – not seek to give the law to the Party from the top. The same applied to Mosley, who had come in at the top, like Cripps. Mosley was right in wanting an activist policy in regard to unemployment, in the world-depression that held the Labour government in its grip 1929–31, and wrecked it as it wrecked the Weimar Republic in Germany. But Mosley should have stayed with the Labour Movement, if he wanted to be effective: his time would have come. Instead of that, he went out into the wilderness to form a New Party on his own – there was no sense in that – joined by such voluble geese as John Strachey, Harold Nicolson, and the cackling Catlin. Anybody with any sense could see that he was heading for Fascism – and that was no go in this country. So Mosley's energy and drive, his demagogic gifts, were not merely wasted but led to the criminal folly of lining up with Mussolini and Hitler.

What is one to think of such people?

Yet, when Mosley's memoirs came out, *My Life* – he might as well have called it, *Mein Kampf* – he was hailed by the ex-Trotskyist, Muggeridge, as 'the only living Englishman who could perfectly well have been either Conservative or Labour Prime Minister'. The ex-Trotskyist, A. J. P. Taylor, sounded off, 'Mosley alone rose to the height of the challenge ... an astonishing achievement, evidence of a superlative talent.' Dick Crossman considered him 'the outstanding politician of his generation'. All these people wrote rave-reviews of Mosley's book, regardless of the evil course he had taken – and these people were supposed to be men of the Left! Though no longer a man of the Left, I should be ashamed to write such rubbish. These people – *New Statesmen* types – are fundamentally irresponsible. No wonder Ernest Bevin had such a distrust of Left Intellectuals: when Labour came into its own, after the war, he said he 'wouldn't have them in the Cabinet: you can't trust them.'

Long before, early in the thirties, I have never forgotten a walk round Magdalen with G. N. Clark. An early friend of G. D. H. Cole, he had been through some of Cole's gyrations and turnabouts. He said to me, 'the disastrous element in the Labour Party is its Intellectuals.' Brought up short at this, I experienced one of those sudden moments of illumination when one *knows* that, however unwelcome the thought, it was true. Cole could not bear the responsible leaders of the Labour Movement, Attlee and Bevin, any more than Crossman could. Neither Cole nor Crossman had much political judgment – and Attlee had his own shrewd estimate of Cole: he called him an undergraduate still, in politics.

These journalists were far more prominent misleading Labour people, who needed above all responsible leadership. I remained solidly with the Party, as a matter of intellectual conviction rather than of any emotional satisfaction. My emotional life was elsewhere, and of a very different complexion. I was rather close to Morrison, whom I admired for his chirpy good sense. His importance after the disaster of 1931, was that he was the only Labour leader in any position of power, as Leader of the London County Council. As such, he did a first-class job. I wanted to see him leader of the Labour Party. Here I was wrong in preferring him to Attlee; no-one could then have guessed Attlee's later development – in the end, he turned out a near-great man. Churchill had an amusing joke on it: 'if you feed a grub of a wasp on royal jelly in time it turns out a queen.' Bevin intuited these unsuspected qualities – but then he was almost always right.

In the leadership of the TUC in those days he had an able partner in Walter Citrine, another man of judgment and responsible outlook. These were the men to go by. I find that this term I was meeting Citrine through John Fulton at Balliol, another sensible Party man, who later did a good job in piloting the early stages of the University College at Swansea. A man of administrative experience in the Civil Service whose early death was a loss to the Movement was E. F. Wise, a heavy-jowled man, rather like Geoffrey Dawson to look at. He came to stop a night when speaking at Oxford. I entertained a lot – All Souls was certainly convenient for the purpose. I spent another depressing evening when I went to speak for the Labour Party at Abingdon – a forlorn hope, where a Ruskin don, who lived in a depressing old house in the main street and was rather prissy in manner, was the Labour candidate.

It was all uphill work, discouraging all the way, ending in nothing but grief of the spirit. I was neglecting, or at least thwarting, my true vocation.

Other acquaintances were more after my heart. Tea with the Robert Bridges's on Boar's Hill, the quiet, Waterhouse interior with the tousled lion of a Poet Laureate sloping in from his impenetrable study for tea. Dinner with the hospitable Buchans at lovely Elsfield, with its memories of Dr Johnson and his Bodleian friend, always made me a little nervous in spite of their kindness. Then there were the Bucklers at 1,

Bardwell Road, most indefatigable of hosts. Willie Buckler – scholarly, emaciated, with nervous manner and hoarse voice – was a Greek epigraphist, pupil of the celebrated Ramsay. He was an American expatriate of old Baltimore stock, a character out of Henry James, half-brother of Ambassador White. A more notorious Greek scholar was R. M. Dawkins, of whom there was a cult at Oxford. He had been a victim of Corvo, since he was well off and had some tastes in common. When Dawkins did not come up to the scrounger's financial expectations, he described him to the life: 'the blubber-lipped professor of Greek', whose conversation was an alternation of 'snarls and screams'. This was exact: I often could not make out what Dawkins was saying amid his gurgles and giggles in the breaking voice of an adolescent satyr. He was an odd phenomenon, this Cambridge engineer who had taken up the more unsuitable aspects of Byzantine folklore and was intimately acquainted with the folk life of the Greek islands. His appearance was in keeping: straggling sandy-grey hair and moustache, scraggy neck which emitted his silly screams. But for the gold-rimmed spectacles he might have appeared as a dancing goat on one of Beazley's Greek vases. Improbably, he had been left a country house with a pack of hounds in North Wales by a Fellow of All Souls, Doyle: an odder rider to hounds could scarcely be imagined.

I never fell for his charm, and had no time for cultivating mere eccentricity; so I was never one of his favourites. Relations remained friendly, however – until the skies darkened over appeasement. Dawkins had no political judgment, and belonged to the type of cosmopolitan playboy who had a good time in the thirties. So he became a rabid Chamberlainite; I had no idea of the depths of this until I learned how much he disliked my outspoken views. I mention this only to show what the atmosphere of the time was, and how determined those people were to enforce their mistaken line. When the inevitable upshot came with the war, he came round and tried to make amends by presenting me with the rare book he had written under his first names, Richard McGillivray, on Norman Douglas. That was his ambiance: Norman Douglas, Corvo, the Greek islands. I was not amused by him.

After the end of term a hefty bout of examining for the

Oxford and Cambridge Joint Board descended on me. This was a quick way of making a little money, and in those years I always stayed on into the torrid atmosphere of Oxford in July to get through this chore. In those days the Junior Fellows of All Souls received the magnificent remuneration of £300 a year, plus rooms, service and dinner. It was considered such an honour to be a Fellow of All Souls that we should never have dreamed, in those gentlemanly days, of getting up at a college meeting to ask for a rise in salary – let alone claim housing allowances, family allowances, travel allowances for writing one's book and, on top of that, asking the College to purchase books for one's research. So, instead of scrounging, I set out to add to my modest income for myself, by work – teaching, examining, reviewing, writing articles, eventually books. I preferred to be independent and, in later years, the half-time Research Fellowship with which I was content made much the smaller proportion of my income, while leaving me free half-time to work in the USA.

Before the deluge of examination papers descended I was taken over to Chequers, with a small party, by Lionel Curtis to tea with Ramsay MacDonald, then Prime Minister: it was the only time I met our revered Leader. Talk about Personality Cult – you have no idea what veneration there was for Mac-Donald among the lower echelons of our Movement. All the greater was the fall from the heavens in 1931, the dismay and grief when he deserted to become head of the appalling 'National' government. It was all a miserable introduction to practical politics.

Lionel had some project to put to the Prime Minister – he was a projector, full of schemes, some of them good ones, like his campaign against 'Ribbon Development' in housing. (I don't know what practical use Chatham House was.) Millionaires and big industrialists were easy prey, for they had generous minds; he could do nothing with academics – too small-minded. I remember Robin Dundas describing Lionel as a great bore. Well, like all eminent men Lionel could be a bore, but what a small-minded bore Dundas was, with his adolescent fixation on the boys. I never once heard him say anything of the slightest interest.

This was typical of a fairly general attitude at Oxford

towards All Souls. There was much envy of the College's distinction in its public figures, archbishops and viceroys, cabinet ministers and leading lawyers – the one thing I regretted was that there were not more literary men. Maurice Bowra, for one, was anti-All Souls – sheer envy, the more because Wadham was then a small college and poor. Even Charles Henderson once gave voice to this; Bruce was never friendly towards us. Oxford was full of people who had sat for All Souls and not been elected, and that was it. One encountered this childish envy, as I encountered anti-Oxford feeling at the London School of Economics, or even among Cambridge men – like the anti-Harvard feeling in other American universities. Very human, and silly.

One result was that the History Faculty would not appoint us junior Fellows of All Souls to University lectureships, intended as an encouragement to research for full-time teaching dons. This meant that I was never asked to lecture in the History School at Oxford. The reader may find this odd in someone who became a leading authority on the Elizabethan Age. As G. N. Clark said one day, 'if you don't have to lecture, why do so?' With my usual acceptance of authoritative guidance, I never put myself forward; my attitude was what it has always been in these matters: their loss, not mine.

Later on, when Sir Arthur Salter succeeded Adams as Professor of Political Theory and Institutions, he made me his deputy, to lecture on the theory, one more push in that direction. These lectures were always well attended and received with lively interest, though they were a bit of a bother to me. Thus I took my share in examining for the Diploma in Politics and Economics. This Diploma was for people who were not up to the standard of the Final Honour School. One year the Economics paper, set by Lionel Robbins, was of such an absurdly high, even post-graduate, standard that nobody could answer the questions, which made it almost impossible to assess the candidates. Samuel Butler in his *Note-Books* has something to the point here: 'One man who entered for the Chancellor's Medal [at Cambridge] declined to answer any of the questions set. He said they were designed to show off the ingenuity of the examiner rather than to test the judgment of the examined.'

Everything conspired to involve me in the field of politics, which was not really mine; it engaged my mind, but not my heart. Later on, when Humphrey Sumner was Warden of All Souls, having made his old friend, Ernest Jacob, Chichele Professor of Modern History – a medievalist, when we already had a medievalist professor in Galbraith – Sumner came round to ask whether I wouldn't try for Professor of Political Theory. By that time, I certainly wouldn't – I had had enough of the subject, and didn't want to be a professor anyway.

I have observed all through my life that, where my fellow-humans have been ready to hinder me at every such turn, it has worked out very well – I ought to be grateful to them. It has prevented me from wasting my life on third-rate jobs which anybody can do and left me free to fulfil myself. It is as if a guardian angel stood at the gate, and every time I attempted to turn aside from my own true vocation, stopped me in my tracks. I am grateful to the angel, but hardly to the humans, all too obvious in their motives. And if anyone would now like to know why – it has given me a perfect alibi for not doing anything for them.

Even within the gates of All Souls there was an inferiority-complex among some of the academics towards the public figures and the function of the College in public affairs – notably with Pares and Woodward, both of whom should have known better. They were hostile to Coupland, a protégé of Curtis, who had recruited him out of the rut of a teaching Fellowship in ancient history, into the history of the British Empire and Commonwealth, a new field of promising work. Coupland became a brilliant historian, whose books on the history of Africa, India, Stamford Raffles and Java, Wilberforce and the Abolition of Slavery, had far more life and significance than Richard's on the 18th century Sugar Trade or Woodward's prolonged engagement with sterile diplomatic history.

They were jealous of Coupland's hobnobbing with pro-consuls and having them to stay in College, travelling about the Empire and serving on the Indian and Palestinian Commissions, etc. They didn't like the public figures in College, and would have got rid of them if they could. This was not my attitude; I found the public men far more interesting than academics, and besides there was so much more to learn from them. Why couldn't they see that, and learn? G. N. Clark, watching the in-College game from Oriel saw that, though I was the aggressive Labour man in theory, in practice I was ready to compromise, Richard not. Pares was a purist, a 'sea-green incorruptible'.

This came out in his writing of history, which was even more purely academic. An element of father-complex entered into this. Because Sir Bernard Pares – responsible for much family unhappiness – was a fascinating lecturer and writer, Richard, though scintillating himself, deliberately withheld from this field for the dull, academic grind. Not even like Namier, whom he admired, whose brilliance occasionally came breaking in. It was silly of Richard, and self-defeating; but he wouldn't take telling from me, I was his junior and – so far as research was concerned – his protégé. He worked like a beaver for some years at all the available archives – in Britain, the USA, the West Indies – and at length came up with a manuscript of half-a-million words. It wasn't a book, which should have an organic life; a beginning, a middle, and an end. Namier and Clark worked at this quarry, and ultimately excavated two books out of it, a couple of *English Historical Review* articles, with something left over.

Richard was secretive about this, as he was about everything (he had reacted against his gay undergraduate life). I tried to read *War and Trade in the West Indies.* My interest was engaged only when Richard described the personality of Governor Trelawny, important in the story; this admirable character-sketch showed what Richard could do if he chose, but he at once switched off, to become dull and unreadable again. When I asked him why, Richard replied that he did not think that that was history! His was a deliberately chosen academicism, refusing to fulfil his gifted nature in his work. A mere tyro at research myself, compared with his professionalism, and lagging behind with an inferiority-complex encouraged by all the fuss made about research, I did not dare to tell him what I thought. Shortly I followed him into the research world – Public Record Office, British Museum manuscript room, Institute of Historical Research in the evenings: what a strain, we were killing ourselves, I led on by Richard! However, from my first work of historical research, *Sir Richard Grenville of the Revenge* (just republished again after forty years), our paths diverged.

Richard was not pleased that my first work turned out to be a biography since historical biography was not much approved of at that time by the academics who called the tune. One of them was Namier, though he spent his last years ploughing the sands with innumerable biographies of insignificant parliamentarians. I remained innocently unaffected by the prejudices and frustrations of the professionals, since I wasn't one of them. And it was largely accident that drove me to write that biography. I was soberly engaged in building up a picture of Tudor life in Cornwall, when I found myself noting everything I came across about this controversial Elizabethan. There had been no biography of him, a singular gap for so famous a figure. Shortly I discovered why: practically all the personal material had been destroyed; no private correspondence, no letters to wife or friends to help to bring him alive.

Besides this there was a technical difficulty: the documents in the Calendar of State Papers dealing with his important South Seas project, anticipating Drake's voyage round the world, had been misdated. This preliminary obstacle had been cleared by an admirable West Country antiquary, R. Pearse Chope, of Hartland in North Devon. I went down to visit him, and thereupon made life-long friends with the Stucley sisters, Betty and Priscilla, who were descendants of the Grenvilles. Betty took me all over that wonderful countryside, with its iron coast, its towering cliffs and precipitous gorges, and introduced me everywhere to the places Grenville had known, some of the houses still occupied (then) by descendants of people he knew.

Maddeningly I found that all the archives of his town of Bideford had also been destroyed. What was I to do to make the book real? I took a leaf out of Macaulay's note-book and set myself to describe the places, and the people from their tombs or their portraits, precisely as I had them under my eye. That would help to bring them alive, in the absence of intimate personal material. It helped to make the success of the book when it came out – though how I longed for a touch of Pepys, or even such letters as Grenville's cousin, Ralegh, left!

Sir John Squire – generous 'Jack' Squire of *The London Mercury* – had intended a biography of Grenville. A Plymouth man, he told me that in earlier days he had often swum out to the Breakwater. Sabotaged by drink, he once spent an afternoon in my rooms swigging a whole bottle of sherry. But he could never have written the book: he was a literary man, not a historian. When it came out, he did not fail to crab it for its apparatus of historical research; I did not trouble to see him again, not my type anyway.

Nor had Pares been right about it. It is a good idea for a beginner to start with a biography, easier to write than a general historical work, the chronological form being given. If I hadn't written *Grenville* first, I might never have been able to accomplish a portrait of a whole society, if on a small scale, in *Tudor Cornwall*. And if I had not had that experience I should never have been able to cope with a portrait of Elizabethan society as a whole in my trilogy. G. M. Trevelyan came over from Cambridge to encourage me in the big undertaking much later: I have never been more grateful to, or more encouraged by any man, except Eliot. These were two great men.

But I anticipate. Sunday, 7 July 1929 was the red-letter day on which I was wafted into the presence of our Leader. We were quite a party, and MacDonald was at his best as host in an Elizabethan country-house: the Highland laird in him, full of courtesy and natural distinction. What was wrong with that? After his desertion of the cause much was made, by Harold Laski and others, of his seduction by 'the aristocratic embrace'. I never took part in this personal vilification of him, though as strongly opposed on political grounds as the rest of the Labour Movement. MacDonald's tastes were another matter. A Celt, he was a man of distinguished sensibilities. It was a tribute to these, and to him, that he had the sense of fine living, neither ostentatious nor vulgar; that he appreciated pictures and literature. I remember with what interest he showed us round the pictures at Chequers, to this day I recall the Ferdinand Bol that specially appealed to him.

It was touching that this handsome man, who had had so impoverished a youth, should have discovered his own true nature in things of beauty. There was nothing of that in Ernest Bevin, a simpler and perhaps bigger man. Both he and Mac-Donald were illegitimate, like others among the early Labour leaders – Keir Hardie and Jimmy Thomas too; this had sharpened their wits along with their resentment.

It would be a mistake, unworthy of an historian, to under-rate MacDonald's abilities because of the bathos of his declining years. The truth was that he came to power too late and in untoward circumstances. He would have made a good Foreign Secretary, given the chance. He had instinctive skill as a negotiator: McTaggart of Cambridge said of him that 'his hands were literally calloused with wire-pulling', and Roger Makins told me that he had often seen him at international conferences never giving a point away. The pity of it was that owing to his romantic personality, his looks and his aura, his spell-binding appeal to Labour audiences, he was made leader and became Prime Minister in 1924 and 1929. Arthur Henderson, sensible boiler-maker as he was, would have been better as Prime Minister: his was a simpler personality, with less conflict within himself; he was more integrated – no split within – and therefore more reliable.

After tea and the pictures we went for a walk up that springy turf of the hill – Buckinghamshire chalk country, summer Sunday evening (were there church bells?), nearly fifty years ago. MacDonald led with a little group around him, Lionel and I bringing up the rear, others strung out between. Lionel's scheme was to waylay the Prime Minister at a favourable moment on the way up. He sent me ahead, as a scout, to arrange the movement. In this I conspicuously – and not altogether without malice – failed; for, seeing the others turn back before reaching the top, I turned back half-way too; the whole straggle moved back in reverse direction, so that Lionel never waylaid his prey. I was secretly amused – the visual turn-round down the hill looked rather funny, and so did Lionel's dismay. But he never gave up.

Geoffrey Dawson told me a story of Lionel's pertinacity in pursuing Prime Ministers – first Baldwin, then MacDonald, then Baldwin again and MacDonald once more – for an 'honour' for some tycoon who had contributed, expecting it, to one of Lionel's good causes. The reward Lionel had faith-fully promised was not forthcoming; the tycoon protested and was assuaged with further promises. Still the 'honour' did not materialise; the tycoon grew impatient, protested to Lionel, who in the end got it for him. Part of the secret of his technique was never to ask for anything for himself; people, and he too, thought he was above such things, but he would like to have been Lord Kidlington. And why not? Worse men, who have done less, have fared better.

As for me, it was the inner life that always counted most – or, though I did not know it – counted all in all. I find notes for a 'Poem on the Garden', and thought that I had at last found structure for it: as 'a scene on which my consciousness of time is projected. There I see the days, the seasons, the years pass; the changing light pass over the palace [this was the wonderful front of Queen's Library I could see from my rooms in the Old Quad]. It is time objectified, in which I watch my life passing. And yet, though it typifies change, it is the one thing unchang-ing in my life.' I watched the garden intently: 'the boughs of white apple-blossom, nid-nodding noiselessly in the wind; while the great chestnut tree spreads its crinoline above the lawn.' I had forgotten the poem, but I find that it is there in *Poems of a Decade*, 'The Garden', the theme and all the phrases I had carefully collected.

Now it was Whit Sunday:

Coming back from Common Room after midnight, I stay a little in the dark angle by the tulip bed. They catch my eyes in white light, pallid driven creatures ceaselessly active though no wind drives them. I lean over and see that they are all moving and stirring, all those white ghosts of flowers. I take now one, now another in my hand and stroke them gently, thinking of Adam. Somewhere an owl laughs in the stillness. After I let a flower go it goes on swaying drunkenly: all in unceasing motion, as if whispering in some shadowy dance unknown to day. Later – though up late, I am down early and catch the garden while the sun is still in the east. Tree-shadows point to me across the grass; slowly they wheel round to their more familiar place, until at noon there will be only direct plots of darkness under the trees. Light coming from the east gives an uncommon effect to my day. I am up early enough to see the sun brilliant upon the other side of the quadrangle, which all day rests in shadow. Already the grey mass of the gate-tower has crept along to the south-west angle, and will shortly eat up the unwonted brightness. Now the trees begin to let in the sun, the chestnut to throw its crest up into the day. A bishop appears in the garden; he admires the purple irises, walks round by the old curve of wall, flecked by dappled lights. When he has gone the tabby cat steals out from under a cushion of ivy, stalks in the tracks of the bishop, carefully smelling the ground, and flicking the dew off hind paws with a pretty gesture of disgust. The common day has come.

I do not remember whether I ever wrote that poem, though there is one about Jeremiah, the tabby cat. There is even a note for the preface to a volume of poems, though it was years before I could bring myself to publish one. I was bent on watching, trying to catch every moment of significance on the wing.

If only I could catch something of the changing lights of day upon the palace-front, something of the clarity of the leaves on the trees in spring, something of the magic of bells ringing at evening over the hills of childhood; something of the divine dissatisfaction of remembering him, of the agony when I awoke and found he was gone from my life; something of all this caught in movement and petrified into art – then the problem of poetry would be solved.

Evidently, like other poets, I was in love with the idea of being in love. But I had friends, of whom I was fond, to keep me company – especially David, Richard, Charles, and Bruce. We were all young and childish enough – David the most mature and sophisticated, Richard, though intellectually precocious, the most childlike and sweet. Here I was in the gateway of Wadham, waiting for David, his pretty rooms just around the corner on the left; Maurice's diagonally across the quad on the right, up against the Hall. 'A sudden wind rushes through the gateway stirring all the notices on the boards like dead whitened leaves. They are caught on the underside and flap upwards wildly, but are tethered; after a few efforts in vain they subside into being but college notices, not wind-blown leaves.' How familiar a sight! but I do not recall anyone recording it. Obsessed, I wanted to record everything.

Here is Bruce, safely entrenched with a tutorial Fellowship at last, at Magdalen. The Oxford sky was blown about by bells all one day; Bruce, on a new peal starting up: 'Hullo! They're beginning it all over again, about the King's Accession.' A frog-pond at Magdalen held a horrid fascination for Richard and me.

The horror of it! Around the edges these inseparable couples fixed in the vice-like clutch of natural necessity, sometimes killing each other, squeezed to death; the small male embracing the inflated body of the female with tight, muscular, sub-human arms. At the bottom of the basin loathsome swollen females waiting their turn to be impregnated, barely distinguishable from the mud sediment in their stupid ecstasy. On the surface a floating mass of gelatinous spawn, each jelly a nucleus of black life. Here and there among the leaves the bodies of dead frogs, exhausted by that embrace, flung aside from their single purpose in the scheme of life.

It can be seen that I was in revolt against the natural necessities of life; this took shape in a poem later:

> Nature I hate, and what's unnatural choose
> For rule of life, rather than hourly lose
>
> The sense of separateness from the common world,
> Admit a likeness which I never willed
>
> To all that's human, similar, and mean...

'The pond teems: even the goldfish are astir with desire. Here and there a red fish is pursuing a pale whitish one, for a moment establishes contact, and then loses it again. What a month is May.'

Like Swift, I fed on my disgust with the facts of life. Lionel, older and wiser – and who had met this phenomenon before with T. E. Lawrence in College – disapproved of this Manicheeism. For myself, since I could not avoid recurring illness, I made a point of it: I fancied that illness sharpened one's sensibilities and the edge of one's mind: if so, that justified it.

One obsession was for a poem on the end of the world, '*Finis Mundi*'. I do not know the psychological explanation for this obsession. It may have been partly a reflection from *The Waste Land*, which meant so much to all of my generation. Scraps of notes exist:

The World Dead. The body of this death. The sharpness of death. Thou shalt break the ships of the sea: through the east wind. The great towers that stand like a cliff, imagine them in that ultimate day swaying and rocking and crashing to the earth . . . in that last minute when the trump shall sound and the dead wake . . . I saw the world crumble before my eyes, the buildings slowly sink into the earth; where there had been tall towers, delicate spires, filigree of stone, the city's long lean roofs, there was only a heap of stones and, underneath, the fleshy worms working silently.

Silence descended everywhere, for the last man had gone. Who or what succeeded? Rats – not Proust's victims, but the inheritors softly scuffling. More notes exist which I cannot lay hand on; but I remember a vision of St. Paul's, dead and deserted, a fine grey ash lying over everything.

This obsession recurred, I was faithful to it for a long time, without ever finding time to write the poem. I don't know what accounted for it – the remorseless repression, some obscure revenge of mind or body for the strain imposed upon them by the determined will? (Lovely and tragic Diane Abdy apropos of Cyril, whose precocious *réclame* I envied: 'He doesn't have your advantages. You don't know what you could do with women if you only tried.' That was later; but at no time was I going to compete: I did not even by the movement of an eyelid betray that I had heard. Beautiful Athenais Russell: 'He's *too* inhibited.' But I agreed with Arthur Balfour about marriage with Margot, who married Asquith and ruined him: 'I rather fancy a career for myself.')

I played up to Richard's child-like cult of ducks – he had a psychotic terror of all other birds, understandably atavistic considering that they are descendants of the original lords of creation, the giant flying reptiles. At Magdalen his ducks were trying to imitate the calls of a thrush: 'this is the time of year when they get curious ideas into their heads and make odd noises.' Or they were 'piping on their molehills in the meadow of fritillaries.' 'In the afternoon after rain the tree-trunks take the light as if they are human bodies.' This is followed by a line for *The World Dead*: 'the frozen architecture of the mind.' In the garden 'the tulips under the wind strain like dogs at the leash.'

I had a cult of my room as of the garden. 'I come back to find here and there a book has been touched, replaced a bit out of line. Mainly eighteenth century. On the window seat Swift's

Letters and *Gulliver's Travels* lie askew; at the bottom of the
chestnut bookshelves it is Murray Wrong's little history of
eighteenth century England; above, it is a biography of Law,
the financier. Who can it be who has paid me a visit?' In those
days one never thought of 'sporting one's oak', locking one's
door: everything was left open. What a world of difference this
fact lights up between that good society and our sick one! The
emancipation of the people, which we were advancing – and
behold the consequences: a world of violence and mistrust, of
betrayal of confidence, of insecurity and anxiety. We did not
know what we were doing, for we did not know what people
really *are* by nature, freed from discipline, direction and control – out of order. Now at Oxford, or anywhere else, one
couldn't dare to leave one's doors unlocked. Undergraduates
thieve from each other, quite apart from the general increase of
insecurity, the vast army of professionals on the prowl, so that
one has to live surrounded by precautions, burglar alarms, the
police on call. What a contemptible society, with the people on
top!

The eighteenth-century clue told me that I had received a
visit from Mark Thomson, a West Country friend who
became a professor and even a good eighteenth century
historian. A dearer friend was a Geordie, Tom Lawrenson,
from undergraduate days at Christ Church. 'Tom, arriving
for supper, remembers that he must get some fruit to carry
to a girl in hospital. He goes off to the Turl or to the Market.
Seized with an idea, I fly to the window and shout into
the quad, "Bring two for us." Tom, caught at the gate-
corner: "What? Peaches?", surprised at the extravagance. I
shout vehemently, "Yes." They are to be the triumph of
the feast.'

O sancta simplicitas! We were both working-class boys; in
spite of the public luxuries of All Souls, I clung in my private
life and tastes to the simplicity of my upbringing. One result
was that, small as my income was, I was able to support my
parents in part, and still had something left over. I even saved a
little 'for a rainy day', and note that I was beginning to invest
modest sums. The attitude of a younger generation has totally
changed with the triumph of Keynesian economics in inappropriate circumstances, at the wrong time – they would

have been appropriate in the thirties. A temporary member of the College of today's generation was able to inform me, when I said that I never stayed in hotels that I could afford to stay in, that my attitude towards money was quite out of date and irrational. Himself was able to depart the College leaving a considerable sum of debt. This is what is meant by debit economics. To clear myself of the charge of being irrational, I should say that money is not an end in itself, but it gives one freedom, freedom of movement; it gives one independence, independence of other human beings (a vast advantage); it gives one command, one can command the things one values, books, pictures, music, travel. Of course, *they* do manage to command these things – at others' expense, and partly mine: through penal taxation of what I work hard to earn. After all, it is *my* earnings, not theirs, bloody slackers, incessantly striking: they don't want to work.

I regret to think that I should have been a portent of today's contemptible society ...

Along with notes for poems I find others for the politics book I was mistakenly going to write, *Politics and the Younger Generation*. No inferiority complex in this quarter – as there was about writing history and poetry – would there had been! For of all subjects politics is the one that requires experience above all. Youthful books on politics are not much good, and mine was no exception. Eliot was encouraging, took it seriously and published it – I can't think now why he did. Pushing me into literature would have been better, though it may have been that, from the publisher's point of view, there were plenty of promising young writers; few enough to write intelligently about politics – certainly not from a Marxist point of view.

What with the various pressures upon me, and incessant work, then adding to it a political candidature, I was living under much strain. Beneath all was my obsession with Adam. Letters were constantly passing between us – all mine lost in the German catastrophe, while I have kept all his, now a figure in history, commemorated in Germany for his part in the Resistance. No one knew anything about the entanglement, except him and me: I kept it to myself, my confidant my Diary and the *Buch des Lebens*.

The wind in the trees makes the steady lamps twinkle like stars, one red, one white. A shudder passes through the garden; they wink across the dusk to where I sit watching, waiting.

Now is the room, the moment past, insentient, unruminative. The half-hour chime of St Mary's competes with the sedate old lady marching upstairs of neighbouring New College.

Now it is night in Richard's room [this was to become mine years afterwards]; the clicking of a typewriter contradicts sentimental thoughts. Tulips in a jar hold up their scarlet bowls to the lamp. Yet they were there straining after the sun that day when you and you were here, my friend and his friend with the lovely alien eyes.

Who was this? I rather think it may have been Hasso von Seebach, whose name occurs as dining with me. And before I went home to Cornwall, Adam sent his uncle, von Schweinitz, to dine. Belonging to a diplomatic family as they did – their father Bismarck's ambassador to Russia – one of Adam's uncles had an apartment in Schloss Bellevue, (had this been the Crown Prince's?), the other in the Kaiser's Schloss, of which Adam and I were given the freedom when I went to Berlin that summer. Along with this passionate friendship, I was keen on keeping up my contacts with Germany.

The Diary records the strains of repression, a scene of jealousy headed 'Ugly Light'.

I go into Blackwell's just at closing time, when the assistants at the hot end of the day are all in shirt-sleeves. The accustomed dark young fellow comes, half man, half boy; a gipsy complexion, liquid black eyes, a cob of lighter brown hair curls over his forehead. He goes off, leaps up the iron staircase in two or three bounds, limbs neat and close-fitting. I always notice him, self-contained, self-confident, and distant. I go in search of Perry's *Biological Interpretation of Value* at another counter. A girl comes in from the back, pale, vapid, coolly self-conscious among all the young men. A moment later, looking up from my search, I see her at the top of the iron staircase, flattened against the wall, quite still, thighs outlined against the books. The young assistant approaches her with a quick movement, eager eyes burning with an ugly light: his whole being concentrated in the dark eyes, predatory under the cob, body thrust forward, a gesture, an approach. She is quite pale, offering herself. I turn back to *The Biological Interpretation of Value*. Here is how nature provides for her biological purposes – her priorities in values: not *mine*.

A much later note says: 'Contrast Isherwood. While the Auden-Isherwood group made no such difficulties for themselves, I *created* difficulties for myself.' Here was one reaction to be expected from a young, highly sexed temperament, bent on frustrating itself. Why? It was partly that I had had to encounter so many obstacles all the way along from childhood that I became fixed in the habit of creating obstacles to surmount, and this pattern has remained throughout much of my life. Today, when life is almost over, and passion spent, I see the episode in lighter, more Proustian terms. I am reminded of the narrator watching the Baron de Charlus making his way in the hot siesta-time of afternoon across the courtyard after the personable footman.

Ulcers, coming and going regularly, were I suppose another result of the strain. Here is an entry, after a night of agony.

5 July, 5 am. When I look out from the dark and shuttered room, where pain haunts the crevices, the world unconscious is caught unawares and goes sailing onward to the oblivion of day. In high wind all the world of cloud spins onward to the east: I seem to watch the secular motion of the earth. The wind is in the tall poplars, stirring them to their own music, suggesting unknown worlds. Now it strikes down the mantled walls: they shudder like a summer cornfield. The wing of the palace is poised in grey sleep, under the reticent roofs. All the world has the appearance of dream, unawakened and unaware.

Other such notes were written at dawn, after nights of pain, the sensibilities exceedingly sharpened by it. It seems that I had some idea of a book, *The Room*. Reading Virginia Woolf and Proust, I was much influenced by both. The Note Book has a word from Proust: 'there is always less egoism in pure imagination than in recollection.' I see today that this applies to Proust himself as against Shakespeare. Though I have devoted so much time to studying Shakespeare, as an addict of memory I place myself under Proust's protection: he is my patron saint. In fact I often think of his withdrawal from society to give himself up to his research into the past, in my retirement here in Cornwall to give myself up to remembering all that past, re-creating it from Diary, note-books, letters and the *Buch des Lebens*.

2

Adam von Trott:
Portrait of a German

All the while, intense if not impassioned letters were going to
and fro between me in Oxford and Adam in Germany. I still
find it, nearly fifty years afterwards, the most difficult thing to
get right in a long career of writing – heaven knows I have
waited long enough! For one thing the relationship was so
complex. We had made a profound impact on each other in
that short space of time: it *was* love at first sight. But what kind
of love? And what could be made of it? On my side, there was a
residual defeatism from the first. I was convinced that no-one
would fall in love with me – perhaps this was another aspect of
my Manicheeism. I accepted beforehand the fact that Adam
was dominantly heterosexual, as I was not; on the other hand,
the thought of physical relations was strongly repressed in me,
conceivably more so than with him, who cannot have attached
the exaggerated importance to them that I did. So there was an
impasse from the first, a denial of satisfaction: we were
high-minded with regard to each other, and I was too
proud.

I recognise how difficult this made things, and how complicated (Betty Stucley said 'mixed up') I was – but so was he, in
a totally different, irretrievably German way. How easily
Auden and Isherwood took these things! Neither Adam nor I
could or did. What was to come of it all? Even Wystan dis-
cusses the nature of love, quite complicatedly, in that prose-
poem about his relationship with Chester Kallman, when they
were both middle-aged. Adam and I were young; I was a few
years older, but all this was new territory for me: nothing like
it had happened to me before, and I was willing to explore at
least. So, evidently, was he.

It would perhaps be too egoistic to go into it simply as part
of my story – though we were both being formed to some
extent in the crucible of the experience – if the subject had not a

certain external, wider significance. It was in a way symbolic of the difficulties between England and Germany, between an Englishman – though I was not all that English, or (a) things might have been easier, or (b) I might not have been so responsive – and a German, for Adam was irreducibly German. (His own people killed him.)

Adam was more conscious than I of this symbolism in our relations: he mentions it in his letters. A vast amount of material remains in those – where all mine were destroyed; so it should be possible to present a portrait of a remarkable German from the inside. That is, if I am capable of it, for the psychological complexity is Jamesian. Then, too, Adam never dated his letters – just like the vague boundlessness of the German mind; it is a task as bad as historical research to have to put them in order from half-obliterated post-marks, all with the square head and wooden features of old Hindenburg staring out on the stamps of that tragic past before the deluge.

That April I had sent him the poem, 'The Progress of Love' and received a long reply in German, pages and pages of those long wandering sentences so characteristic of the German mind, of which even then I could not wholly grasp the meaning. '*Dein Brief und Dein Gedicht haben mich sehr bewegt und doch sind vielleicht Traurigkeit und Freude alle Worte, die ich über diese Bewegung sagen kann.*' However, one thing was clear: '*Dass Du mich und unsere Beziehung anders sehen und empfinden musstest als ich.*' That was no surprise to me: I always had expected that the relationship would appear differently to him. '*Oh, nenne diese Spannung zwischen innerer und äusserer Welt nicht abstrakt, denn auch Du kannst das Leben nicht nehmen wie es ist.*'

I must have advised him to 'take life as it is', instead of the perpetual doubt, the beating from side to side which was to be such a theme of his letters, the constant zigzagging from confidence to despair, the lack of a settled foundation, which in the end I couldn't stand. I recognise that it expressed the hopeless insecurity of the Germany of the time, but also it betrayed itself as something endemic in the German mind: the absence of the plastic bonds among Latins or the sensible empiricism of Anglo-Saxons. It wore me down in the end – among other things. '*Dein Erlebnis war die Offenbarung, die in ein sicheres und zielbewusstes Leben fiel, mein Erlebnis enthüllte den tiefen Gegensatz und Zusammenhang zwischen dunkelster Verzweiflung und göttlichster Freude.'*

There you are; that became the gramophone record: the endless veering between deepest despair and divine joy. All very German: it was like the Hegelian dialectic incarnate in a human being – very uncomfortable to live with. Others have said that Adam had a gift for making himself – and others – unhappy. In that, very German too. Then what was the point of going on? Well, to put it on the lowest practical plane, beneath our high-minded exchanges – he wanted to learn English and England, I wanted to learn German and Germany. I must say he got the better of the exchange (or was I in part responsible for his terrible end? I have sometimes reproached myself; there is a later poem about that – for it is in my poetry that I have expressed my secrets.)

Even so, I learned much: I got a window into the German soul, which very few English at the time possessed – and in consequence they had no understanding of the Germans or knew what to expect when Hitler came in. I did – though I did not intuit all the horror. I knew Adam's mind so intimately that once, after 1933, I could put the question: Why do the Germans have to give themselves up to such hysteria? (Witness the hysteria and neurosis in their literature.) Adam admitted: 'At bottom they feel so null that, if they did not work themselves up into hysteria, they would feel nothing at all.'

It was a terrible answer, but it explains a lot in German history and in the tragedy that ensued. But how dangerous in a whole people! What a contrast with the contentment of the French, sitting down to a 'bock' in a café, satisfied with the good things of life and the finest country in Europe! Or the English, at least as they were – they have since undergone a degrading change – satisfied with their cottage and garden, with country and country sports, complacent and pleased with life as it is (or was). The Germans – never satisfied, always upheaved and upheaving for something beyond them: the Hegelian dialectic in action. They had tried to bring it off in 1914–1918, and they were to try it all over again in 1939–1945. From 1933 it was one furious preparation under Hitler for the second attempt. And his was a marvellous achievement in the psychological, as well as in the material and military, preparation for it. He had the German people, or the strongest forces in the German people, and their mind and will, behind him.

After this early and disheartening hint of our separateness –

And in our loves a separable spite –

his next letter showed how anxious he was to hold on to me. It was addressed from his uncle Schweinitz's apartment in the Kaiser's palace, the Königliches Schloss – which no longer exists, reduced to rubble in the war. Adam had given his uncle a message for me. 'After all, haven't you some positive hopes about the future of our friendship? Our friendship and, let me say, love', he went on to say, had a kind of exquisite craft, 'the main point of which is that nothing right can be done by one alone, but together.' Adam was reading some of Hölderlin's writing during his madness – 'you know he died after forty years' madness.' It made him 'terribly sad too that I may lose you, or might have already lost you, not being able to speak the language of your heart and mine, and living far away.'

Now he wondered 'what use writing has in our case, although I find some rest and comfort in this imagined conversation with you – yet I should not treat it too much from my point of view.' Why so much unrest and discomfort? I could not understand it in one so young, and of incomparable looks and prospects. He longed 'to forget the fatal individuation into which we are born'. Wasn't that very inviting? What did he want? Perhaps we were too sensitive about each other's feelings to say, 'I wish that you would feel that you could tell me everything about us without hurting me.'

Well, exactly: I was not going to say anything to hurt him, or he me. I held intuitively to leaving some things unsaid, trusting to luck or intuition or the way things would come right, or not, on their own. Adam was one for endless analysing, probing where it is better not to probe. I didn't want to possess him, body or soul – he may have feared that I did. To be frank, proselytiser as I was, I think I wanted him as a disciple, someone who would could take on my ideas, which were being formulated, all too inadequately, in *Politics and the Younger Generation*, and put them across in Germany.

He next wrote from his student's room in Pariserstrasse 54; I don't know what is left of the Berlin we knew (when Ernest Bevin wished me to go and lecture there during the Air-Lift, I refused to go). A silence had elapsed on my side. On his, 'as I have noticed before: every time when my heart is more filled with new experiences, it turns more devotedly to you – sure to find more understanding (of course!) but sympathy too, more than anywhere else.' This was, perhaps, taking me – never one to be taken for granted – a little for granted. The new experience was, as was to be expected, a girl. He was encouraged to make that admission by a passage in Jean Paul Richter, whom he much admired, to the effect that 'love lifted up the wings of friendship.' But which was which? Jean Paul was decidedly not my cup of tea; nor was German literature as a whole. I was inexpugnably French in my sympathies and tastes, even my convictions. Hölderlin and Jean Paul – madmen!

The new experience brought him no more satisfaction than before. 'I am pretty sure that this new story will end unhappily, for she is engaged to someone else, and there seems little hope that her favours [!] to me will ever exclude that fact.' I should have thought that, with his ravishing looks, the 'favours' would have been on his side. Oddly enough, he does not seem to have been very successful with women; perhaps they saw through him better than I did – love is at least partially blind. He felt that she did not take him seriously (as I did, too seriously). He needed my sympathy more than ever. 'She is very beautiful – I am sure you would like her; everybody thinks us brother and sister, but she is two years older.'

No wonder the poor boy could not make up his 'mind about us two'. How far did he understand me? His intuitions were prodigious – that was what had knocked me over; but analysis in the German manner wouldn't get him far. 'How curious that more than ever in the last weeks I have thought of you, my dear, and loved reading your lines in *The Criterion* [some phrase or other directed against reactionary medievalism with Eliot in mind] as no remedy for the current ills of industrial society. I shall take up the subject of Marxism seriously, it is practically the intellectual creed of an important part of my people.'

After my weary chore of examining I was taking the night train home for vacation. At the ticket-office I was thrown together with a good-looking Swedish cadet, whom I helped out in German over his ticket. He was on his way to Falmouth to catch his ship. While waiting we watched a station cat clamber down on to the rails, I a bit alarmed for its safety. The young Swede, to reassure me, crouched down his shoulders and made stealthy motion forward with his hands. This was rather endearing. Separated by his travelling first and I third, we met again at Swindon. The last I saw of him was his gazing after me to the end of the corridor, where I was being shown into my sleeping compartment alone.

Waking up at Lostwithiel, I noted 'the trees by the river and I crying out over them, "Oh lovely, Oh lovely" to the unawakened dawn. Seeping mists under the trees in the woods asleep. A field of clover sloping steeply. To be home again! The trees are more lovely; the fields greener; the gorse more golden; the birds sing sweeter; all the land is a dream.' A very different aspect of home-coming was my mother's invincible Cornish dialect. Looking out of the window at the skies: 'The 'ebms is lookin' ferly full.' Me: ' 'is, the 'ebms isn't lookin' very 'ebmly.' Mother: 'The 'ebms is lookin' wicket.' Actually, her speech was extraordinarily vivid, expressive and uncompromising. I have many notes of it.

Here I was, approaching St Dennis for a dreary political meeting (what a way to spend a summer evening!).

The squat tower appears on a hill with a girdle of wind-beaten trees. Up a winding lane, and in front of the churchyard a little God's acre surrounded by walls of huge granite stones off the moor. Inside, a stone Bible open at Jeremiah 47: 'The word of the Lord that came to Jeremiah the prophet concerning the Philistines...'

In the ghastly years that followed I often had reason to think of the prophet Jeremiah. 'Only the sound of a loud clock, and the noise of the winds besieging this exposed place like a fortress.' In fact, the church is in the midst of a primitive encampment, the thick stone wall around – folklore used to say you could drive a carriage round on top – the revetment of the caer (round camp).

Crossing the acre, a lark is lyric over the moor; a cuckoo shouts from within the church enclosure. On a headstone, the name Phillemon Best; and a family whose father was killed in the Sudan war, then all three sons lost; last, the old mother left, at eighty: 'Safely gathered in.' Inside the church, two primitive carvings in the tower-arch: one of an archbishop, chasuble and cross, I suppose St Denis; the other with archaic angular wings.

Today, one cannot get inside the church, locked against vandals. That did not prevent them stoning the windows of the poor little place, a year or so ago. Behold the progress of the idiot people, to which I devoted myself in my ignorant young days – now everywhere out of hand. In the corner of the eating-house where I gulped a snack, a grandmother was reading aloud about so many New Zealanders coming to England. (Today, it would hardly be New Zealanders!) 'All due respect to Mrs N., but I was afraid she was going over there to make a fool of herself.'

So much for the Labour meeting: I haven't the ghost of a memory of it, sheer waste of time. But I used to note down the words of wisdom that fell from the lips of the people. Once, when holding a meeting in our rooms at St Austell, above the Market House, we couldn't hear ourselves speak for the harmonium in the street outside and the voice of Mrs Mingo lifted up in prayer and praise. I went down to expostulate and ask if it couldn't be lowered a little. The good lady paused doubtfully, and considered, with finger on lip: 'Well, you see – the Devil is abroad, and the word of the Lord must go forth.'

Meanwhile more and more letters piled up, reams of them. Adam was beginning his law studies in Berlin; after a silence arrived a portentous letter from Grabow near Magdeburg, where he was staying in a 'pretty castle' belonging to family friends. As usual he found no contentment there (I should have made the best of it): he wrote from 'the disappointing reality of this bright and tasteless sleeping room with its pictures of old Emperors and flowers. They feel obliged to entertain me, while I deceive them in their vain conversation in thinking of you, and this afternoon it gave me some joy in this noisy society that you may have thought of me too.' He wanted me to 'promise to have confidence in my devotion to you and to those hours we were together.' Letters were a poor substitute for our 'understanding without words'. He had noticed a saying of David Hume in reading Nietzsche:

> And from the dregs of life hope to receive
> What the first sprightly running could not give.

Dregs of life, at his age and with his beauty! His letters were hopelessly full of doubt, *Verwirrung* and near–despair. I had evidently written to him to keep 'busy and happy'. The second seemed to be impossible for him – incomprehensibly. He had had a dream of me in my room at Oxford:

> I remember those two blue chairs, but there was a slight alteration, i.e. a long yellow chaise-longue [psychologists note! no such thing in my chaste room] at the wall where Van Gogh and your friend's picture of your Cornwall landscape hang [i.e. a Christopher Wood]. You were in a dark suit, and with your earnest eyes standing at your writing table. Suddenly I was your pupil – a thing which, by the way, I always loved to be, as I know that my brain still lives in the shadow of a very bad education.

It seems that I was laying down what I considered to be Shaw's place in English literature. Adam replied with Hölderlin, who expressed most passionately the depths and heights of friendship. Such were his 'fantasies of loneliness'. There was more about his girl-friend, a fellow law-student, 'who has helped me a lot, but I don't know if my difficult nature doesn't trouble her more than is just . . . You know the thing which only a woman can do for you, if you have lost it, is to repair your relationship to other people – and I wanted her to lead me back to you. Has she succeeded?'

At the time I took all this seriously and was anxious to help all I could. What strikes me today is the inextricable egoism of it. The poor girl! While I was to promise to have confidence in his devotion to me: 'I feel rather awkward in confessing *our* experience has become connected with the life of my heart.' He promised to write 'simpler and happier letters', as I had advised, sending him Katherine Mansfield's stories, suggesting that he might translate some – evidently as occupational therapy. He replied with Hölderlin: I *must* read him in German. I dutifully did: admiration for the poetry, none whatever for the mad enthusiasm, the lack of sense. Rather typical of my feeling about German literature, and symbolic of our relations. On my side Shakespeare and Proust, Shaw and Eliot and Katherine Mansfield; Adam replied with madmen like Hölderlin and Jean Paul, Kleist and Nietzsche, whom I could not abide. I thought these tutelary deities bad for him, as they were: they reinforced his irremediable *Deutschtum*.

Distracted by his Berlin life, no doubt distracting enough, he felt that he couldn't stand it much longer. Often as he walked the streets, looking into people's faces for some sign, or in the bus, phrases from my letters or from the poem, 'The Garden', accompanied him. 'Do come to Berlin in the autumn – you know I not only think it the most wonderful thing but the most necessary for our friendship.' There followed the familiar lapse into doubt that I might be disappointed in him.

Very well, I was willing to make a trial.

His next letters were rather sweet, bothering about finding suitable accommodation for me in Berlin – neither of us was well off, and he was anxious lest I should be disappointed. His own student lodging, next door in the Olivaer Platz, must have been very simple – come to think of it, I never entered it. He entertained me in his uncle's apartment in the Kaiser's Palace – I suppose he thought it a suitable return for All Souls. We each had an inferiority-complex: I about my working-class home in Cornwall – it served its purpose for me, but not for my friends. Nevertheless, true aristocrat as he was, he had not a trace of snobbery.

He enclosed for me a charming snap of himself with a younger brother at home on the porch at Imshausen – I had forgotten how many snaps he sent me, to fortify my devotion. One letter is yet another analysis of the nature of love and friendship, for what use that was – I didn't hold with eternal analysis in the German manner. Take things as they were and make the best of them, without for ever probing! I think now that probing, self-doubt, self-torture were German forms of satisfaction. Not for me. I also see that my own confidence in myself was a source of attraction to him. And, of course, *then* there was the added assurance of the security of the English background, in contrast to the Weimar Republic. *Nous avons changé tout cela!*

Nevertheless my junior – and pupil – was more experienced in the ways of the heart than I was, and certainly knew how to hook me. 'Oh, A.L., don't you believe in me?' Was it my fear of the absurd 'which makes you renounce just at the doorstep of that – yet only dreamed – province which we could enter hand in hand?' Evidently I had given a hint of my defeatism about personal relations, a contingent renunciation beforehand, while still exploring. Perhaps only a Henry James could do justice to the complexity of the situation – he was a past master at renunciation, and expectation of defeat. 'After considering all those numerous difficulties of our friendship, after all I found it has – at least for me – so much the divine glamour of a definite change in my life and of yet unknown possibilities that I should love to do what I can to holding you by me!'

I was hooked – but only contingently. It was just as well, for a postscript made a significant and searching point. 'Tenderness and sensuality' were not to 'deceive us about this last step towards the Wonderful which two men can make together with burning passion, while the man and the woman get lost in that union the consequence of which is "satisfaction". I don't want "satisfaction", do you?' That was pretty clear: ordinary heterosexual satisfaction was an end in itself. The absence of such simple satisfaction prolonged our affair and kept it on this high level of enthusiasm, for in its nature it was incapable of the easy resolution of 'satisfaction'. This I was as ready to renounce as he; for, after all, love and sex were not synonymous. In the animal world love was not the same thing as sex, and did not go very far along with it – as anyone can see.

Next, 'I am so much afraid that you will not like Berlin and me, and somehow depressed that you won't say it if that will be so ... Though Berlin is not inspiring, people do say that nowhere you could work better than here. Anyhow, if you come, you must and will finish your book and your other work; do you want them rob you into Parliament? I am so proud of you, though *very* jealous.' Here was an unmistakably German touch. 'P.S. Oh what a wonderful poem you have made! Oh, that I only knew English better!' His English was immeasurably better than my German; anyhow, I never liked the language, while he had had an English nurse and spoken English from his childhood. He was so fearful of my not liking Berlin that he had thought of our meeting in Weimar – perhaps that has its symbolism too. 'My few friends you will not find a happy company, and my place is just a simple student's room.' Characteristically, 'in the days when I rejoiced most about your coming, at the same time fear assailed me that all would remain a dream, as it always does when we hope most.' (Does it?) 'But now I am thinking less and trusting more . . . I bring all my tiredness and desolation to you who have greater confidence and faith.'

Next, 'nothing makes me happier than the expectation to have you here and to recall those hours when we first met and left each other . . . The time we were together seems like a lost paradise.' However, he had found a new friend, a 'labour-poet', with whom he was going into the country on Sunday – *Jungendbewegung* and all that. In Berlin all was confusion and the 'dark activities' going on in his mind. However, on his desk was a picture of the Founder's Tower at Magdalen, with a snap of me: 'one of the only fixed and clear points in this intellectual *tohu-bohu* is my belief in our friendship and the consoling thought of our mutual devotion.' He had been out looking for a room for me in his neighbourhood, 'this bad Victorian part of Berlin where nothing is older than 1890'. He had rejected several and at last fixed on one nearly next door to him, 'a room with a piano, good desk, sofa, etc., relatively the best, though not in the least adequate to the reception this country ought to prepare for your first visit to its capital. But, mind you, Berlin is not Germany, and what she is like you will only see when later you will come and see me at my home in the country!' A PS added that it was only a bed-sitting-room, 'but you can also have a prince-like bedroom at its side with a huge bed, etc., for what they take one mark more, i.e. 5 marks per day.' I opted for this prince-like bedroom, with its enormous bed: I recall the ineffable German sentimentality of the cherub-children at its head, the incitement to proliferation worked in pink tapestry. Many hours I spent in it, reading Tolstoy's endless *War and Peace*.

This abode of domestic bliss was apparently in the Uhland-strasse – I do not know whether even the street still exists. At this last moment there was his familiar doubt whether I should be 'as happy about our seeing each other again as I am'. It certainly was remarkable to have kept excitement and expectation at that high pitch for so long. But he was 'afraid to think too much of it for fearing the trick which fate usually plays off on our imagination'. Well, well: why not take things as they were? Anyhow, I was on my way.

Nothing in the Diary of the intense excitement of our time together in Berlin, only entries recording later the top moments of emotion recollected in (very far from) tranquillity. But, as usual, the *Buch des Lebens* registered life as it went along. The railway journey back to Oxford: 'at Par masses of purple flowers – campion or willow-herb? – on the mudflats, the wind tossing in the feathers of the little plane trees.' A moment of life caught, before it vanished. A thought crossed my mind: 'the absolute disinterestedness of a man becomes absolute interestedness.' I must have had Lionel Curtis in mind. 'The friendly tinkle in the interior of a bus that passes: a tiny universe on its own, alien, unknown.' 'Birdsong from the hidden depths of trees.' Arrival in Oxford, Sunday evening: 'when I come into the quadrangle, the wind-blown bells are everywhere. I cannot find them: they play a game with me behind the four walls and over the roofs. Now I think that that sweet octave is from St Peter-in-the-East, now from All Saints. The winds blow them in from all quarters into the quadrangle, empty but for a bewilderment of bells: the essence of all English Sundays.'

'Reading West station: catching this sprawling lout of a town on the hip: strings of suburban brick and young men playing tennis in cramped backgardens.' At Didcot: 'the locomotive *St Austell* shunting by: what can that be an omen of? A greeting from home: the last time I saw that engine must have been as a boy, at the level crossing at Tregonissey Road.' 'Winchester Cathedral: Bishop Gardiner's chantry, carving already full Renaissance. What an extraordinary England – so full of belief and finding complete expression in religion. It's that that is so impossible now.' The Tudor historian-to-be conscientiously noted down chantry after chantry, monument upon monument – till I came to Jane Austen's grave. The inscription gave me some pause: 'She openeth her mouth with wisdom, and in her tongue is the law of kindness.' Was that quite right? I did not associate Jane with the milk of human kindness.

'Winchester: Georgian red brick and tiled roofs. Evening, and swallows wheeling over the chestnuts in the garden. The people in the hotel, in groups of twos and threes, walk inanely down the gravel path, between fussy geraniums and bustling begonias. The spirit of Jane Austen presides over Winchester: no doubt of it.' Here was the tower of St Michael with St Swithin upon Kingsgate: a lawn bordered with boys'-love, a clump of gillyflowers and tall hollyhocks. At the Barracks:

men playing in the empty yard; bugles over the hillside. Evening: the Close deserted, the failing light flutters raggedly across transepts and tower, lifting the vast mass of stone off the earth into an aery world of the imagination. Sunday morning: on the Southampton Road all the dowagers going to church, prayer book in hand. A squad of the Hampshires turn up a side street. Oh the atmosphere of a county town! The meadows of St Cross: what more English in the world? Sitting in the porch, I listen to the Naaman story, first Lesson for the day: 'Are not Abana and Pharfar, rivers of Damascus, better than all the waters of Israel?'

Much taken with Bishop Morley's Restoration palace, Wolvesey, after the damage of the Civil War to the Castle, I watched a hawk hovering, 'like a ship rising and falling upon some unseen wave'. I reflected upon old Bishop Fox, retiring here from Court and politics, occupying himself with repentance and prayer within sound of his cathedral-bells – and the contrast with Jane Austen, the poise of the domestic scene in those reticent Queen Anne houses: two spirits of Winchester. On leaving my hotel, I remarked on the new arrivals: a well-to-do bourgeois, with a horde of females, telling them what a funk he was in during the war with twenty cwt of sugar stored in the house. Then, looking intently at his dog: 'If only we men could put on the expression that dogs sometimes put on, there isn't a woman in the room who'd be safe, I often say.' There was the average man; and the average females discussed the matter with feeble seriousness.

The journey by sea to Hamburg gave me the chance to write some notes for *Politics and the Younger Generation*. The stars of the Conservative Party at Oxford were very dull luminaries. One was the diplomatic historian, R. B. Mowat, the boredom of whose lectures had driven me frantic. I derived consolation by comparing him with G. D. H. Cole, whom we considered brilliant; or placing the veteran Marriott beside R. H. Tawney. It was 'unintelligible to me that men of our generation can be Conservative – except from self-interest, or when unaware of political issues. But when one comes across a young man from the working classes, who is self-consciously Conservative, it needs looking into.' I proceeded to look into a case I knew: 'poor, acutely proud, intelligent, and intending to return to the land he came from as an agricultural worker. He was conscious of the superior intellectual appeal of socialism, but distrusted intellectualism. Needless to say, he is now a university teacher.'

The bright younger generation of Liberals were 'many of them professional politicians before they were out of the cradle.' This referred to such people as the young tribe of Foots, all of them then Liberals like their father Isaac Foot, leading light of Cornish Liberalism. They were dismissed as 'representing no tendency at large in the country. The almost general tendency is for working-class sons to be solidly Labour when they come to universities, etc.' This seems a fair forecast of the way things would go with my generation.

Nothing odd or eccentric, or even radical, in my taking this line – though it was thought so at home in backward Cornwall, smothered as it was in Nonconformist Liberal humbug. Again and again I was to be told as a political candidate there, 'If only you wuz a Liberal you'd get in flyin'.' But there was no point in being a Liberal, even in 1929; it was simply a fossilised survival: the political expression of Nonconformity – and Nonconformity was a cause very far from the heart of someone brought up a rather High Anglican. Thus, in a backward area like Cornwall, I was doubly in a minority.

Since ordinary human beings are incapable of seeing outside their particular environment and take its colouring, an Isaac Foot was the representative figure of Cornish Liberalism. I got to like him as a private person later, but couldn't bear his public idiom as standard-bearer of Nonconformist Liberalism. The little chapels out in the china-clay district were virtually Liberal recruiting stations in my time: notices of Liberal Party meetings would appear pinned up in their porches. I knew Liberalism was all over and done with and, as a propagandist, engaged Isaac Foot in controversy to that effect. Once I succeeded in pinning him down to answer the question: did he ever expect to see a Liberal government again? I knew well that any intelligent man would have to say No, and never expected that Isaac would be such a fool as to expect to see a Liberal government again. I was simply flabbergasted when he replied, Yes: he fully expected to see a Liberal government. He was a good fellow – but one sees what fools politics makes of us all. It was nonsense even then to think that there was any future for Liberalism: why didn't they see that?

Sir Francis Acland, who was MP for North Cornwall, in succession to Sir Donald Maclean – his son, the Cambridge Communist, now in Moscow, had this propitious Liberal background – saw that by this time the Liberal Party was just a survival from the past. As Labour candidate in Penryn and Falmouth I had an understanding with him that we would not attack each other in our respective constituencies, and I would try and keep a Labour candidate out of North Cornwall, hopeless from our point of view anyway. One could get no such understanding with Isaac Foot; Acland described him to me as a 'hard-bitten party man'.

Though a solid Labour man, I was more willing to compromise. As Chamberlainism, appeasement, betraying our friends to make up to our enemies, selling the interests of Britain – I was not alone in thinking this, Bevin and Churchill, Eden and Macmillan thought it too – developed its full horror, beside myself with anxiety, I was willing to cooperate with anyone to get rid of the incubus. A chance of winning the seat at St Ives against the Tories in full support of Chamberlainism presented itself. At a by-election Isaac Foot put up as a Liberal against the Chamberlainite. Will Arnold-Forster and I succeeded in getting the Labour people to support Isaac; we wanted him to make his appeal as broad as possible against Chamberlainism. Lloyd George offered to come down and speak for him. Isaac wouldn't have it; and instead of standing on the broadest platform of Collective Security against Hitler and Mussolini – i.e. a Grand Alliance against the aggressors, which was the only hope – Isaac wasted his breath on the wrongs of Nonconformity. He lost the election; it was the end of his political career and he had only himself to blame.

What was sickening was that a chance of a blow against Chamberlainism was lost. In the thirties the stars in their courses fought for Chamberlain and Franco, and Hitler and Mussolini. It was heart-breaking – unless you were a politician, and I suppose a heart is a superfluous organ for a politician. But the great-hearted Churchill confessed that the night that Anthony Eden was sacked by Chamberlain, he spent in sleepless anguish of mind. This was the atmosphere of the time, on our side at least – while a Tory government in Britain played Hitler's game, and people like Unity Mitford let him think that the country was rotten from top to bottom and he could get away with anything – as he very nearly did.

I arrived in a beflagged and gay Hamburg, everybody out enjoying themselves beside the Aussen and Innen Alster, the two lakes which were the feature of the city – to be smashed to bits a dozen or so years later in the war which the course of events brought down upon us. Eighteen thousand people died in Hamburg, many of them drowned in the underground shelters when the waters burst in upon them. Politics was deadly serious in the thirties, when these events were incubated. Yet you cannot imagine the frivolity, the good time had by the middle and upper classes, the complacency, the unawareness! (They are paying for it today.) General de Gaulle once said to Attlee that politics were too serious a business to leave to politicians – and de Gaulle is someone whose attitude I largely share (temperament too, for he was much of a Celt), in case anyone finds my line about politics odd.

On my way to imagined happiness I had a brief break in Hamburg, with the *Buch des Lebens* for company everywhere, so that those vanished moments can be brought back, half a century afterwards.

12 August: moment in a restaurant. A young waiter with exceptional freshness of complexion flirts with a girl behind the counter. The

music progresses from extreme sentimentality to a shrill wail. A forlorn young man up in the gallery performs with a perfunctory pianist. The clock moves a hand with a sudden jerk that takes me by surprise; I was on the point of taking a *Kuchen*. The music stops; nobody claps; I take a fresh fruit cake. Outside, a tram-bell rings, a man pauses in the act of raising a glass to his lips.

Dutifully I went on with my impoverished education in pictures with a visit to the Gallery: I record a few, for heaven knows what has survived the tragedy of our time. A series of medieval Hamburg pictures had two of St Thomas Becket: one of the martyrdom, another *Die Verhöhnung* (*The Mocking*), one of the pursuers on horse-back having cut off the Saint's horse's tail, flourishing it in his hand. I observed that Hamburg painters of the seventeenth century, with names like Matthias Scheits, were an inferior offshoot of the Dutch School. Eighteenth century society exposed itself with *Bürgermeisters* and ruffed senators –

like Venice, but oh what a difference! Rooms and rooms of atrocious nineteenth-century painting – with an unexpected oddity; a Herkomer (I thought of his vulgar portrait of Warden Anson at All Souls), *Zither Abend im Atelier*. This must be the picture praised by Huysmans in the Salon of 1879: a moment of recognition, a gathering of men listening, a big window, night outside over the fields.

What a contrast in the French Room! I still remember two superlative pictures: the finest Renoir I have ever seen – woman and girl riding on horse and pony in the Bois de Boulogne, full of motion and contrasted rhythms, greens and greys.

Picasso's absinthe drinker puts all the modern Germans in that room in the shade. The insistent rhythm of the woman's shape doubled into a half-moon, carried on by the round table and the round world of lighter green surrounding her: a submerged, subaqueous world of dream consciousness, eyes shut, figure unaware ... A recognisable Vlaminck, a mountain landscape, blue-greens, bridge and hill crowned with castle, sweeping brushwork his signature-tune.

What an extraordinary, inexplicable thing it is, come to think of it, that among hundreds of painters one should be able to recognise one man's handiwork! Even such a tyro about painting as I, am able to – though when I get back beyond 1500, say, I am somewhat lost. Significant historically, for the whole keynote of the modern age is the release of individuality. So how foolish it is of mere critics to decry the importance of the personal – C. S. Lewis, for instance, calling it 'the personal heresy', with whom the personal bulked so largely, no–one more so.

Here were Sisley landscapes, an early Cézanne of the Seine bank, carts unloading, horses, men, a crane; a series of three Delacroix,

a marvellous one of a tiger, crouching before a python, tawny striped against vivid green jungle. A Manet of Nana at her toilette, watched by gentlemen of the seventies; a Monet of Waterloo Bridge [to be destroyed by my friend Herbert Morrison, against the protests of 'the long-haired gentlemen' as he described them to me]; a brilliant Renoir vase of flowers; and three Courbets, think of it, though not his best.

All the Germans were on pilgrimage to the Hans Thoma, whoever he was, neglecting the Courbets. 'God, what are all those industrious German pictures, miles of them, compared with this one room crammed with works of genius? The date of the superb Renoir is 1873: what did it matter losing the war of 1870–1 when one looks at that?'

A judgment of youthful enthusiasm – for, of course, losing the Franco–German war did matter: it announced the full entry upon the European stage of Bismarck's Germany, set upon the course that was to wreck the twentieth century. I was on my way to meet Adam who became one of his country's victims; my French sympathies were unmistakable, but I was out to learn about Germany from the inside. I learned.

Again, in the Friedrichs-Museum in Berlin, it was the French, Spanish and English rooms that held me. I did not know then that many of the pictures had been scuppered from the disgraceful sale of paintings, as well as furniture, from Blenheim Palace by Winston's uncle, the 8th Duke. When Lord Randolph visited the Gallery he was furious to recognise the pictures and objects from Blenheim, sold by his brother. Again, I don't know how many of these unoffending objects survived the catastrophe the Germans brought down upon themselves – but I noticed a couple of admirable Zoffanys: one of Dr Hanson of Canterbury, an old man with a staff, under a spreading tree; a fine full-length Gainsborough portrait; a Raeburn of a Presbyterian worthy in full gown and bands, candid and clear. An exquisite woodland Watteau – but 'liberty under a charm, the woods of Versailles before the deluge.' I liked best the splendid Zurbarans, a painter who spoke specially to me (as do Tiepolo, Patinir and all the French Impressionists): 'an interior of a monk's cell, with crucifix and brilliantly coloured books – what an exquisite colourist when he lets himself go, out of his usual sombre tones!' What is it like so much about him? I think it is the precision, the firmness and realism of the depiction: *things as they really are,* the beauty of the actual brought into the light of day. Perhaps thus specially an historian's painter, as is Bronzino: both favourites also with my historian friend, McFarlane.

3
Berlin under the
Weimar Republic

Berlin under the free and easy days of the Weimar Republic has
been much written up by my contemporaries. We have all read
about Auden earning his keep shovelling snow in the streets,
buying himself a workman's cap – a significant gesture, to
disguise his unmistakably bourgeois personality (he was sick
into the cap in a cinema: was that perhaps no less significant?).
We have heard all too much about *Mr Norris Changes Trains*,
and now Isherwood is coming back yet again to his old vomit.
Then there was Stephen, then Goronwy, then John Lehmann,
Uncle Tom Cobley and all.

What a lot of attention they have received, directed upon
themselves like a nozzle from a fire-extinguisher! I was there
before them, but have kept silence till now. Yet, looking back
over it, I cannot but think that my German experience, my
insight into what was happening and involvement in what was
coming about, was much more significant than theirs –
entirely owing to my relationship with Adam. I do owe that to
him – that tragic experience in every way, that has never left
my mind (in which I hoarded it up), and still moves me. I owe
all this to his memory.

Arrived in Berlin, 'I am seated in a café, across the street
from the Schloss [now utterly vanished], with flower-beds
and traffic between. The vast town has no historicity as other
capitals have. It does go back to Frederick the Great, but there
is no real continuity beyond Frederick William IV, though
there are earlier buildings.' This added to the Kaiser's
inferiority-complex about London and Grandmother's Windsor; and he could not abide everybody making for Paris (who
wouldn't?), ignoring Berlin – so important and powerful, so
vulgar and nouveau, and so ugly. (All the same it did have a zip
in the air, then). Nothing the Kaiser could do could alter
matters. When Uncle Bertie went annually for his cure to

Homburg or Marienbad, with his exotic entourage, the
English Court was always referred to as '*The* Court'. Intoler-
able! everything ministered to this psychotic peacock's complex, which dangerously reflected the psychosis of the Germans about Britain.

Characteristic of Berlin was the Dom, a hideous Lutheran
cathedral not far from the Schloss, scene of the ministrations of
the Kaiser's favourite Hof-Predikant, a foremost preacher-up
of aggressive German nationalism. The Allerhöchste himself
was not averse to taking his stand in the pulpit to preach the
same gospel. Nothing was beyond his conceit. Consuelo Van-
derbilt, whom I was to meet years later in New York,
describes him in *The Glitter and the Gold* on his visit to
Blenheim, lecturing them all on Marlborough's battles and
how they should have been fought. To think that Harry Elmer
Barnes and other American Revisionists, who did so much to
undermine the authority of the Treaty of Versailles, should
have been taken in by his flattery in exile in Holland!

Adam had free entry to his uncle's flat in the Schloss, from
which the nymphs and Imperial Highnesses had departed; we
went up there in the evenings when his day's work at his law
studies was over. We roamed the corridors and rooms at will. I
was particularly taken by the Kaiser's study, and made a note
of his books, since a man's books give a good index to his
mind. They were half German, half English; part theology,
part history and politics. There was the copy of Winston
Churchill's life of Lord Randolph, which he had presented to
the Kaiser at the Army Manoeuvres of 1909. Here was Bishop
Boyd-Carpenter's *Communion of Prayer* – he was a favourite
with the family – and Matheson's *Studies in the Portrait of
Christ*. *The Creevey Papers*, Greville's *Diary*, *The Correspondence of the Princess de Lieven*, testified to his common interest in
the early nineteenth century history of Britain.

The Future of Greater Britain and *Across Africa* reminded one
of the other side: the jealousy of Britain which possessed him,
in which again he was representative of his people. He could
never forget that he was Queen Victoria's oldest grandson: if
his mother, Vicky, had been the son, instead of Uncle Bertie,
he would have been enthroned at Windsor and Buckingham
Palace. ('Saki', killed in the 1914 war, wrote a brilliant account

in *When William Came* of what things would be like if the Germans won, the *Pétainisme* of Society. It would need a few changes of name, like that of the Victoria Memorial to *Grossmutter Denkmal*, etc.) William detested his mother and what she stood for: representative, responsible government in Germany on the English model. With that, there might have been no war. Vicky herself foresaw the disaster that would overwhelm Germany and the Hohenzollerns from the disastrous course on which they and Bismarck were set. The simple explanation historically is that the German upper classes, and the directors of their policy, held that the only way to maintain their hold on power, against rising social-democracy, was a successful war of conquest. So they made their gamble in August 1914.

I was amused to note – what should please Graham Greene – that Edwardian signature-tune, Rider Haggard's *She*. The Poems of the Princess of Schleswig-Holstein, in princely leather, reminded the young historian of the war against Denmark in 1864, which had announced Prussia's career of aggression; a history of the war of 1866 against Austria carried on the story. Shelf upon shelf of Ranke's volumes, of boring writers like Gustav Freytag, and the German classics looked untouched since placed there.

'What an atmosphere!', I commented. 'Those bookshelves portray the man more than anything else. And the big writing desk made out of the timbers of Nelson's *Victory* – on which the Kaiser signed the order for mobilising, at five in the afternoon of August 1, 1914.' The German action, in spite of all Sir Edward Grey's efforts to keep the peace, started the war. We now know from Fritz Fischer's documentation – what historians of common sense knew all along – that the Germans thought they had a favourable opportunity in July 1914, when they might appear not responsible for launching the war: such a chance might not recur.*

Actually Grey was a man of the utmost scrupulousness of conscience, who thought of the war (rightly) as the lights of civilisation going out, and tormented himself for years with the thought whether there might not have been something more he could have done to avert disaster. Given the German

* See Fritz Fischer, *War of Illusions, German Policies from 1911 to 1914*, and *Germany's Aims in the First World War*.

mentality, and the will to war of their militarist classes in control, there was nothing he could have done – except let them win. And then, to have been traduced, as he was, by aristocratic irresponsibles like Bertrand Russell and his claque of Cambridge pacifists! Leftist as I was, I did not fall for this rubbish after I had seen Germany for myself.*

The public parts of the Schloss were open to tourists, and I recorded the Americans entering upon their European patrimony, as Henry James would have done. The historic core of the huge building went back to the eighteenth century, and there was attractive rococo from the time of Frederick the Great, one round room in particular, green painted panelling, frilled with gold. From these we moved into the late Empress's suite (stupid 'Dona' of the family photographs), into hideous Wilhelmian marble and gilt, 'Better taste,' said the Americans; 'you see, it's later.' One of them to his female, looking at a Sèvres vase: 'Take it home with you.' 'Wish I could; but I shouldn't know what to do with it.' The attendant opened a glass-door to display the *Beleuchtung* – 'Does that lead down into the kitchen?' A more romantic soul thought it a secret staircase. 'How all these attendants regret the old régime, like the charwoman on the staircase of Dublin Castle!' In the Kaiser's private apartments the appalling pictures had been taken down from the walls and stacked behind the doors, waiting for his return. Here he was on display in every picture, silly eagle outspread on glittering helmet, waxed moustaches ferociously upturned, vast-bearded old men bowing reverently before the puppet. No wonder his light head was turned. (He was still alive at Amersfoort, and remained so until his place was taken by a real man of the people – some members of the Imperial family went over to him.) At the writing-desk the telephone wires were cut, as at the Armistice in 1918, the ends still loose. Everything spoke volumes to the attentive historian-to-be.

So did the pictures in the Kaiser Friedrichs-Museum – I had plenty of time on my own while Adam worked. Here was a portrait of Charles v, by Christoph Amberger, an Augsburg painter, 1500–1562, from what was to become my period – the Emperor then a pallid young man of thirty-two, with sensu-

* See *A Cornishman Abroad*, Chapters 2–4

ous red lips that couldn't meet because of the Habsburg jaw. Amberger also painted the cosmographer Sebastian Münster, whom I would encounter years later when researching for *The Expansion of Elizabethan England:* a curious picture, marked feeling for the subject, the face covered with white down. I had fallen for Altdorfer on my first long stay in Germany, part of my education in German painting. I found myself responsive to the early painting – Altdorfer, Michael Pacher, especially Dürer and the younger Holbein, and even the tortured Germanità of Grünewald – but couldn't bear the sentimentality and coarseness of their nineteenth century, the Arnold Böcklins and Lenbachs, the crudity and violence of a Louis Corinth (on whom I was to have indirect light later, through a nephew.) Did he disappear in the maelstrom?

Best of the Altdorfers was a small Crucifixion, with a dramatic coloured sky, dark thundercloud and underwing of bright yellow. Loveliest the Dürers – the Leonardesque woman, with rosy light brown colour on face and breast, shadow on throat; hair dressed close to the head, straight parting in middle, gold chain round neck, line of water, sea or lake, behind. Hieronymus Holzschuher: old man with grey ringlets streaming down forehead, fear and mistrust in the puckered eyes; and Jacob Muffel, another old man, clean-shaven, broad brow under little skull cap. Frederick the Wise of Saxony, whose protection of Luther had such importance in the history of Europe: an extraordinary face, half pedant, half robber; a swarthy type, black beard and glaring dark eyes.

I was educating myself. How to define the distinction between Dürer and Holbein? I found it difficult: both had such astonishing power in the rendering of character. Dürer had more response to pure beauty, from his experience of Italy, fount of the Renaissance sense of beauty; but I did not appreciate the element of ethical uplift in him. No idealism in Holbein: the rendering of things as they really are was enough for him. Here Kaufmann George Giszge was rendered like a medieval Fleming in precision of detail; the glass of flowers, coins in the box, pattern of cloth, the bills and receipts: the feeling was in the clarity itself.

I developed an appreciation of German painting of the Renaissance, none for the School of Fontainebleau contemporaneously. Germany was then at its best, a pattern of city-states, prince-bishoprics and electorates, under the nominal suzerainty of the Holy Roman Empire. Even then, the *furor Teutonicus* broke out in the Lutheran Revolution that destroyed the unity of Catholic Europe, split it in two and let in the Turks up to the walls of Vienna. Hence the Thirty Years War which put Germany back for three centuries, Bismarck said, and made her so fiendishly anxious to catch up in the twentieth century. Once more, the result has been to divide her – and Europe – from top to bottom and let peripheral Russia into the heart of the Continent. Whose fault? – the German incapacity to play their proper part as the keystone of the arch, which they were strategically placed to do.

Europe could live with a federal Germany that was 'a tesselated pavement'. Those were the circumstances also that were most propitious to it culturally: the smaller states where flourished the Bachs, Haydns, Mozarts, a Heinrich Schütz, Beethoven, Schubert; or Goethe, Schiller, Hölderlin, a Lessing or Winckelmann. The concentration of Germany from the 1860s onwards on military and political power, the obsession with *Macht* and *Macht-politik*, aggression and expansion, has been as sterilising as it has been disastrous. Not least to Germany, now split in two, and likely to remain so, since experience has shown that nobody else in Europe can live safely with a united Germany. It need never have been necessary if they had known how to play their part properly or behave decently.

Along Unter den Linden was the baroque Zeughaus, the Armoury, one of the better buildings of ugly Berlin (so much appreciated by Wystan and Company: they responded, in one way and another, to its physical charms). Here were mementoes of Germany's wars – the prolonged resistance of Vienna and the south-eastern Mark against the Turks – which had inspired Rilke. A splendid Turkish tent came from the siege of Vienna in 1683: rose-red interior with patterns in green and blue; above, a bronze Crescent, dreaded symbol. Decorated saddles had come from Turkey and Egypt, presents from Mehemet Ali; the huge key of the city of Adrianople given by Nicholas after the siege of 1829. Frederick the Great appeared on 'Condé', the horse he rode in his last years – so like him, with his cult of everything French, to name his horse from *le grand Condé*. For all his unprincipled rape of Silesia, setting the course for successful German aggression, one finds Frederick among the more sympathetic of German figures. *

For all my dislike of everything modern Germany stood for and my increasing realisation of the danger she was to civilisation – unlike the Leftist claque in Britain who had a cult of Germany (but Spender and Lehmann were half-German, Crossman a quarter-German, Brailsford dominated by a German wife; Kingsley Martin had no such excuse: he was just an ass, braying away in the *New Statesman*) – I admired the sculptor Kolbe or a painter like Franz Marc. I was much struck by Kolbe's *Tänzerin*, of 1912, 'the ecstasy and languor of its rhythm, hands drooping, feet instinct with sound, poised at the beginning of movement. Someone passing treads on a loose board and gives a slight tremor to the figure – as if the frail boundary between the poise of art and the motion of existence had been over-stepped, the dancer waking into life.' I was perpetually on the *qui vive* for such moments, much influenced by Virginia Woolf as a writer; still more by the gospel of art as the redemption of life – Proust, Joyce, Bridges – which has remained my constant creed. I regard it as man's redemption from the mud.

All the same, never more so than when in Germany, it was France that spoke to me. 'The French rooms in this gloomy palace [the Museum] are superb. Three Cézannes, an exquisite landscape of 1880, a narrow high building like a mill, a pond, a tree, much greenery and many sandy paths.' Two still-lifes: the familiar black bottles, fruit and cups with thick blue patterns, a white cloth with folds at corner. I recognised the inspiration of a picture by Isobel Codrington I had recently seen at home. I was possessed by the aim to render in words what I saw in pictures, as well as in architecture or landscape, or what I heard – even the impossibility of rendering music in words. Perhaps I had been influenced, in my self-education, by Rimbaud's aim of transposing experience, transmuting the bounds; it was still more the desire, from whatever it came, to arrest the moment. That too has remained with me all my life: a constant amid all the flux of experience. A Degas sculpture of

* See my *Homosexuals in History*, Chapter 6.

a dancer certainly gave me a transposition of feeling: it almost made me physically sick. The surface was coruscated as if lacerated by disease, and the hair arranged with no back to the head, a hole where the back of the head should be! I could not get the image out of my mind for days, and have never forgotten it.

To compensate there was a brilliant picture of women in conversation, soft browns and blues, a sharp perspective of heads over a patterned table cloth. A Gauguin of 1889 showed a farmyard by a stream, a woman sitting against the bridge, pigs in foreground, rounded forms of trees bright-green-dark, and the farm chimneys – all a swirl of colour. Renoir's *In Summer 1870* – what a date to show up here – portrayed

a luscious brunette, black hair falling over naked shoulders, untidy bodice, stripey skirt, all in green shade of vividly coloured leaves. A Renoir of fourteen years later displayed a more complex subject, *The Children's Afternoon in Vargemont*: a table before a window, nurse-girl knitting with one little girl, doll on knees. An older girl on an Empire sofa has a blue check dress spread out concertina-wise. Children in blue, nurse-girl in print frock with pink dots; heavy patterned table-cloth, with bowl of red flowers before window, afternoon shadows on polished parquet.

Oh, that vanished summer afternoon of 1870, before the Prussian blitz burst on France!

This was accompanied by a big Manet, *In the Winter Garden, 1879* – after France's bitter experience, which ushered in the modern era, Commune and all. 'Does Huysmans comment on it?' Evidently I had been reading him, as Baudelaire earlier and Gautier's art-criticism.

Two figures dramatically posed: the woman in a corner of a garden seat, the man virilely bearded leaning over to her, lust in half-closed eyes. She appears undecided and passive, parasol defensively across knees, tight-fitting dress invitingly spread. [Manet paid the price for his fixation on women.] The décor – exotic garden plants, full of impulsive, though not sinister, life.

Four Monets included the *Place St Germain l'Auxerrois, 1866*, which specially spoke to me: a plain cloudless sky, giving the effect of a hot thundery day (the Second Empire advancing to its doom). A river-scene at Verneuil: those poplars familiar among all the Impressionists, almost a signature-tune, an island, puffs of white cloud and shadows in the water: a visual equivalent of

Le vierge, le vivace, et le bel aujourd'hui.

Here I was, lost in my dream of France in the 60s, 70s and 80s of last century, in the midst of the overpowering Kaiser Friedrichs-Museum. I record these pictures because I don't know if they survived the holocaust of our time. Many more works I noted for a rainy day: Rodin sculptures, Sisleys, Pissaros, Harpignys. I was to own an Harpigny later, a characteristic *Crépuscule*, orange-tawny sunset, sepia wash, violet blob of a figure. A Renoir of 1881 was uncharacteristic: a chestnut tree in flower above the curve of a river, an explosion of brilliant colour. I much preferred early Renoir to later, those acres of rosy flesh upon blowsy floosies leaning forward out of the picture; and early Monet as against the flux and imprecision of the façade of Rouen cathedral or enormous expanse of *nymphéas*. Manet's house at Reuil appeared, looking on the garden in summer: a *tour-de-force*, white lilacs in a vase, brilliant greens and blues relieving the whites.

I was a good deal alone – Adam was so occupied with work (and was there a girl around the corner?) – not that I minded that. He had thoughtfully provided me with an alternative, thinking I might be lonely: a large, hulking fellow. Was he called Hans Fink? I used to call him Hans Sachs, though I had little use for him, Adam so occupied my mind. Hans was a good fellow, a fellow-proletarian, a Communist or near-Communist. Was he the 'labour poet' Adam had written to me about? He kept a friendly eye on me, though I was not encouraging. I wonder what happened to him? killed by the Nazis, like Adam, I suspect, or lost in the war they let loose all over again.

Alone: the sensation of being first to take a seat in a large theatre – so different from when alive with the bustle of people – now like a church, only more vast and depressing. Hundreds of rows of red plush, expectant of the crowd and only one man to the feast. Now is the chance to remember what Adam told me at Potsdam, the big green dome far off in the train – later at night on the Paraden-platz, in front of the Stadt Palais. The house on the opposite side of the square was where he was born. In the mornings his mother used to close the windows, on account of the dust from the troops drilling.

Waiting there, arm in arm, we listened to the hour chime from the church-tower and play one of the old Lutheran hymn tunes. When he was there last with his mother she cried at hearing the familiar chimes out of the past. For all her memories, and for her brother who had written from the Front that it would be heaven enough if only he could hear the Potsdam chimes again. He never did, for he never came back.

Here was one example of the price Germany was prepared to pay – and inflict on others – for her aim to dominate Europe.

'We went through Sans Souci together – the place echoing Frederick and Voltaire at every step – through the suite of apartments Frederick decorated for his gilded captive,' and the room in which the hero-king (Voltaire's 'amiable whore') died. Surely Carlyle must have known? Two clever, malicious monkeys. But what taste! What exquisite rococo interiors – French, of course.

'We tailed along at the end of the crowd, to have the rooms as much as possible to ourselves. Suddenly, left alone in one room before passing on, we heard a clock strike with silvery reminiscent chime, as if keeping watch from the years when the palace was lived in, and the echoing footsteps were not those of mere sightseers. At the end we stole back over the apartments alone, savouring their desertedness, though having to hurry for fear we might be locked in with Frederick and Voltaire's ghosts.

Now the theatre is filling, and all the hum of chatter and tuning up is in full swing.

I had been waiting for Adam: we were to hear Strauss's *Die Fledermaus*. I noted Adam's fear – fear, mistrust again – that 'he may come into my room and find it empty and I am gone.'

Notes for *Politics and the Younger Generation* follow. Where my contemporaries, like Ralph Fox, and my juniors, like Christopher Hill, were ready to swallow Communism whole, I was wrestling with it, trying to work out what I really thought, and not commit myself a millimetre beyond what was true. Both Ralph Fox and Christopher gave themselves – and a bitter price they paid for it. I spotted an element of the feminine in their attitude intellectually, and once much offended Christopher by diagnosing it for him. They wanted to find a body of thought they could subscribe to, without thinking things out for themselves. Just like those clever asses, Ronnie Knox or Evelyn Waugh, who found the answer in the Catholic Church. In this respect I was at bottom a Protestant, determined to take nothing on trust from anybody.

Ralph Fox admitted as much to me, when he wished that, instead of taking Modern Languages at Oxford, he had done the History School: it would have given him a firmer intellectual equipment, a foundation for thinking for himself about Marxism, etc. I was deeply influenced by Marxism, became quite well read in it and collected a small library of Marxist books, rather rare now, since a number of their authors were bumped off by the Comrades. Ralph's was rather a feminine mind, in keeping with his literary sensibility.

My relationship with him was one long wrangle. He had swallowed the crazy Communist line of attacking Social Democracy as the enemy – think of the criminal idiocy of it! In place of thinking, he adhered to the Communist slogans at the time – Social Democrats were Social Fascists, Social Democracy was Social Fascism. In the Berlin tram strike of 1931 the Communists lined up with the Nazis to defeat the Social Democratic workers. Can one imagine anything more lunatic? I used to shout at Ralph – can't you see that it won't be the Communists who will win? It will be the Fascists, the Nazis. As of course, it was.

I was only at the beginning in politics, but at heart I was already on the road to despair – with one's own side such idiots, and our enemies having all the political sense, the sense of power, no illusions. When these issues came to open war in Spain – the Spanish Civil War, the announcement of the greater conflict to come – the Communist Party sent Ralph Fox to Spain to become a martyr, deliberately. He did not want to go. He wrote me a letter, which I have kept among my archives, asking me to find him a job in Oxford. I tried his own college, Magdalen – in vain; I tried Warden Adams at All Souls – no response. Ralph went to Spain, and was shot on the Cordoba Front, by Nazi aircraft.

Well, people must pay the price for their follies. That I am telling the truth of the matter no one will doubt who knows the inner story of the Spanish Civil War, and how the

71

Communists murdered their own comrades. Or as they did on a more monumental scale in the purges in Soviet Russia in the thirties. Though both Ralph and Christopher had nice natures, it was impossible to respect them intellectually. *Human beings are what they are*: neither Jonathan Swift nor I could say worse of them than that.

I was not engaged in saving my soul by giving myself to a faith – I suppose Ralph Fox had a Nonconformist background like Christopher – I was trying to think things out. Wrestling with this, in these ominous circumstances, the clouds constantly lowering; the people who believed in the best causes riddled with ineffectiveness and liberal illusions, the malign forces of Fascism and the connivers with Fascism all too effective; ourselves wasting energy in constant disputes, misled by the utter irresponsibility of our own intellectual organs like the *New Statesman*. When what the Labour Movement needed above all was responsible intellectual leadership – it got Harold Laski and John Strachey and the Left Book Club, which circulated its claptrap in thousands. Well, it was all not very good for a recurrent duodenal ulcer.

Here was the kind of thing that occupied my mind in Berlin, instead of having a good time with 'Mr Norris' or the boys.

'The strength of Nationalism is far stronger than socialist theory recognises, stronger even than before the War, increased from the hatred aroused. It has this much justification, that the social life of a nation is a sufficient world in itself, which one doesn't need to go outside.' I should have made the qualification, 'which ordinary people don't need to go outside.' The restriction does not apply to the educated, let alone the elect. Even then, I made as I always have done the proper difference – a chasm in understanding, sensibility, intellect – between ordinary people and the elect. I note that at the end of his life Auden arrived at the same point – it took him a long time to get there: I had known what the people were from the start.

'What is Socialism to do in these circumstances?' i.e. the overwhelming strength and appeal of Nationalism – which was annexed and exploited by the upper classes. At the time, all I could think of was to support the League of Nations as an arbiter of national differences, and indeed the hopes placed in the League should not be disconsidered now, because they were destroyed by the rise of the Fascist thugs, and the connivance of the upper classes in the western 'democracies' at the time. And we hoped that the internationalism of the Socialist outlook – of Marx, Jaurès, Lenin – offered a better hope.

Here, I think now, socialists of the thirties were caught in a dilemma. As a matter of practical politics, why should we have let the Tories have all the good tunes? In those days patriotism was an effective appeal (it still has its validity, rightly understood). The Tories exploited it for all its worth – the Union Jack, the monarchy, the Empire: they were all *their* assets. No wonder they were in a perpetual majority. But why were we so ineffective as to let them? Why not stake a claim for ourselves? In fact, we were the *people* of Britain: we had as much right as anyone to put ourselves forward as patriots, and not allow this strong psychological force to go by default.

But they *did* – fatuous ineffectives as they were. The Jack Jones of the day – there always seem to be Jack Joneses for the Labour Movement to carry round its neck – called it 'Waving the Union Jack before the Union Jackasses.' They should have claimed it for themselves, instead of allowing the Tories to win every trick. (Their ineffectiveness, the congenital ineffectiveness of the liberal-minded, constantly gnawed at my guts.) A really great Labour man, Ernest Bevin, was a patriot. Similarly with regard to the British Empire. Though a Labour man, I was all in favour of the Empire. Even a Radical pacifist like John Stuart Mill had admitted that, in a world convulsed by wars, within the *Pax Britannica* this much of it enjoyed peace. The empire-builders at All Souls were strong in their belief in *trusteeship on behalf of native races*. They had every reason to be proud of the achievement of such men as Lugard – who used to visit us when he came home – in Nigeria. When the British withdrew, the blacks killed each other in hundreds of thousands. As in India. Can anyone suppose that the people of Uganda are better off under the thuggery of an Amin? As against Harold Laski and Company, I was a believer in the trusteeship idea of the British Empire as a force for good, in a world where there was all too much bad.

The book that occupied my mind was not to be taken up by the Left Book Club – nothing of mine was. And when I wrote a little tract of some significance, *Keynes and the Labour Movement*, Victor Gollancz was foolish enough to turn it down. This essay had an urgent argument: that the implications of Keynes's economics brought him close to the Labour Movement; if he wanted to make them effective he should put himself into relation with the mass-movement that could give him fulcrum and leverage. This was a Marxist line (cf. Lenin: 'Politics begin with the masses'). Why wouldn't Keynes see it? I kept on urging this on him throughout the thirties – see the essays collected in *The End of an Epoch*. I believe it was intellectual snobbery, more than anything, on Keynes's part. He was snooty about Marxism; he thought he knew better – which, in pure economics, he did. But this wasn't a purely economic point; as with Marx himself, it was politico-economic, and Keynes's Liberalism obfuscated its significance. He went on being a Liberal, when there wasn't any point in it. He should have joined his intellectual powers to the mass-movement of Labour: it would have increased the effectiveness of both in the discouraging circumstances of the thirties – and Bevin would have welcomed him. Why could not this cleverest of men see the point? One despaired. (De Gaulle: *'Pour agir, il faut espérer.'* I gave up hope. With 1939 the future had to be fought for in the lives of millions. It need not have been, if they had had any sense.

Gollancz turned down my book for the claptrap of the Left Book Club. I at once went to Macmillan's, Keynes's own publishers; Harold Macmillan, being a Tory, was not such a fool: it was the beginning of my long association with the firm, profitable to us both. To explain his motive for not taking my book, i.e. that it was not in keeping with his Leftist Socialism, Victor Gollancz asked me to lunch at the Savoy, where I had never been. I did not much approve. He invited me down to his house for a weekend, with the allurement of a swimming pool. I thought all this inappropriate for a Left Socialist. I had no intention of going; my own tastes were simple, and I was not very sociable.

I met him only once again. We were on the deck of the *Queen Mary* (now laid up, I believe, as a fun-fair on Long Beach), saying farewell to New York. I was no longer an active Labour man, but a successful author. Gollancz was very friendly, and pressed me to call on him in his private suite: he was, of course, travelling First Class and I, as usual, Second Class. Once more I registered the fact, and laughed to myself. Needless to say, I did not call. I disapproved of his ethical campaign after the unspeakable German extermination of the Jews, falling over backwards to forgive the unforgivable. He was a good sort, though he need not have striven so officiously to earn the description of him by one of the (female) asses in his firm as 'that Jesus Christ-like man, Victor Gollancz.'

A further note for my politics book inquired:

whether the problems of history and historical concepts, sociology and economics, were not the most real and pressing, the purely metaphysical no longer of interest. It is the laws of social development, the inner relations and movements of society that engage our minds. Look at the popularity of Spengler and Keyserling [all the rage then], or even Tawney; and the constant growth of argument around the M.C.H. [as we fondly termed the materialist conception of history], Marxism and Croce – all witnessing a shift of theoretical interest. Even when the old metaphysical problems are raised, one is conscious of their unreality; they arouse no interest or excitement. The intellectual battleground seems more and more to revolve around a. history, b. the new physics.

Naturally, there was a reaction here during the second war, with so much suffering of mind and body, in favour of C. S. Lewis's nonsense-problems of pain, and similar concerns – though all that has now had its day. And the Wittgenstein boom? I should have thought that the sainted Wittgenstein had emptied metaphysics of significance. I respected more his musical and engineering gifts, his facility with his hands, as against Bertrand Russell's uselessness, who could hardly make himself a cup of tea, and had no music in his soul. I noted, sceptically,

the tendency in one's mind to give the character of necessity, almost of predestination, to what one knows – if one stands apart – to be fortuitous. Meeting someone one likes, perhaps falling in love, and afterwards wondering how life can have been without that experience, one tends to conclude it was fateful. [Or, as simple folk say, it was 'meant'.] Again, if something goes wrong with one's plans and one is disappointed, then later it comes right, possibly better *because* of the change and the disappointment, one thinks that all has been arranged for the best, especially that it is *arranged*. But one knows in one's heart that it is not so: it was only for consolation in loneliness of mind that one allowed oneself to think so, or that the chances that come our way belong to any scheme of things outside ourselves.

Adam's week's work over we went off for several days into Saxony and 'Saxon Switzerland', the Erz Gebirge. 'First night in Dresden – the most beautiful of German towns, a German Florence, smashed to pieces by Anglo-American bombing during the war.' (Well, they asked for it, didn't they?) 'My room high up in the roof overlooking the Hof; Adam's at the back looks towards a high church tower' – one of those elegant baroque spires one sees in Canaletto's paintings of the city.

My room is charming in half-darkness, lit only by a paper-shaded lamp. Pleasant print curtains with a frill, a window-box and two bold red flowers staring at the moon – one might be inside a picture. But I see them though their backs are turned to me, red, dark-red, like summer darkness. The moon, high and full, lights up the low buildings along the street of the Prinzen-Palais, the forlorn shuttered stables, the black masses of trees in the Garten. The occasional footsteps of passers-by rattling on the *pavé* bring back the Boule d'Or at Bourges, provincial quiet after the incessant noise of Berlin.

In the Gallery I made for Holbein's splendid portrait of the Sieur de Morette: an expansive Henry VIII type, grizzled beard, fur coat, black sleeves slashed with white, background of puffed green silk; a hard type, with cruel expression. A clear contrast with Dürer's Bernard van Orley: a young man in light brown flesh-tones, high cheek-bones, wide placid eyes: painted with sympathy and delicacy compared with Holbein. The contrast was becoming clearer to me. Holbein's portrait of Sir Thomas Godsalve and his son, 1528, made for a double rhythm and cross patterns. The family likeness was caught: rough English types, bony noses; the son's submissive yokel appearance, unintelligent, not without charm. Father with hat on long grey hair, son's auburn and without hat, looking out of the picture with expression of filial deference. Who were they, the Godsalves? Officials of Henry VIII's Court, of course: sensible of them to have had their portraits painted by the first painter in the country.

When the Second German War was over, I wished as some

reparation for the irremediable cultural damage the Germans had done to collect from them the Holbeins of Henry's Court – the Jane Seymour from Vienna, for instance – and bring them together once more in London where they were painted and belonged. The English, as usual, were too high-minded and conventional to think in such terms.

The same might have applied to Van Dyck's charming portrait of Charles I's children: the eldest boy in saffron satin, two others in silcer, the youngest holding his brother by hand and arm; two King Charles spaniels completed the group on either side. A portrait of Henrietta Maria showed her in white satin against an orange-tawny background; right hand holding some roses in the cup of the hand, her left twitching a fold of dress. There was Lely's copy of Van Dyck's portrait of Charles, in half-profile at a table with high crowned hat on it. All in black satin, except for lace and deep pointed collar; star on left shoulder, blue ribbon on neck: the usual expression of distant inhuman dignity. Another English picture one could have done with at home was a Raeburn of Lucius O'Byrne, Bishop of Meath; the head reminded me of Archbishop Lang at All Souls, dark, deepset eyes, shrewd face full of character: head set against a dark red chair contrasting with clerical black.

Incomparable riches graced the Dresden gallery, silted up from the art-loving Saxon kings – what a pity Saxony could not have absorbed Prussia, instead of Prussia swallowing half Saxony! Here were Vermeers, Mantegnas, Botticellis, besides the too celebrated Raphael *Madonna* I did not fall for: stale with being too much looked at. Three Velasquez portraits, Rembrandts, Francias, a Zurbaran of a Papal Election by St Bonaventura, two Ferdinand Bols, to remind me of Chequers and Ramsay MacDonald; a Guardi of a Papal blessing in the Piazza at Venice to carry in my head with a favourite in the Ashmolean. A Guercino of St Francis specially appealed to me: thundery ragged blue clouds, like Magnasco, St Francis in a corner, a violin being played to him, some angel from the clouds.

My own personal taste was forming, the slow way, laboriously, as with so much in my life – where everything came to others without (or with) asking, fell into their laps, like all the fruits and fun that fell into Cyril Connolly's, or Maurice Bowra's, or John Betjeman's. The painting that I *liked* most, that appealed to me naturally, was not the grandest, either in the high Renaissance – Raphael, Titian – or Baroque Rubens or Rembrandt, but the rococo painters of the later seventeenth and eighteenth centuries: Guercino, Guido Reni, Tiepolo, Magnasco, Piazzetta and such. Thus my favourite galleries were the Dublin National Gallery, the Ashmolean at Oxford, the Walters at Baltimore and the Wadsworth at Hartford, Connecticut. Second, however, to the French Impressionists whom I venerate in the Chicago Art Institute and elsewhere.

On the way out from Dresden to Bastei by bus – Adam's long arm extended along the back of my seat – we passed a villa with several wings and green shutters where Weber composed the *Freischütz*. We were going through country fought over by Frederick the Great in the Seven Years War; then, over a distant range of hills, whence Napoleon conducted the Dresden part of the 1813 Campaign. 'I think of a circle of camp-fires on the horizon, and the trails of the armies across this much fought-over part of central Europe.'

I had been with Adam to see Strauss's *Aegyptsche Helena*: 'thinking of him, and suddenly realising that he knows more about life than I, and the hopelessness of it'. We arrived at Bastei, at 'the enormous Gasthof on top of the limestone hills, with a perpendicular drop of 300 or 400 feet to the Elbe. All the good Germans were drinking their beer out on the high terrace, drunk with the altitude. The walks and steep places had been made straight, regulated and brought into bourgeois order. Oh for Germany of the romantic years, of Schiller and Hölderlin, Schubert and Weber!'

What did we talk about so much when we were alone together? Adam was fundamentally political; he was much interested by my political ideas and very encouraging about my politics book. I was ambivalent, as much interested in literature as in politics. I don't think Rilke meant as much to him.

A good deal of Rilke's poetry is the versification of such experiences as I have collected in this Note-Book. His attitude to passing experience, mainly visual, his commentary on impressions has much in common with mine. As far as poetry is concerned, it may become of no more value than a verse-diary à la Ruskin; only occasionally the experience may have uniqueness and so value as art.

For my December article which Eliot was pressing me to write for *The Criterion*, I read Lenin's *The State and Revolution* – intolerably dogmatic work that it is.

Criticise the Communist contrast between the deterministic present and the Communist concept of freedom [1977!] as too categorical and quite unhistorical. The process of extending freedom is continuous. I do not assert that it is regular – the Fabian 'inevitability of gradualness'; but the process makes headway under capitalism – as well it may lose ground under Communism. The contrast comes from too rigorous adherence to the dialectic; it obscures the truth.

This is perceptive enough, years after, of how things were and would turn out – when luminaries like Gide were seeing, if only briefly, Soviet Russia as the New Jerusalem, the old Webbs were taken in, or an intellectual ass like Sartre could see the concentration-camp of Stalin's Russia as the exemplification of human freedom! One need pay no attention to a buffoon like the Red Dean of Canterbury, who preached the same gospel to thousands through the medium of the Left Book Club. How sane Ernest Bevin was, confronted with this intellectual rubbish! It may be seen that thinking things out for myself provided a sound defence-mechanism against nonsense. Only today do I learn that bright young Oxford men of the next generation – after I had had enough – Tony Crosland and Healey both fell for this Communist nonsense. No wonder they hadn't much use for me. Healey I never knew (I suppose genetically Irish), Crosland came now and again to see me; I found him pretty cool: now I know why.

On the hillside at Bastei I slightly sprained my ankle. Adam sat on the railings protecting us from the immense drop to the limestone rocks below, dangling long legs over the precipice. I could not bear to see it, though I admired his coolness. He had no physical fear at all. All sorts of thoughts passed through my mind. Germans have plenty of physical courage, little enough moral. Adam was to prove that he had moral courage too – more of both than I. But how paradoxical that someone of such extreme nervous sensibility should have no nerves at a 300 or 400 ft drop! All my English friends would have quailed, some with no head for heights at all; it meant nothing to Adam, this sense was left out of his composition. I made him draw back. I have sometimes wondered whether there wasn't something symbolic about the episode.

He certainly walked along the edge of a precipice by taking part almost openly – how incompetent they were! – in the Generals' Plot against Hitler in 1944, while serving in the German Foreign Office. When Hitler came to power in 1933 I knew that all our hopes were ended. *He* was no liberal ineffective; he knew all about power, and would hold on to it to the very end. I warned Adam that all our hopes were over, and in Pitt's words, after Austerlitz: 'Roll up the map of Europe!' Wait for a better day – after all, there was the Frenchman who, asked what he had done during the French Revolution, answered: 'I survived.'

I suggested to Adam that he give himself up for ten years to writing a companion volume to a masterpiece of German historical writing, Burckhardt's *Civilisation of the Renaissance in Italy*. What a wonderful subject it would be to write about the culture of the German cities at their best: Augsburg, Nuremberg, Cologne, the Rhineland; Dürer, Holbein, Erasmus; the geographers and scientists, Sebastian Münster, Mercator, and the cultural extension into the Netherlands and England, the circle of Erasmus' friends, More, Colet, Linacre. I should have liked to tackle the subject myself. Adam refused: he said he could not do it. And indeed history and literature were not his subjects. Politics became the breath of life to him, his gifts (like Lionel Curtis) those of a contacts-man. This led him into the twilight world of the foreign service under Hitler, conspiracy, and the drop from the butcher's hook in Plötzensee prison.

Perhaps it was inevitable – it is too terrible to think of – given his nature and upbringing, and given the hopeless incompetence of all and every opposition to Hitler, military or civilian; aristocratic, middle class or working class; conservative or liberal, Catholic or Communist. Communists died in hundreds at Hitler's hands; why didn't one of the idiots, who was going to lose his life anyway, get him? It would have saved the lives of millions; for Nazism stood or fell, lived and died, with Hitler. *He* knew well how to deal with every kind of opponent: what a man he was! I much admired his sense of power, a man of the people: no ineffective, lily-livered liberal, the worst enemy of their own good causes.

This is the cleft stick we were caught in in the thirties. I diagnosed it again and again: the total ineffectiveness of the people who believed in the best causes, selling the pass to the malign forces who were all too effective in prosecuting the worst. Why couldn't they see it? When Munich approached, it was the *New Statesman* – along with *The Times* – that sold the pass by advocating the break-up of Czechoslovakia! The suggestion was planted on the *New Statesman*, and the stooges fell for it.

This was the path we were to tread step by step all through the thirties. Hitler used to say that he walked 'with the certainty of a somnambulist.' Those of us who lived closely to all this in the thirties can never be the same, it made such an indelible impression on our minds. I still dream of Hitler, and I was interested to learn at All Souls that Rohan Butler does, editor of our Foreign Office documents, who knows all about it from the inside. In my dream Hitler is still alive and there, in power. He hasn't won his war, but there has been a compromise peace, and I realise that this is terribly dangerous: we may have the whole issue to fight over again.

Strangely enough, this is much what Adam's position came to, as a front-man in trying to make peace with the Allies. He was a patriotic German; a compromise peace would have left Germany – a 'respectable' Germany, without Hitler – in a position to dominate Europe. So the offer put forward by Adam and his group, the Generals and other good Germans, was not one to be accepted: it would have been fatal. Christopher Sykes, in his biography of Adam, does not have the political judgment to appreciate that.

The way things were to go pulled us apart long before this fatal terminus was reached. It was just as well that my love for him had a contingent reserve about it. 'Coming back in the bus from Bastei to Dresden, I could watch the changing expression of his face reflected in the glass-pane, as we went through the dark forest, the queer effect of the trees in quick motion reflected upon this beloved head.' One day from Dresden we went out to Moritzburg: 'a hunting Schloss among the lakes, full of duck and waterhens. A square building, tall with red roofs, turrets at the corners. Pine forests – and Swift, Stella and Vanessa under the trees. Later: reassured about Adam's greater experience of life.'

Back in Berlin, I was 'on my way to the Tiergarten, to read Shelley's letters on a bench under the trees; the day so full of sun and breeze that even the Wittenberg Platz looks beautiful. A large expanse of stone with a fringe of trees, but the sky is bright blue and merry with white clouds, even the leaves falling do not make the day autumnal. The surfaces of the new houses gleam and glitter, balconies wide open to catch the sun.' Shelley was describing the English cemetery at Rome, with no intimation of the Fate leading him and Keats to lie there: 'one might, if one were to die, desire the sleep they seem to sleep.' He considers politics superior to poetry – as Byron did, who desiderated political activity more than the fame of being a poet. I noted Shelley's unexpected admiration for reactionary Coleridge: Shelley regarded his *Cenci* 'not inferior to any modern play, with the exception of *Remorse*.' No one but Coleridge was fit to translate Goethe into English. He also thought that 'Hope is a solemn duty, which we owe alike to ourselves and to the world.' Oddly enough, this is a Christian view. The events of the thirties killed all hope in me; I merely survived.

Adam told me how he had gone down to see his old English nurse in a Kent village, to which she had retired. He also missed the train and, arriving late, couldn't find the house in the long village street. Two hours late (couldn't he have asked where she lived?) he saw her waiting at her gate, a little woman, oldish now. She had kept his dinner warm for him, kissed him, and everything was as when he was a child and she in charge of him. He recalled everything about her: she could never speak German, yet got her way very well. She took command of the situation one day when Adam was taken into the Ministry of Education, where his father was Minister, and the boy got his large head caught between the balusters. No-one knew what to do: she ordered one of the balusters to be sawn off.

She had saved money in the years with the family, and invested it, on their advice, in German funds. All was lost in the inflation. She could never quite grasp what had happened, but thought that the money must still be somewhere. It was hers: she had saved it, it couldn't have been stolen. So the family thought of taking her back for her last years, to look after her child, Adam, now a grown man. She was making him socks, as usual, for his birthday: would he like them plain or coloured? Poor old soul, she could have had no conception that the inflation had been largely gerrymandered by the German industrialists and financiers, bent on defaulting on reparations. The innocence of Keynes, and the Cambridge liberals!

We were back in Berlin, for our last picnic supper in the Schloss, having bought our things in the stores and prepared it.

Adam was so exhausted, poor child, that he couldn't eat anything. He lay on the sofa while we talked in the darkness. The life of ordinary humans pursued its way in the next room. The airman occupying it was dolling himself up excitedly to entertain his woman: a small, sanguine man full of nervous energy, and more so tonight. From the next room we heard occasional chat, then whispers, then all fell quiet on that front. We left.

I find notes for a night-sonnet. Going through the night with the thought of Adam, 'each time waking up into the empty night, realising that the thought of him had been in my sleeping mind. Outside rain has fallen, lights gleam under windy trees; over all, the old stars and the white soldered moon. So the heavens go round wheeling like a ship into the day and the awakening of the sun.' Another note was for a poem, 'The Death Mask', macabre, considering what was to happen: was it an omen? 'Tie up the dropped chin and close the loosened mouth, once beautiful and quick.' One poem I did complete –

> I fell asleep and dreaming of your lips
> Upon my lips...

though in all the years we never once kissed. I did summon up courage to print that poem when, after the decade of agony resolved itself in the war, I at last committed myself to publishing *Poems of a Decade*.

Our stay together at an end I devoted myself to storing up every scrap of those hours, unparalleled in my experience, whatever they had been in his. (Friends told me after the war that our relationship made an indelible impression upon him, among all those others.) 'These evidences I'll shore up against

the inevitable ruin that Time will bring upon us and our love.'
And so it was.

In the train at the Friedrich-strasse Bahnhof was a photo-
graph to accompany me of Sans Souci, where we had been
together in the quiet of that summer evening. Then,

in the train drawing near to Oxford, I fell asleep, and heavy raindrops
came beating on my face in my dream. How expressive of sorrow
this was – like some vain consolation offered from the external world
to assuage a dumb, half-conscious grief. Back in Oxford, I read
Hölderlin, hearing in it all Adam's voice. I know now what it ought
to be like to be loved: one should feel enfolded in the warm strength
of another's feeling. One should feel more confident about one's life,
it should mean strength and reliance.

4
Labour Candidate

Homeward bound in the train, I was put off by *l'odor di femina* in the crowded summer compartment (I should travel first class in a non-smoker to myself, but only bureaucrats and Trade-Union bosses can do that nowadays). The horny-handed son of toil has a note *à la* Joyce: 'a smell exudes from their twisted hair and their bodies, under their arms and from their bodices: sweat, rigor vitae, lactescence, the torrid essences, the languescence of woman. Women should always wear perfume.' Simone de Beauvoir has a riposte to a similar reaction of Montherlant's – a favourite writer, with whom I see very much eye to eye: neither of us in sympathy with the demotic world round us. And I was on my way to becoming a Labour candidate!

'Coming into Cornwall: mists upon valley woods, green of hills, the milky opal of the sky. The high ridge carrying the road from Lostwithiel to St Blazey with telephone posts, like spikes along the back of some prehistoric monster sprawling over the valley.' Home: 'the huddled houses down the hillside, dark blobs like a flock of sheep penned in for the night. Silence, and the flitting of domestic lights behind closed windows.' Faithfully I went up to the pilgrimage spot of my boyhood, where I had spent so many ecstatic evenings reading and dreaming: Carn Grey. That I was, paradoxically, not out of touch with my own people and had no difficulty in making contact, may be seen from the scraps of conversation I had with them.

Mrs Brenton, very deaf, comes along the white road in her clean afternoon apron, carrying a jug of milk and wearing her best smile.

'Hullo! Where've you been to? Haven't seen 'ee for a long time!'

'Been away. Just come back from Germany – Berlin, you know where that is?'

'Yes, tha's where the Keyser's to. Did'ee see'n?'

'No. Gone away now.'

'Aw. Where do 'ee keep yourself? Be 'ee to a school or a college?'

'Yes: college – in the university.'

'What do 'ee learn? Shorthand?'

'No.'

Mrs B., disappointed: 'What then?'

'All sorts of things.'

'Well, you ben't married yet?'

'No. Too young.'

'How long since you've been wearin' glasses?'

'Long time – years.'

'But you're gettin' grey.'

'Yes, getting old.'

Mrs B., launching out with the news: 'You know Fred Bartlett over, 'ee that lived just under the Stack – well, 'ee's gone dead. Died last Sunday in town, taken there sudden. 'Twas his heart. (Fixing me as I look vague.) *You d'knaw Fred Bartlett?* He married Miss —— down 'ere to Trethurgy – whatever was she called – I knaw 'er name as well as I knaw yours. A brother-in-law of 'ers married Miss Pascoe, you knaw Mrs Dustow's sister, tha's livin' in behind Jack Jinkins' shop.'

Now I swim up to surface: I do know Jack Jenkins' shop – who is there that doesn't? Cigarettes and sweets, top of Tregonissey Hill. I extricate myself: 'Well, I must get on and see if the Rock is still there.'

Mrs B. grinning, 'Aw well, saam as ever!'

Such was my testimonial. My mother's talk was far more vivid, even further gone in Cornish dialect, and extraordinarily expressive: it brings her sharply before me as I transcribe it from the Book of Life. 'They'm always ready to jase [i.e. chase round: she was crippled with arthritis]. But I *can't jase*. So there.' She quotes Grandmother Vanson, an equally abrasive personality. 'Tes so windy, 'tes enough to blaw 'ee up Callin'ton Downs. Shut the doors – else 'twill blaw me up on Callin'ton Downs.' This shows the district grandmother came from – Duloe-Looe.

On our butcher: 'He is the most deceivingest butcher I

ever...!' Mr Folly the milkman, to whom she was confiding this information *sans phrase*: 'Aw! tch, he's wuss than that!' Somebody was 'always the last shoe in the shop.' Old Mrs Goodman, impecunious but ladylike, dolled up with frills and flounces, invariably scrounged a cup of tea.

M.   ''ave a cup of tea, Mrs Goodman?'

Mrs G. 'Well, I don't like to be personal, Mrs Rowse, but I *would* like a cup of tea.'

I garnered a good deal of Cornish folklore before it quite died out. M., making her bed: 'Tedn goin' to be no fine weather: the tie is so heavy as lead.'

In a good mood she would repeat folk rhymes with which old people amused themselves on winter evenings before wireless and TV had set in to fill up the vacuum.

> I had a bonnet trimmed in blue –
> Why don't you wear it? So I do:
> I do wear it when I can,
> When I go out with my young man.

> My young man is gone to sea,
> When he come home he'll marry me –
> With a bow behind and a bow before,
> And a bow behind the kitchen door.

Then there was the well known, 'Old 'oman Whiddle-Whaddle jumped out of bed.' Or:

> Grandmother, she
> Was the age of eighty-three,
> One day in May
> Was taken ill and died.
> After she was dead
> The duty will was read:
> How they chittered, how they chaffed,
> How my brothers and sisters laughed
> When the lawyer did declare
> Granny only left-a me the old arm-chair.

Or again:

> Last Saturday night
>   I lost my wife,
> And where do you think I found her?
>   Up in the moon,
>   Playin' a tune,
> And all the stars around her.

FATHER: 'I'd rather hear they old toons they used to sing and play, and dance to, than what they play now – there's no tune in it.' [Just what I think of Boulez, for example.]

MOTHER: 'They used to sing and play purty little things, when we wuz young.'

FATHER: 'You could dance to what they used to play: form up couples an' dance through the village, light as a feather. Now 'tis like draggin' their life's out.'

This goes back more than a century: it must have been like the village life Hardy knew.

I resumed my solitary walks. I was in the cut cornfield on my way to Trenarren – little knowing that this favourite terminus of my evening walks would be the terminus of the evening of my life. That cornfield is enclosed by the ramparts of a late Celtic encampment, Castle Gotha, well sited for the lead-silver lode running down the cliff to Silvermine Beach below.

The half-breast of hill to the skyline has been harrowed after harvesting; the strange sunset light reflected from a cloud has a strong colour effect in lavender and dust-gold, combed earth and ruffled stubble. Suddenly from behind the hill the sun lights up through the haze of cloud: I turn round to find the further cornfields on the cliff swimming in gold, as if an electric light had been switched on in a dark room. Beyond the cover the peninsula opposite gleams with varied colours out of rosy haze across the blue ground of the Bay.

I wasn't always alone. My school-friend, Len Tippett, and I went for jaunts about the county – good preparation for an historian of Cornwall. We went one September day to remote St Keverne, near the Lizard, where the Cornish rebellion of 1497 against Henry VII's taxation began. With taxation at a moderate rate in 1929, I was more interested in the memorial to 'Officers and men of His Majesty's Seventh (or Queen's Own) Regiment of Hussars – Major Cavendish, Captain Dukenfield, Lieut. Waldegrave, and 61 non-commissioned and privates, who in returning from Spain in *The Dispatch* transport unhappily perished in Coverack Cove, 22 January 1809.' There hung an officer's sword. Nearby a tablet to the *Primrose*, lost with 126 men, displayed still the ship's gudgeon.

Tyrant! the barrier of thy rage, the deep,
Aids thy fierce boast, and English mothers weep.

Here was Hardy's Peninsular War – one could hear the Trumpet-major's footsteps echoing until they could be heard no more on the fields of Spain. At St Anthony-in-Meneage we rested

in the garden between church and river, the inflowing tide running up slowly. A boatman told us to go up to the thatched cottage with the green gate and tell Granfer that 'enry sent us along and he was to row us across. Under the shadow of the tower a modern woman with long ear-drops smoked a cigarette from the top of the farm gate. A small dog chased a hen up hill and down dale, with various women trying ineffectively to stop him. The commotion did not disturb the enormous village sow sleeping by the water-trough, nor the lady with the ear-drops, who descended from her perch to tickle the sow with arched foot. Was this apparition a witch?

Now loomed my candidature: 21 September was the Selection Meeting at Truro. I had forgotten that I had a rival, until Penderel Moon reminded me, an Anglo-Indian of some distinction: Sir John Maynard. He was the candidate favoured by Transport House and the local constituency officers – and he would have been more useful to the Party, in the House of Commons, with his knowledge. However, it was a democratic election and the china-clay delegates from the St Austell area, solid for me, tipped the balance. The Party Officers swallowed their disappointment and manfully set themselves to introduce me around the constituency.

September 1929: Labour hopes were high; the Party had the largest number of MPs in Parliament: no-one could have imagined the catastrophe of 1931 – from which I have always dated the end of hopes for Europe: eighteen months later came Hitler to power – real power. The Liberal Party, because of Nonconformity, was still ahead in Cornwall, with a sitting member, a carpet-bagger: he had topped the poll with some 15,000 votes, the Tory next with 13,000, the Labour vote was 11,000 – rather good for a backward area. The main block of Labour votes was constituted by the dock-workers at Falmouth. Their Trade Union leader, Jack Donovan, was a tall dark craggy type, high cheek-bones and complexion, prognathous jaw and big teeth. I could sense that I wasn't his choice; however, he was a good fellow, in Bevin's good books and, in the end, having stuck to my guns through two disastrous elections, 1931 and 1935, without giving up, Jack rather warmed to me.

My first tests were meeting the Truro officers, followed by an evening meeting at Falmouth. The Party had a full-time agent, one Alford, and it was a job to raise his salary: we were dependent on Christmas bazaars and socials, and the poor chap was full of schemes for raising a bit of cash. He was an honest sort, with clacking dentures, North Country accent and rather rat-trap interests. He lived in a cottage out west of Truro at Hugus, old mine-country, by name Tomperrow, with a stream at the bottom of his garden. It was the prettiest thing about him: however, we jogged along together, never an ill word, and the old boy was pleased by the letters I wrote round to the stalwarts.

Falmouth was unfamiliar territory, and all the Labour councillors turned up. One, in particular, I have never forgotten: silvery Councillor Butler, with club foot, ex-headmaster, who had been Mayor. In the course of talk with this sympathetic figure, he stumbled on something: he referred to someone with 'a cross-bench mind ... I wonder whether you will not develop a cross-bench mind', the wise old man said. I had one of those moments of illumination – what the Cornish call a presentiment – that this was precisely what would come to be.

Next evening a Labour social at St Austell; the evening after a series of propaganda meetings out in the western china-clay area, St Stephens, Treviscoe, Nanpean – and walked those miles home. The eastern china-clay villages, Bugle, Roche, Penwithick, Carclaze, were dominantly Liberal. How I hated those out-of-door meetings with their casual groups at village corners, speaking against the traffic and the visible unconcern of the men, as the years went on and my anxiety about Germany and Europe mounted. Nothing one could say or do could make the fools listen. If they wouldn't listen to Churchill, it was not to be expected that they would listen to me, as I warned them of the wrath to come.

Father D'Arcy's description of his propaganda for the Faith

in Hyde Park came to mind: four men under an umbrella in the rain, of whom three were already converted. Mine weren't even converted or willing to be. I still think of it at the road-crossing in Bugle, whenever I go by: a dozen or so china-clay workers lolling against the wall, one or two giving the impression that they were there by accident or only half there – when their bosses and the chapels, which were the centres of their community life, were Liberal. I always detested congealed Nonconformist Liberalism.

Nuances of class differentiation were significant in the split between Liberalism and Labour. The better off Nonconformists, like the Foots, were Liberals, that is Wesleyans, Congregationalists, Baptists, most of the town Chapel-folk. The lower class elements – Primitive Methodists, United Methodists (in fact Disunited from the main body), Bible Christians, were apt to be Labour. None of these popular religious or, rather, social phenomena elicited my sympathy. The well-heeled Wesleyans were in process of moving over to becoming Tories – witness the arch-humbug, Baldwin himself. The 'National' Government provided a heaven-sent opportunity for these people to cross over. When I got back to All Souls, Archbishop Lang – much more my type – asked me about the situation: I reported it as I saw it. 'Just as I thought,' he said sagely.

The prime task for Labour in Cornwall was to bring home the futility of going on being Liberal. My grand-parents had been Liberals in the days of Gladstone, but these were not the days of Gladstone. A Marxist could explain the situation. In the nineteenth century, with thousands of small individual family concerns all over the country, shops, businesses, crafts, industries, they were typically Free Trade in economics, Nonconformist in religion, Liberal in politics. In the twentieth century most of these individual concerns had gone out: now large-scale industry and multiple shops, where the managers and rentiers were Tories, the employees Trade Union and Labour. The social and class foundation for the Liberal Party had collapsed: no point in its going on, a corpse encumbering the political scene.

I once put the point to Powicke the historian, a Manchester Liberal. He said reasonably, 'I dare say you are right; only it's terribly hard if you've been a Liberal all your life.' I could sympathise, but there was no point in throwing votes away, misdirecting energy, keeping a number of able men out of effective service to the country, either as Labour men or Tories. The country needed them, there was not so much ability on the scene that people could afford to waste it – still less today, when far fewer men of ability go into politics.

The leading figure in the village of Trethosa was a splendid old chap, Sam Jacobs. In his seventies he was a fine upstanding figure: ex-Indian Army, he had spitted his man on the North-West Frontier. He was the sort of fellow I admired and oddly enough, he took to this aesthete-intellectual. When he died I wrote a tribute to him in our *Cornish Guardian* – which pleased Alford. However, here was the inner man.

25 September. Oh! God, sitting in the squalor of the agent's office, I come upon the letter I wrote from Dresden, 'Zinzendorf-Hospitz-Vereinshaus'. I remember what pain those letters gave me, writing them in the stuffy little Lese-saal while waiting for Adam to come down to breakfast. He arrived late with sleep still in his eyes, not the happiest of mornings. But what wouldn't I give to recover the lost days and be there again with him now!

Instead of that I had my first public engagement as candidate at a comic affair, the Duchy Oyster Feast at Port Navas on the Helford River. Here was the oyster fishery belonging to the Duchy; gathered in a marquee for lunch were the Duchy officials, the Mayor of Falmouth in fluff and feathers, and an ancient alderman who made an amusing speech about oysters, who didn't open their mouths except for some useful purpose, etc. I was expected to open my mouth – but, alas, I can't bear oysters *au naturel*, and there wasn't much else to eat. I felt like the donnish Bishop who went down to St Hilary for Bernard Walke's induction. It took place on a Friday – and Friday was a fast-day; so Father Walke laid on a feast of oysters and white wine. The Bishop was a tee-totaller and couldn't bear oysters. This was my predicament at Port Navas.

Dr Marion Phillips, a regular Party propagandist came down to speak for me at St Austell. A formidable figure with an outstanding bust, she was Australian. When G. D. H. Cole was getting married, he received a wedding present of a large protruding quart-jug: 'Just like Dr Marion Phillips', he said – and indeed it was from her.

Out in the western clay area obtruded a type I came to detest: one Percy Harris of Carpalla, where he was a large frog in a very small pond. He became too big for it and, because he couldn't get his way in the local chapel, he took to pontificating at the Bible Christian chapel in the town. He was, of course, a pompous Liberal. I didn't detest the Tories – I expected the country gentry and their tenants to know their own interests. It was Liberals like Percy whom I could not endure – their self-satisfied Nonconformity, the moth-eaten clichés with which he would answer me back in the local papers. I never liked being answered back by the half-educated (I still don't, about Shakespeare or whatever). I put him into verse as 'Pompous Parsifal' to amuse our youthful team.

For I had good friends, and we formed a team. These friends belonged to the first generation from the secondary (now grammar) schools, several of whom had been able to get on to a university, others not. One of the dearest of these friends was Claude Berry, a gallant personality, of an endearing nature, and a gifted journalist. The descendant of generations of Padstow boatmen – his grandfather had been drowned in ferrying across that dangerous strip of water – Claude would have had a career in London, if his health had not been impaired in the war. (His younger brother was killed by the Germans.) After the war Claude became a Lobby correspondent in the House of Commons; he had a flair for interpreting news. As a schoolboy I was a follower of his articles. A tubercular tendency drove him home to Cornwall, where he became assistant-editor of our local paper, the *Cornish Guardian*. He chafed under the régime of its owner, who belonged to just the type of public Nonconformist Liberals who were top dogs in Cornwall in those days. Most uncongenial to us younger university folk – so provincial, so self-complacent, such humbugs. I preferred Tories any day, particularly High Church Anglicans with a sense of the arts.

Claude got out of step with his boss, and moved from Bodmin to Truro to become assistant-editor of *The West Briton*, the oldest of Cornish newspapers, which went back to 1810. Here, too, he had for proprietor another of those irremovable Nonconformist Liberals who decorated the Cornish scene like so many up-ended sarcophagi. We detested the type. One of the significant changes has been the subsidence of Nonconformity – scores of chapels folded up. When I was a boy a dozen Nonconformist chapels were a feature of our town, and scores littered over the clay-area, with their ugly angularity. Some of them have become fish-and-chip shops, others Bingo halls: such is social progress.

Claude could not come out openly for me, but he saw to it that I had a fair deal in his paper. Our relations were affectionate, and I admired his gallant personality. I can see him now: that compact, slightly huddled figure, the shapely head, dark eyes blazing with eagerness and intelligence, the eager voice collapsing into a boyish laugh. When we set up our own monthly paper, he and his successor at Bodmin, gave us valuable help, even though – with those Liberal worthies in power – it had to be *sub rosa*. Think of it, and what we had to put up with!

I had to put up with endless insults for daring to be a Labour man at all, in a backward, narrow-minded area, and I didn't take that very well from inferiors, who should be taking their line from me, not I from them: I regarded that as an inversion of the order of nature. The third-rate should listen to the first-rate – in every sphere – whether history or literature, science or politics or, for that matter, Shakespeare. (Though a Labour man, I had no illusions about democracy.) It can be imagined how intensely I resented having A Cornish Childhood attacked by one of these friends, on the orders of his editor. He was at once – in accord with a practice I later regularised – demoted from being a friend to being an acquaintance. I had no thought at the time that the book would become a classic, hailed thirty years later – too late to give me any pleasure – as 'a masterpiece'. I knew only that I had put my best into the book and that it was authentic and sincere. It was to be expected that it would be attacked by enemies, but I wasn't going to put up with its being attacked by friends. (Stephen Spender, who had been something of a friend, didn't acquit himself very well either.)

One of my circle down here who was involved in the *fracas* over A Cornish Childhood, said to me the other day that these people couldn't understand me. Very well, they should try; the third-rate should try to understand the first-rate – good mental exercise for them. As Flannery O'Connor says, herself a writer of the first rank: 'A writer should never set himself to satisfy the expectations of the third-rate.' Quite recently, a Cornish literary journalist with whom I was on friendly terms made the mistake of lining up with other mere journalists to question my findings about Shakespeare. They do not qualify to hold an opinion on these matters – any more than I do on the insides of my motor-car. But I don't lay down the law on the insides of a motor-car: I expect to be told by those who know. The notion in a democratic society that everybody's opinion is as good as anybody else's is nonsense – most people's opinions are of no value whatever.

Other friends of my generation lent a hand. Fred Harris, of neighbouring Tywardreath and Fowey Grammar School, went up to Oxford, where he was a pupil of David's at Wadham. He came down to a life-long career in adult education with the Workers Educational Association. With much public spirit and in spite of the handicap of ill health he devoted a lifetime to good works – County Council, social service, the Royal Institution of Cornwall, what not. A closer friend, Noreen Sweet – we have been loyal friends all our lives – was away most of her time at her work, teaching and examining, and later married; but when here, in vacations or at election times, she lent a hand. A girl of natural distinction, she meant to come to Oxford. Without warning the cuts of the 'Geddes Axe' in education came in 1926, and she was almost stranded. However, she made it to Reading, where she had an idiosyncratic Oxford acquaintance of mine, Hugo Dyson, for tutor. Ethel Magor, from Foxhole, was a good sort: a mass of dark auburn hair, buxom figure, a winning smile. A most loyal spirit and a generous helper, she later made it to Oxford, if only to Ruskin.

We were a team; we pulled together; no quarrels; I have never forgotten any of them. In the Book of Life I find a couple of 'Maxims for Politics' of this date: 'Never to surrender oneself, but always to keep one's inner integrity. To be kind and friendly: but if one must attack, to attack one's opponents.' This was a different inflexion from that of the Left

Intellectuals, who spent most of their time attacking their own Party. (They are still at it: they never learn – though apparently Healey and Crosland, even Dick Crossman and Michael Foot, apparently did.)

One more engagement – St Stephens again.

In the Recreation Ground six men are working with a will, digging up the ground. What makes them so active? Is it common effort for the village? – They are making a bowling-green for themselves. Though nearly October, a hot summer sun over fields, a high hill beyond the village, deep green a background for ploughed fields, a deserted engine-house half way up. And Adam? Perhaps I am more content, even 'resigned', a favourite word of his.

On coming back from Germany I set myself to record what fragments I could salvage from our time together – 'so that I might have something to fall back on, in case anything should happen to him or to our friendship.' There follows an analysis of what kind of love there was between us – rather naïf, thinking:

that we can make nothing ultimately of it. But might not something be made of an *amor intellectualis*? At the beginning he felt the same passionate impact as I, and was the first to write; without that first move on his part I should have forced myself to forget. Several times, at Neu Babelsberg and our last night in the Tiergarten he said that he was sure the future would bring him nearer to me, that when he got rid of his present uncertainties he would come closer to my point of view.

He never did: he was too irremediably German – hence his fate. I always believed that mine, a more common sense English line would have been better for him. But 'he fears a relationship in which he would be passive.'

Doesn't that encapsulate the whole character of German policy towards Britain from Bismarck to Hitler? And wouldn't it have been better for Germany if she had been content to fall into a partnership in which the senior and more mature partner took the lead? It would have saved Germany from disaster and Europe from the civil war which ended its primacy in the world. Europe could have lived with a Germany which was content within its boundaries and to cooperate in keeping the peace in the way Edward Grey hoped. Instead of that, the Kaiser had the impertinence to describe this civilized statesman as only fit to be a provincial country gentleman.

And here was German egoism: 'in our last hour together before leaving, Adam said that he believed I cared for him more than anybody in the world had cared before.' Even here there was some incomprehension – for my attitude was a contingent one, contingent on response and good behaviour. That is what the Germans found impossible to understand with the English. (Today it doesn't matter any more: our world was ruined.)

At home I was reading Henri de Catt's *Memoirs*, which brought back Moritzburg, from a visit of Frederick the Great.

We set out in a motor coach from Dresden, after a long wait in the boiling heat of the Altmarkt. We talked about dialects of home. Adam is on good terms with the village youths and can talk their dialect with them; his young brother, in reaction against the family, always speaks dialect and won't speak correct German. [He came to see me after the war: as tall as Adam, but dark.] Sweltering in the bus, full of courting couples and lone young women off into the country, we crept along the north bank of the Elbe at a snail's pace. Arrived at the Schloss, we sat on the low wall of the avenue, looking across the lake and the marshes that almost surround the castle. Into the woods, over paths and ditches, I told him the strange story of Swift and Stella and Vanessa. Was it a parable?

This encouraged him to tell me about his girl-friend in Berlin, in whom he was, as usual, disappointed. (He was born to disappointment of his hopes, like all Germans.) He got sympathy from his women, but they didn't really care for his heart-searchings: these were not serious matters to them. Nor did he care sexually for this 'bourgeois girl'. He was rather chaste where women were concerned: he had only once had a woman, and that a long while ago. The other students in Berlin and people like Hans all did: he did not. How high-minded we were! What *did* he want? At this late date, I am reminded of Moeller van den Bruck's summing up of the Germans: 'We are a problematic people, made to create problems for ourselves and for others.' 'On our way back to Berlin in the train, people passing up and down the corridor were

97

interested in us, he said and suggested we drew down the blinds of the compartment. But one didn't need to shut out the world: our inner world of feeling was enough for me.'

At home I was making myself concentrate on writing my politics book. 'However, I feel more resigned about him since I got my mind back into the groove of my work. [Work is the only anodyne.] *There* lies the future for me. I recognise that we have some special relation, but it is impossible to define it: better to let it take its course, naturally and without forcing it. I see that I could argue myself into anything I want: better to reserve the faculty for arguing other people into things they don't want.' That meant politics.

He could see from my attitude towards England that, though critical, I loved my country. It was possible to be content in England and with its potentialities, it was so highly organised a community, its traditions and values so firmly established. But what was there for Germany? Or for a German like himself in that environment? He hated Berlin life, yet that was what the future of Germany was going to be like: shallow and materialist, talking about art but never caring for the values of life, or understanding them; godless and pleasure-seeking, subsisting on American money, yet holding on to power so that people like himself would never get a chance of changing things.

This was a remarkable outburst from so young a man, prophetic in its way. Yet the future was to be far worse than he feared. 'What was there for Germany' indeed? The short answer was – Hitler.

I didn't sympathise with this lugubrious outlook at the time. 'It makes me uncertain of his capacity to rise above the situation, and to help form the new order. Yet he has intelligence enough, and understanding, and subtlety; he needs only strength of purpose.' Today it is I who now condemn myself for naïveté: my 'strength of purpose' owed itself largely to the security of the English background, which Adam appreciated correctly. That security has vanished with the society that engendered it: today we are all at sea. It is true that his disordered Germany shattered it – but for that, the transition to a new social order in Europe would have been given more time, we could have moved into it more gradually, with less violence, perhaps even without a relapse into barbarism. I recalled my arrival in Berlin.

He was for a while so moved that he lost his command of English. At the station I caught sight of him at once, tall above all the others, and with that nervous turn of the head as my compartment glided past him. Coming through the streets and the Tiergarten he was as excited as a child. At such times he seemed so much younger than I, at others I felt that he was more mature and disillusioned. I can see him now as he sat astride the bedroom chair, glass door open on to my balcony. He offered to wait in the other room till I was ready – I was less affected emotionally and felt master of the situation! We lingered talking until we had each found footing, then went out late to dine at one of the little Russian restaurants he likes to go to. [Berlin under the Weimar Republic was full of Russian *émigrés* from that other barbarism.] I felt oddly uncommitted, half-amused when we recovered the fulness of sympathy we had found at once at Oxford. It enabled me to lay down a programme: we would be apart by day, while he worked and I saw Berlin, and devote the evenings to each other, the best time for friendship.

So it worked out, though we broke into it with trips together. Out from the little station in the Savigny Strasse, not far from the Kurfürstendamm – the centre of the café life of Weimar Berlin – through the woods of Charlottenburg and Grünewald, where Rathenau had lived, before his murder by the Frei Korps reactionaries. The *umgebung* of Berlin was not unattractive, sandy wastes and coniferous heaths, glimpses of water and lakes – but I couldn't bear to go back there again, after the earthquake that has supervened. 'Across the fields was the green dome of the big church' – today I think of the Oath sworn to Hitler, so ingeniously manoeuvred to confuse the 'consciences' of the Generals in the conspiracy of 1944 in which Adam was involved.

From the house in Potsdam where he was born, the family moved to Unter den Linden, where he lived till he was seven. He never told me about the blight upon his father's official career and the persecution he suffered at school because the Minister had fallen from power – so typically German. He was more attached to his mother, strong in character and religious devotion. He had sent an Indian friend to stay at his home, with whom his mother had found common ground in their religious sense and their liking for Browning. He supposed, rightly, that I didn't care for Browning any more than I should

99

approve of their religious line. [Göring: 'When I hear the word Browning, I reach down my revolver.']

Going over Sans Souci with the tourists must have been odd for him, for when his father was Governor of Potsdam the various palaces were in his keeping. 'We talked about national qualities; he thought that there were Roman qualities in the English, and that I had the self-discipline to sacrifice what was not in keeping with my deliberate plans.' I think now, too late, that I was foolishly willing to sacrifice far too much.

The budding historian derived satisfaction from the sense of life Frederick the Great's relics gave. I collected together in mind the plum-coloured coat and satin waistcoat from the Zeughaus, his flute and music stand from the music room, his books and papers; here the alcove with his bed, there the writing desk towards the window, the chair he died in. 'A vivid sense-impression passed over me when Adam went over to the alcove and bent over the rope to look down on the celibate bed.' At the other end was Voltaire's room, decorated with parrots and flowers on the panelling. What a background for an historic friendship! I joked about being Voltaire to Adam's Frederick. He thought not: after all we both meant to be politicians, he too urging me in that direction. He became one – and see what it did for him!

We wandered out into a formal garden in front of an Italianate palace, I suppose, the Neuer Palais.

Adam wanted to find a spot free from passing people: he wanted to talk more intimately. He has the gift of leading one into such intimacy: I couldn't achieve it. It crossed my mind that what he could do so easily with me, he must often have done with others. He told me more about his family and the influence his elder brother had on him, the anxiety the extraordinary course he takes causes his father and mother. Having survived the war, he has arrived at total disillusionment, thrown up everything, no occupation, gone to live in a peasant's hut in Bavaria. A favourite pupil of Max Scheler at Heidelberg, he gave up in despair of its leading anywhere. He discourages Adam from following any career and reproaches him for leading a life of compromise.

Here was one more wreck from the collapse that had overtaken Germany: I think that this brother had peasant-Communist ideas and had gone back to the people as a way out. He was a disturbing influence on Adam, pulled this way and that; 'perhaps he was looking for an elder brother in me.'

Our letters tried to bridge the distance and keep going the illusion of being together – I can only skim them here, he wrote to me at such length. Our relationship was for him 'the one fixed point in a changing and unreliable fate around us.' He had been over again the walk we had taken one night into West Berlin, autumn already in the air. On his way home to Hesse he had had a couple of photos taken for me, still there in the envelope, looking thoughtful and sad.

An immensely long letter reached me from a forester's house in the woods, where he was reading Proust. 'How much I missed you at Coburg. My fellow-traveller for whose sake I went there was so poor a companion compared with you – there was a growing antipathy between us.' Was he never satisfied? Could he never learn to take things as they come, and make the best of them? I couldn't understand it, and before the end I felt I couldn't stand it either. The scenery around the Prince Consort's Coburg was charming, 'if only one had been alone or with you.' He was so sensitive to atmosphere that he couldn't write to me from his mother's room – it was full of the mood in which he talked to her, impossible to say anything straight or direct. The simplicity of my proletarian background left me no time for these upper-class complications – I went straight ahead.

I always fall for telling you things which seem to me most significant in the evening. But the feeling that 'you already know' is one of my great drawbacks. But that this is far from being a more intellectual matter you have shown me so many times – this I feel goes down to the very bottom of my devotion to you ... I am afraid that I am to remain your debtor ... The belief that you must have thought my intellectual life extremely vague and unreliable was awfully depressing – the more so as I thought it would now be impossible that you should find a true and equal interest in my affairs, which, as you had seen, might change tomorrow into quite a different direction.

Yes, indeed: up and down, to and fro, here was Hegelianism incarnate – how I disapproved of it and of its appalling influence on him, merely creating more uncertainty and insecurity. (I am reminded of what Renan wrote of Amiel: *The Hegelian*

School taught him his complicated ways of thinking and by the same token rendered him incapable of writing.') It was true that I could not pretend 'a true and equal interest' in this German state of mind – it was like a portent of the German demand for *Gleichberechtigung* with which we were to be confronted by Hitler. Was it really equality of treatment they wanted? I do not think so.

Adam was aware of the symbolic character in our relations before I was. 'In the whole difference of the foundations and natural roots from which our two lives spring (England–Germany!) there will ever be and must exist divergent effects in our outlook and action, though not in principle. There will always be an enormous need of confidence on your side.' Wasn't this, come to think of it, too demanding, too German? I had no respect, let alone liking, for the Hegelian mentality – my attitude on that was classically summed up by Santayana;* nor could I conceive of any equality with that disastrous frame of mind. What good did it ever do the Germans? A curious thought has just struck me: may it not be that – as the result of the holocaust and the disaster to the old Germany – the Anglo-Saxon attitude of mind has, in fact, at last prevailed in (at least) West Germany?

But what we have had to go through to win the argument!

As for me, he felt that 'I was perhaps the first to whom you felt capable to tell more about yourself than to the other world around you'. Here he was right: I had had reason enough already to be on the defensive, having met with envy and obstruction at every stage, even from one's nearest friends at Oxford. One didn't get that from Adam, with whom I could be completely open. But he was afflicted with 'the fear that this first real friend in the end would turn out an inadequate one.' As to that we would wait and see. 'You may think that I am attempting to analyse what is not to be analysed.' I did. He found my letters 'somehow altered. I wonder how you look addressing your voters?'

In October he was back in Berlin, as was his brother with whom he was trying to come to an understanding – he had always been a Bohemian, had no money, was living in one

* See his penetrating diagnosis in *Egotism and German Philosophy*, inconceivably ignored for third-rate works on the German mind.

hideous room and only now attempting to get in touch with newspapers and periodicals. 'Coming down the Uhland-strasse, looking up to your two windows, I was touched by gratitude and devotion to you! The Russian sculptress of Richard Hare [subsequently his wife] said to me today: "*Wenn man einen Engländer als Freund hat, so hat man ihn für sein ganzes Leben. Sie sind so treu!* – May it be so with us, my dearest!" – But I was not all that English; my friendship, it would be found, would depend on how things worked out, that is on the other: it could not be taken for granted.'

His next letters plunged back into despondency: 'how ever could you love a creature like me?', etc. Up and then down! I tried to counteract this Germanic swinging to and fro with reading in French and English. I sent him books. His comment on Eliot's poetry was illuminating: it expressed experiences which he had not thought capable of being put into poetry – here was the reason why it meant so much to our generation.

I described this perpetual swinging to and fro (the Hegelian 'dialectic', ugh!) as the 'Berlin malady'. He replied with an interesting letter, defending himself: mutual independence and being ourselves was a precondition of any intimacy, i.e. Germany was not giving up being German. And then, 'I would not let you part from me even if you wanted to.' Between Germany and Britain an element of struggle was involved; not on my part, for I could not conceive of giving way to a state of mind I thought detestable in itself, and bad for him. Here was the Hegelian dialectic with his brother again: 'our meeting is always extremely exciting for me and always hostile.' An Englishman would prefer it less exciting, and less hostile. His companion at Coburg had been a political journalist called von Gordon, a connexion of Lord Aberdeen. Adam had found him disappointing; he would call on me if at Oxford, 'politically he is a quite interesting specimen: but after all he is a fool'. Then there was 'the old tyranny' of falling for a girl again at Imshausen: that had followed him like 'a secret wound, which makes one pathetic and ridiculous at the same time.'

Was there then no-one and nothing that was satisfactory? Apparently I was cast for this rôle. He followed this up with a shrewd and searching doubt, whether there was 'enough in him to make my life *really*, and not only *aesthetically*, valuable for yours'. That shaft reached home, for of course the aesthetic element was dominant not only in my attitude towards him but in my own nature. It was not only his personal beauty, his extraordinary sensibility and intuitiveness, that seduced me, but the poet's weakness (or strength) of being in love with love. Since my ultimate values were aesthetic, not moral or religious, the core of my nature, how could it be otherwise? Time, I had said, would tell. Time told that his nature was otherwise.

While Adam was in Berlin wrestling with the law, which he detested, I was back at Oxford busily engaged with the chores of teaching, examining and committeeing, and the ritual of my aesthetic life, to which I was now adding the incompatible burden of practical politics.

Autumn evening: an ice-blue sky, and a white reef of cloud, like a glacier broken at the edge of the sea. A revelation of beauty from within the palace: the soaring dome some strange dark flower of the night upon autumnal mists lit by the moon. This beauty I would share with you: it is all disquiet when you are not here!

Tonight at the Musical Club a quartet of young women played Delius and Beethoven. They were unexpectedly beautiful in that audience of men: more delicate, their bodies more sinuous and flower-like; they sat for a moment arranging their flowing draperies before playing, their bodies moving rhythmically. One shadowy figure kept flitting in and out of it all: I seemed to see it leaning over them, taking one of them in his arms, as no doubt in Berlin.

Moonlight in the garden: I look up from the lighted desk to see over my shoulder the brilliant jade-green of a star, a cold ironic steadfastness. I thought of him under the same star, perhaps noticing, in Berlin. Moon-lipped sill of window – in the cold glare of moon and the stony bitterness of the air the trees look small, as if one could reach out and pluck them like bouquets from their shadowy stems.

Assize Morning. A Sunday sweetness in the air because of the bells. I go out into the street, a few onlookers gathered outside St Mary's. The policemen on duty wear their ribbons and new white gloves; two buglers from Cowley barracks by Laud's baroque porch. A chauffeur stands up prosperous and expansive with large lapels to his coat: he is the Judge's coachman. The bells continue from St Martin's all the time the Judge is at prayers. More passers-by collect on the pavement; a car goes by, the lady within raising lorgnettes to view the scene. I cannot wait to see the Judge issue forth in scarlet and ermine: the majesty of the law. Back in my dark-panelled Caroline room at work: the bugles blow in the street, the bells cease.

The autumnal evening is hard to capture, the air downy and soft, sky like peach-bloom. St Mary's spire withdrawn, a few diamond sparkles of risen moon caught in an upper lancet, a lower opening pierced by light through the body of the tower. In the garden the trees droop like peacocks in their autumn finery, the three poplars further off beckon to the orient.

Morning garden where the sun has not yet reached to dry up the dew, the troglodite gardener rakes up the leaves. With long sweep of arm and satisfying rhythm he extends his line of colour, dun, red, lemon, across the grass: swish, swish go the leaves, the sparrows chattering from the refuge of the wall-creeper.

I remember that little gardener, short, powerful, muscular. It was impossible to make contact with him, he had such a protective covering of impenetrable religiosity. He was of some odd sect, I think a Plymouth Brother. But he had an unexpected human side: one of the scouts caught him on a bench up at Shotover with hand under the skirt of a, perhaps, Plymouth Sister.

Tonight the moon is rising through a rent in the cloud, behind the Japanese plumage of a branch. Above the bank of cloud a clear dark sky full of stars. I open the window; after all the rain the smell of earth is strong. Today I wrote to Adam in propitiation for some distress I had caused him: sometimes I feel fated to defeat and despair. Next night: the moon a dull gold plate mysteriously caught in the tree, no longer at the plumy edge. The night is dark and full of nostalgia. The Palace in Dresden comes wearily back to mind, the Elbe that evening we came back content from the Heide and the spires of the churches from the Terrace. Another day the morning wind upon the river as he leaned against the bridge at the bend of the stream. At night a raw, piercing damp, small lights gleaming beyond trees, a dying fire flickering in a window; my breath went out in a white column into the night.

5 November: a grand spectacle on the other side of the garden: a Guy Fawkes bonfire in the inner quad at Queens', the bright flames shining in the library windows, so much smoke I thought the library itself must be burning. Tonight my neighbour, Cyril Radcliffe's Fellowship expired. I wondered who was the other, his mate, whose term ended with his. I asked Penderel Moon, who said, 'It is your ghost.' A cold shiver came over me, his Fellowship night running

out along with Radcliffe's. Even now, it isn't so long ago. My
bedroom was haunted by that poor spectre; but I would not give up,
in spite of my frequent terrors. I told David last week that all that had
meant as much to me as ever a friendship.

Such was the secret background to my life: it can be seen that
the place had an intense hold upon me. The extrovert side was
full enough. I was now writing *Politics and the Younger Generation*: I count that abortive exercise, authentic enough of my
interests of mind, as belonging merely to the extrovert side of
life. So, too, College activities, though they had a charm for
me in those days.

There was Lang's official visit as Visitor of All Souls on
becoming archbishop of Canterbury. For much of his life Lang
– as we called him simply, according to College rule – had been
re-elected Fellow since he remained unmarried: All Souls was
his Oxford home, where he took refuge from his hard-
working life of archi-episcopal chores, when he came south
from York and needed a break from London. On succeeding
Davidson at Canterbury, Lang became our official Visitor and
could no longer remain a Fellow. It was rather a wrench for
him – though how much Warden Pember and Senior Fellows
appreciated this I doubt, for the Archbishop was not over-
popular with them.

He was very archiepiscopal, all in purple on Gaudy Nights,
though willing as Lord Mallard in Common Room to sing, in
that carefully modulated voice, the Mallard Song, one bawdy
stanza being omitted in deference to the cloth. Lang was all
that a prelate should be, natural dignity, all the gifts of bearing
and demeanour, reserve and absolute self-discipline – one
could see that in the tight-shut lips – nothing lost upon those
bright, wary eyes. The tone of the College was far from High
Church – in fact so low as to adhere in the Chapel services to
'Regency Use', northward position and all. The Warden was
an old-fashioned Victorian rationalist, with as good as no
belief at all, but a positive strain of anti-clericalism. He abomi-
nated 'Puseyites', and told me that the venerated Dr Pusey had
once betrayed a secret he had learned in confession. True or
not, I expect the Warden had got this prejudice from his father,
a Christ Church man.

Henson, Lang's senior, was jealous of him; Oman, churchy enough, was a 'black Prot', who didn't see much use for cathedrals. Lady Oman entertained a romantic illusion in her womanly heart that Lang had been disappointed in love: handsome as he had been when young with raven-black hair, a lady of title had been enamoured of him. I had enough sense to realise that that would not have been Lang's line. He had been – platonically, of course – in love with the Scottish laird, Moreton Macdonald, on whose estate he had a cell to which he retired every year in August, for meditation and repentance, to offset his worldliness. He also had a devotion to popular Dick Shepherd, of St Martin-in-the-Fields and of the footling Peace Pledge Union, of Bertie Russell, Jack Priestley and other worthies. This was not the Archbishop's line, who was a statesman. Dick as a young man had chopped and changed so often about being ordained that Lang had practically held him down at his ordination. Many stories are told of their affectionate relations – Dick could do anything with the Archbishop: I found it rather touching.

Underneath the episcopal exterior Lang had sharp antennae where humans were concerned – unlike his successor, large Billy Temple, with whom causes and abstract ideas were everything. A philosopher and theologian, Temple had little sense of the individual: Lang had. He told me that as a Junior Fellow he had thought of writing a biography of Thomas Cromwell; he had certainly written, when young, an ineffably sentimental romance of a Little Lord Fauntleroy kind. At College meetings I used to observe Lang, among all those clever men spinning out proceedings and wasting so many man-hours. Not so Lang. He sat there at the top table, silently going through his interminable correspondence, the pile of answered letters mounting up and up before him. Then, if anything came up touching the Church or its interests, he rose, spoke briefly to the point and sat down again. Never a moment wasted. (In later years I followed his example and answered letters, instead of listening to the chaffer of people who did not value time as I did.)

Lang's only real friends in College were Halifax and Dawson, both churchy, and Dougie Malcolm, a fellow Scot. Dougie told me the story of Lang's 'conversion'. He had not

intended to go into the Church, but to the bar and into politics;
but returning from Cuddesdon one Easter, coming over
Shotover he heard a voice repeating, 'Why shouldn't *you* be
ordained?' He always remained faithful to this inner voice, and
returned every Easter to Cuddesdon, until his withdrawal
from public life.

So many things about him appealed to me – as they did not
to people without imagination; perhaps he sensed that, for he
took notice of me and would tell me interesting things. A Celt
on the Gordon side, he was genuinely psychic. When Bishop
of Stepney, there was an appallingly ugly window in a church,
where the vicar wished that the boys would throw stones
through it. Lang said, would that a storm would come and
smash it! A month or so after he heard from the vicar that a
storm had done so. After that he was rather careful with his
comminations. Another story was even more dramatic –
about a letter he received from a Nonconformist minister,
warning him that he had dreamed of an accident to the Archbishop's car at a precipitous bridge-crossing he had to under-
take that very morning ... Lang was as fine a raconteur as one
would expect from so finished an orator.

But not even a good Churchman such as Cruttwell – Evelyn
Waugh's monster – liked Lang. A friend of the Royal Family,
Lang brought the young Prince of Wales to dine on a Sunday
night, sweeping grandly up to the top table with a gesture,
'Those are the Junior Fellows.' What was there to object to in
that? The Archbishop couldn't have added to the shyness of
the youth by introducing him all round to all and sundry.
Another time he was to preside at some World Conference of
Churches, had dined at the Lodgings, retired to array himself –
and returned in purple and scarlet to make the round of the
drawing room and take leave of the ladies. That Scotch maiden
lady, Miss Adams, commented tartly, 'And to think that my
mother called his mother Hannah!' For, of course, Lang was a
son of the manse. On his becoming Archbishop of York, all
the good wishes he got from his ghillie was, 'Weel, ye've a
gran' fine kirk noo!'

'Prelatical' – well, what else should an archbishop be?
Alterius orbis papa: 'I through whom God chiefly speaks to his
English people' – perhaps this was going a bit far. The Warden

in his *discours de réception* had a fling against 'the divine right of presbyters', giving me the tip of the wink. The funny thing was that this Leftist didn't object: Lang's complex character appealed to me – so much more complex than ordinary men. Like one or two other bachelor Fellows without physical satisfaction, Lang was an insomniac all his life; the chiming of the hours made sleep all but impossible for him in Oxford. He told me that he had trained himself to empty his mind of all worries – and, lying quite still, got almost as much refreshment as if from sleep. What a burden to carry with all that incessant labour!

Naturally he did not react as normal humans did, so he sometimes miscalculated. During the war he had spoken of our enemies in a Christian spirit, then added an unfortunate phrase that he had many 'sacred' memories of the Kaiser: 'vivid' would have been all right, 'sacred' raised hell. He was vindictively attacked throughout the Press. In the course of the campaign of vilification his magnificent mane of hair came out in handfuls; he tried a wig, but it was no good. He ended with a little white fluff around the bladder of lard: this added to the venerability of his appearance, especially with a purple skull-cap, like a cardinal. He would have done well as Cardinal Cosmo, and made a grand figure in the Curia; but of course he would have had to be Pope.

The outcry at his pronouncement after Edward VIII's Abdication should be put in proper perspective. Lang was no prime mover and had no responsibility in the matter, as the populace thought. The Duke of Windsor – incapable of seeing any point of view but his own – continued to blame him for it in various books and articles. The Archbishop was in a terrible fix. As a confidant of the Royal Family he well knew about Mrs Simpson: what was he to do when it came to the Coronation? He prayed that this cup might pass from him. It did, by the adroit handling of the situation by Baldwin. The Archbishop was then pressed to make a pronouncement *ex cathedra*. When he did, with its reference to the Duke of Windsor's 'exotic entourage', there was once more a nation-wide outcry. I should have thought the phrase a mild one for the company the duke kept, of Society tarts, American go-getters and disreputable pro-Nazi industrialists like Bedaux.

At the time I was quite wrong, as Dalton's Memoirs point out – as if there were one's sole appearance in the Labour Movement. I was young, ignorant of the real situation, innocently in favour of 'love having its way', and anything to get rid of Baldwin, an incubus around our neck, as we considered. My sympathies were already half-way with Churchill – even about India. (Can anyone suppose that the suffering millions of India have benefited by the end of the Raj? – now victims of institutionalised corruption from top to bottom.)

Lang was not a reactionary: he had been a Balliol Liberal, keenly interested in the WEA. He had had a tough assignment as curate in Leeds. He told me once that bad as it was to intervene in drunken men's fights, drunken women were worse: impossible to part, with their hands in each other's hair. One way and another, he told me a great deal – about his first notice from Queen Victoria, the timbre of her deep expressive voice, and his first introduction to George V. Bishop Hensley Henson was always unfair to him: he expected to be made archbishop of York, when Lang moved up to Canterbury. Disappointed, he preached in Chapel a sermon I heard, with a reference to his predecessor, Bishop Butler, 'refusing the Primacy because he would not be a pillar of a declining Church', looking across at Lang, head bowed in his hands. I said to Lang, how could Henson expect ultimate responsibility when he took such an irresponsible line? 'Well, exactly,' said the ecclesiastical statesman.

When Archbishop, Lang could hardly say anything without people jumping down his throat; the moment he retired, he became altogether more free and relaxed. My friend David Mathew, Coadjutor to Cardinal Hinsley at Westminster, was the go-between these two dignitaries. Finding Lang reading *A Cornish Childhood*, he asked him what he thought of it. 'Very ... very' – pause – 'interesting': non-committing himself had become second nature. During the Second German War, when the old man had retired, I was walking with a young friend, an American Signals sergeant (not *the* American sergeant all Society fell for in war-time London), when we ran into the Archbishop. He could not have been more sympathetic. He was on his way to a meeting of Trustees of the British Museum. I think if we had gone down on our knees and asked for his blessing, we should have had it. Not long after, on his way to the Museum again, he was struck down. I have always thought his last words characteristic: 'I must get to the train.'

Duty was the prevailing trait with all that generation of older men at All Souls.

I caught the infection from them: duty was a strong element in undertaking the chores I was now engaged in, certainly not pleasure. I put up Creech Jones, Labour spokesman on Colonial affairs, when he came down to speak – nothing very exciting in that, a bromide. I was bidden up to Headington to meet the Daltons, stopping with the Sanderson Furnisses. These were rather well-to-do people, of whom G. N. Clark told me an incident typical of those days for progressives, embarrassed by class differences. They had had a dinner-party, in full evening dress, tails and white ties; being Labour adherents, they asked the servants to join in. It was embarrassing for all concerned, not least the servants.

More congenial was meeting Mary Coate at Lady Margaret Hall, who was writing her book, *Cornwall in the Civil War*. A good historian, she was a dedicated Tory, a devoted teacher, who handed on pupils for me to teach (again in Political Theory!), including her own Veronica Wedgwood. Mary Coate's father had been Vicar of Luton; the vicarage was in the midst of the town and on Saturday nights the voices of the people were sometimes lifted up outside, drunk, swearing and blaspheming. The Vicar would open his window and ring his hand-bell at them: 'My daughters are ladies and I will not have them hear such language.' Thereupon – *O sancta simplicitas* – the idiots would disperse.

Miss Coate had had a spell at Exeter University, during which she enjoyed the friendship of the old Courtenay Vyvyans of remote Trelowarren near the Lizard – fascinating Elizabethan and seventeenth-century manor-house with a rich library of books and a full archive of documents and papers. A regency Sir Richard Vyvyan, a High Tory, was a cultivated intellectual, who kept a diary in Italian and collected Italian books – I subsequently bought a splendid edition of Palladio in five volumes from that collection. With the best intentions, on the approach of war, Miss Coate advised the removal of the archives, deeds, papers, documents to Exeter for safety – in time to be destroyed in Hitler's Baedeker blitz. After the war the library was sold, with many of the pictures and much of the furniture. All part of the universal break-up of our time – at any rate the break-up of all that I care for in it.

Academic life proceeded, with its frequent entertaining in those days. I met Enid Starkie, whom I came to know well later. I find an ambiguous piece on 'Lighting Miss Starkie's Cigarette' in the Note-Book: I did not much like her French way of lightly guiding my hand to the right place, the fluttering butterfly thrill I was given along my fingers. I got the message, but resented the incursion into my privacy. We never became friends, for all her intimacy – which, in regard to her emotional life, succeeded in putting me off the scent. Nor was I a favourite of hers. I did not entertain a high opinion of her, as I did of Mary Coate, good woman, good scholar, no publicity-monger.

Warden Pember regularly asked me to lunch when he had the Buchans, who were good friends to me – and John recommended himself by his admiration for Q. Lawrence Binyon, who came to lunch with me, had been at Trinity with Q. and told me something of interest. Q. had prodigious precocity: he started with more literary gifts than most writers end up with, and was already known, when still an undergraduate, for his light verse, exchanging chaffs and quips with Warden Anson, the leading figure in the University. *Dead Man's Rock,* a Stevensonian best-seller, was written before he left Oxford. Binyon said that they all expected a masterpiece from Q.; as the years went on, no *chef d'oeuvre* appeared, but a succession of lighter-weight books. The explanation was partly, I think, that Q. had to write hard for a living; partly, too, he thought of literature as coming second to life – writing was not all in all to him, as to a Flaubert or a Proust (or even to the author of this book). All the same, in Q.'s prolific output some of his short stories are, in my opinion, masterpieces, and a number of his romances and novels not far short.

End of term. I was on my way home to open Labour Party bazaars at Truro and St Austell, to raise funds (and spend a little of my own on them); and attend the League of Youth, with Alderman Moses, of Devonport. O God, O Moses!

5
1930:
Friends and Acquaintances

Underneath the unnatural repression for a young man full of vitality, my nature was an affectionate one, not at all cool. Here I was on Armistice Day, 1929, unable to work because my companion in the room below, Penderel Moon, had just left for India. A remarkable personality his was – one of the people I have most admired in life – and a memorable career he made of it. A kind of secular saint, dedicated to his job, service to India, of the highest principle, incorruptible – at one point, before the end of British rule, he sacrificed his post for his sympathy with the Congress Party. He came home and I was able partly to fill in the gap by asking him to write the biography of *Warren Hastings* for my series, *Men and their Times*.

When the take-over came Moon had the confidence of the new rulers and was given a tough assignment on the border between India and Pakistan. When brutal British rule ended, Hindus and Moslems won their freedom to kill each other in hundreds of thousands (like the blacks subsequently in Africa). In Moon's area he saved the lives of many thousands, organising trains to take Hindus flying eastward, and Moslems flying westward, to the bosom of their co-religionists. He could have made a fortune like Clive, instead of which he won adulation as a guru. After this feat he became Nehru's right-hand man in the economic development of India.

He had opted for India as a Junior Fellow. All Souls had made a remarkable contribution to India in one way and another, from Bishop Heber to Penderel Moon, via Viceroys such as Curzon, Chelmsford, Halifax; governors and administrators like Sir Arthur Hardinge and Sir Maurice Gwyer; Amery as Secretary of State, Simon and Coupland on their Royal Commission; or so odd and idiosyncratic a figure as F. W. Bain, inspired to write his books by Hindu literature and folklore.* None of these surpassed Moon in the character and quality of his services.

He had been a pupil of the philosopher Joseph at New College, celebrated in his day for the inhuman rigour of his logic. Where ordinary humans were depressed by it, some given nervous breakdowns, Moon took to it like a duck to water. An extremely agile duck, or perhaps more like a frog, slight and electric, leaping and jumping about with excess vitality. He used to try the Josephan logic-chopping – second nature to him – on me, to whom it was very uncongenial: it used to irritate me exceedingly. This did not prevent me from being fond of him, though we were in marked contrast in temperament and character of mind. Penderel was astonishingly rationalist for so young a man; not a rich personality, there was something *raide* and austere, careful and calculating, about him: both Puritan and stoic. He did not suffer from my conflicts and tensions within – he was exceptionally of one piece.

Moon has just gone, his last week-end in College a round of goodbyes for him. I set out to write, because I can't do anything else, and now I can't do that either. I didn't know what to do but gaze out of the window, vainly, just as I ran out into the street because I couldn't resist seeing him away safely. I was too late, the car had already gone. He rushed up at the very last moment to say goodbye, and wouldn't let me go down to see him off. So I waited by my window looking on to the quad; he didn't emerge for a minute or two, then I knew he was saying goodbye to his own room down below, already occupied by someone else – though it will always for me be occupied by him.

Now the bells give signal for the Silence; it's Armistice Day, the dead leaves blowing across my window.

The Silence is over, Tom bell has rung out his deep strokes; footsteps echo in the quad, the buses are running again in the High.

November 18. A week after, and the character of the occupation below has greatly changed. I hear Maurice Bowra's shrill treble laugh alternate with rapid dialogue. A night or two ago a voice was reading a paper to a society, with one joke a paragraph, to judge from the punctuated laughter. The quiet presence of the little Moon was

* Lord Salter was anxious for me to offset *All Souls and Appeasement* with an '*All Souls and India*'; but I had no qualification to write the latter.

114

more intimate and domestic; but he is on the high seas, another takes
his place.

Before he went I wrote him a farewell letter and sent him a
book. He replied typically that, as it was the last hour before
leaving, he had to control those damned lachrymal glands, but
there was some consolation in cold roast goose for lunch.
What was so painful was to watch him removing every trace of
his having been here.

His successor was another of those who had emerged
unscathed, like Roy Harrod, Douglas Jay and Herbert Hart,
from the Josephan mincing-machine – the young Sparrow.
Or was he entirely unscathed? I have sometimes wondered.
For, underneath the Josephan top-dressing, were the gifts of a
literary temperament, emotion, sympathy, even sentiment.
My own gospel is that one should fulfil one's inner nature: this
way lies creative achievement, not to impose upon one's
nature a superstructure not in keeping with it. That way lies
frustration of one's talents, an inhibition upon them, instead of
enrichment and fulfilment. It was on account of this that when
we were younger – no doubt unfairly – I used to call him 'the
Lawyer in Literature'.

It was really Joseph that I disapproved of – so clever, so
logical, and yet missing the larger, more significant points.
These pupils made a cult of him which I reacted against, and
was pleased one day when I managed to score off the prophet.
He had written a book against Marx's *Theory of Value* –
probably correct in its argument – from premises that were
irrelevant, in the result missing the point. One evening at All
Souls he was trotting out the argument which had floored
many persons of feeling, that men talk about 'the *amount* of
suffering people endure, but one could not add one person's
suffering to another person's', etc. I replied that any politician
had to take into account the *number* of people affected: the
phrase 'amount of suffering' in practical politics really meant
that.

For all their Wykehamist antecedents and training, their
having been Joseph's pupils, the new man in the probationer's
room below was very different from Moon; he was much
more self-conscious, acting a part. One day I went down and

was astonished to find him walking about his room, hat on head, scarf wound tightly about his neck, walking stick in hand. When I asked what on earth he was doing, he replied gravely, 'Trying to see what it feels like to be Garrod.' I was still more surprised – as if it were worth while! I regarded H. W. Garrod of Merton as a clever old silly, which he was, talented, but affected, with that lachrymose falsetto in which he uttered his sissy jokes. A good Latinist, he had been frightened out of the field by the uncompromising Housman, and taken to the easier option of Eng. Lit. I do not think that he achieved much in this field either.

It was odd of the young Sparrow to make a cult of these old sillies. Farquharson of University College – Farquie – was another: *the* authority on Cook-Wilson, the logician of whom these other logicians spoke with awe. They told of the occasion when the master was to read a paper at Christ Church after dinner: beginning at 8 pm it was still going on at midnight, by which time he was coming to the end of his prolegomena, most of the audience having disappeared. The old fool! Farquie was another – such cleverness devoted to such minimal ends, or to double-edged jokes for the benefit of the initiates. Warden Adams invited Farquie, when John's guest, to sit on his right in the place of honour. Farquie, turning to us with a smirk: 'What have I done to deserve this?' He considered dear Adams a bore – nothing like such a bore as Farquie. But I was not one of the initiates: I hadn't the time for such types.

My own guests – and I had many in those days – were literary or political. In February I note Spender, then Coghill dining with me – neither of whom became close friends. Nevill Coghill became an intimate friend of Wystan Auden's, his pupil, for all that he got a Third in the Schools. Nevill received his reward – the dedication of poems, testimonials of friendship later, when Wystan became famous. My admiration for Nevill was from a distance, from the vantage-point of an entranced spectator of his stage-productions. As a producer he had a streak of genius, and so was kept out of producing most of his time at Oxford by people vastly his inferiors. I shall never forget the revelation his production of *Samson Agonistes* was in Exeter College garden: the austerity of the first Act, then the voluptuous erotic entry of Delilah upon the scene.

Later on, in all the brouhaha about my first Shakespeare biography Nevill disagreed with me: he couldn't see the point that Mr W. H. was not Shakespeare's man but merely the publisher's dedicatee. Six years later I met him in Merton Street, when he accosted me with enthusiasm: 'My dear Leslie, Mr W. H. was not Shakespeare's man, but Thorp's the publisher's.' I refrained from saying, 'But six years ago you couldn't see it.' After all, better late than never. And when I made the unexpected discovery of Shakespeare's Dark Lady among the Forman papers in the Bodleian – just where she would be, if ever – Nevill wrote me the most generous letter. 'All the time I was Professor of English Literature at Oxford I kept thinking I should look into Forman's mss. in case there was something E. K. Chambers had missed. I told myself I was too busy; in fact I was too idle. You have not been, and have reaped your reward.'

Nevill was far from idle, he was a busy professor conducting his department. I had none of these chores – I had given up teaching: if they didn't require my services, I had better fish to fry. E. K. Chambers never did go into the Forman papers; nor had anyone else, though they had been waiting there all those years to yield up their secrets. What luck it was for me! I made two separate attacks upon them over the years – the first time rather baffled. The second time they yielded Shakespeare's Dark Lady – though I was not looking for her: she was waiting for me.

I was more friendly with Stephen Spender when young and, proselytiser as I was, I was after him as a recruit to the Labour Party. I can see him now, gangling and tousled, retreating over the grass at All Souls from my last attempt upon his (political) virtue, when he announced his approaching engagement to the cause of Communism. How hopeless these intellectuals were, I thought! These were the days when Day Lewis was writing, in Auden rhetoric:

> Hands off! The dykes are down.
> There is no time for play.
> Hammer is poised and sickle
> Sharpened. I cannot stay.

Ludicrous, when you come to think of it! To this genuine working-class offspring these were middle-class juveniles.

Far better read in Marxism than they were, I was at least wrestling with difficulties in Communist doctrine. My Note-book diagnosed 'a fundamental difficulty: i.e. that on the basis of a complicated and hypothetical system of thought Communists demand a drastic line of action. How can they have the confidence to risk such dangerous political action when their diagnosis of the situation is so highly theoretical that, even if a near approach to truth, it cannot command certainty?' Ingenuous as this was, it had its point – even when allowing Communists the best of the argument it did not weigh the balance in their favour. I thought then that the Marxist analysis of society was closest to reality; but, though much influenced by Marx and my conception of history deepened by it, I was no Communist. Those others simply gave themselves to a faith, to learn their bitter lesson from experience later.

In March I was entertaining two Cambridge friends for the week-end, Maurice Dobb and Piero Sraffa, both sweet characters. Dobb remained a beacon-light of Marxism over there for a lifetime and, harmless as he was, must have had considerable influence in impelling his younger generation towards Communism, while at Oxford I was trying to hold them back. The overwhelming consideration was that in Britain the only practical instrument for bringing about a new social order was the Labour Movement.

At Cambridge, where their Labour Club was less strong, the Communists were correspondingly stronger – hence those losses of talented youth, John Cornford and Julian Bell (who attacked me for no reason out of the Cambridge blue), and the misdirection of misfits, like Burgess and Maclean.

My old friend Crowther belonged to this Cambridge grouping, and he brought a real live Russian Communist to lunch, one Tambutsev. I don't remember if this was the Assistant-Commissar who subsequently paid me a visit on his own; once he glimpsed Trotsky's Life (in French) on my shelves, I got no further word out of him: he sat there transfixed, eyes glued to the book forbidden in Russia (Sartre's incarnation of 'freedom'). The Assistant-Commissar was subsequently liquidated. I was taken by the faithful to a reception at the Russian Embassy in Maisky's time, and was presented to the guest of honour, Bukharin, an historic name from the October Revolution – I remember only copper-coloured hair and beard, rather Trotskyish. He too was subsequently murdered. What a society! What hopes of a better world!

More practically engaged, I was off home for the Easter vacation to spend it in a round of political meetings: out in the clay area at Nanpean, at Sam Jacobs' Trethosa, inviting the old boy home for an afternoon with us in our council house. There followed the delights of a demonstration at Bodmin (a hopeless area for Labour), a Teachers' Conference at Truro, and a Chamber of Commerce Dinner in the City Hall – rather a full dress affair with Mayor and worthies, political opponents and the local peer, Lord Falmouth, a Chamberlainite later. What a way to waste an Easter vacation! – I should have spent it in France or Italy, or in Spain before the break-down of civilisation there in bloodshed and destruction.

Significantly, very little of these chores appears in the Diary. At the turn of the year: 'I'm dead tired, I was up so late after a long day, coming home from Truro and then going out to St Dennis and Foxhole in the evening.' I had been writing a poem, but was not pleased with it – 'nothing so good as Auden's play, which has at last been published in *The Criterion*. Four years at All Souls and nothing done: it's hard to know how the time has gone. There's no such consolation as Richard Pares finds in Julius Caesar at twenty-six crying because Alexander the Great had conquered the world at that age.' The church bells at home ringing in the New Year reminded me of that earlier year, 'when I sat up alone with the lamp in the old kitchen at Tregonissey reading the first War Memoirs, Colonel Repington's, and Margot Asquith's. And Germany three years ago, listening to the chorales being played in the square outside the Pastor's house in Hagen.'

As usual I was collecting folk-lore and tales of my people – two or three of them had the same theme as Lawrence's 'The Tinners' Arms', most authentic of Cornish themes. Here was one from my Mother:

Mrs Hore must have been a termagant, led her husband a miserable life, and brought him no children. He left her and went to America, but for years sent her a decent living. She saved on it, a good bit of money. Then he stopped sending for several years, and she lost touch with him. One day, somebody returning from America told her where he was, keeping a pub with another woman, by whom he had a family of young children. Mrs Hore drew out her money, sold her things, and went out to him. She went straight to his address, knocked at the door, which, as luck would have it, was opened by him. 'So I've got 'ee now,' she said. The husband died of fright on the spot.

In a short story one would think this far-fetched; it was in fact authentic, and in keeping with those old folk and their simple ways. Other stories related to my family; one that came peculiarly close connected one side to the most romantic place in Cornwall. Here was cause for trauma that lasted all my life; as with T. E. Lawrence it fortified my distaste for the consequences of heterosexual relations, the vulnerability of women, and cut me off further from conventional family life. That I did not regret, nor, in the end, the story – though there might have been tragedy there. I might never have existed – which would have been a pity, I have had such a wonderful time: I should like those to be my grateful last words – rather like Hazlitt's. Anyway, it made my background acutely more interesting: I was to make a further discovery late in life, which I can have still less reason to regret.

But I notice in the Book of Life the increase of nervous irritability and distrust of people. Once in America I was put through a third-degree inquisition, by the formidable wife of the head of a university institution – the New England type that brought on the Civil War, like a Harriet Beecher Stowe – *à propos* of *A Cornish Childhood*. *Everybody* responds to that book, so I was astonished at being taken to task – 'Why don't you trust people?' going on and on like a relentless gimlet in the endeavour to screw out of me the secrets of my private life. I was affronted at the impertinence, in a cold fury, though I kept complete control. This was what nettled her. Her own life was transparent, clear to the gaze, all too obvious to the beholder – all the more boring. She was a fine upstanding chàracter, a good grenadier, so strong in will-power that she bowled everybody over like ninepins. There was not the least hope of her breaking down my defences – my reasons for distrust of human beings (like Swift's) go much too far back in my experience of them, interwoven in my own nature. Much more interesting, I should have thought, than transparent obviousness.

Already, nearly fifty years ago, I warned myself: 'In giving advice to another, be careful lest you only make your confession to him. It is all the more humiliating when he knows your secrets, and does not act on your counsels.' 'It is a law of my life that I should live to myself. However much I try to establish contact with someone outside, I am thrown back on myself. It seems to be enough, if I make an approach, for the other to withdraw; or, if another approaches, I reject what is there for the asking.' This assumption became a fixed pattern in my mind, 'and never the twain shall meet' – another reinforcement of my Manichee attitude towards life. 'If you wish to be discouraged, you have only to confide your most cherished projects to your friends.'

At home I couldn't bear the racket of the kids playing in the road outside my window – there is a poem about that (dear old Warden Pember commented that he well understood). 'I detest these children at play: all the caterwauling little girls playing at "mothers" and "aunts", trying to persuade the boys to be "fathers" and "uncles", and then the inevitable for the smallest, "You must be the baby." The active little males propelling imaginary machines about, "Ch-Ch", "Gr-Gr", whistling and bustling. All such a disgusting preparation for Nature's purposes. Damn Nature's purposes!' A tell-tale note says, 'Anyone who has had to face the rigours of a proletarian diet' . . . for my digestion had long been ruined, my stomach as queasy as my mind. Nor were scraps of what people were like consoling: I recorded them (like Swift) to feed contempt, perhaps a form of self-torture. In the barber's shop Butcher Stephens, a mountain of his own beef, fits with difficulty into a chair.

BUTCHER STEPHENS: Mornin', Mr Honey.
BARBER HONEY: Mr Stephens in the chair. How is it then?
BUTCHER: Just as belong to. No better and no worse.
BARBER: Couldn't be no worse.
BUTCHER: Which way do 'ee mean? In mind or body?

BARBER: Well, takin' a broad view, like.
BUTCHER: 'Tis broad, and 'tis a very good view.

I had not then heard of Flaubert's *Bouvard et Pécuchet,* but I was already keeping something like his *Dictionnaire des idées reçues,* or Swift's *Polite Conversation,* noting down human converse with a fascinated contempt.

'Oh the blessed relief of getting away from people's tongues! – where there's nothing but the clucking of chicken, the mooing of cows, cocks crowing, and over the moors skylarks singing.' I must have been up at Carn Grey, where there always seemed to be skylarks thrilling in the air.

Clear Easter light over all the leagues of land from the high ground. So bright, every brick, dark-red and crumbling, is picked out separately at the top of the old mine stack; stone-grey splashed with russet up to the cornice of curved stone where the brick begins. Down the valley towards Garker a new clay-burrow, with sky-tip like a ship's mast at an angle. Shadows skim over the brilliant, beloved land, right up to Rowtor on the eastern sky-line, the shadows themselves blue as they pass across the folds of the landscape.

Back at Oxford I would take refuge from the increasing burden of work and worry in solitary walks beyond the Parks and along the Cherwell into Mesopotamia. Here, tired and worn, I had a favourite perch

on a stile under a roof of leaves. In the water-meadows the sorrel is red amid the gold of kingcups; a sudden eddy of wind rises among the long grasses. All the while I hadn't noticed the song the brook behind me has been making to entice me – a rill of sound as it falls over the mudbank and drops down to the bridge. A tiny splutter in the water: a wren is taking a bath among the shallows and cresses. A magic place: it is only after the pulse of motion has worn off that one can hear the small enchantments that assuage and beguile.

Several poems were written along those walks towards Marston – in the measure that attracted me at the time, pentameter couplets, rhymed but separated.

At night, in those rooms gaining more and more a hold on me:

all through the summer night the gentle pattering of rain goes on, beating upon a myriad leaves, the wings of frightened birds, the parched earth. From my gable a steady drip-drip into the lead gutter. A sigh of wind and rain rustles in the corner of mantled wall, bringing to me what unhoped-for memories of lost days and gusts of regret. Within the lighted room it is a friendly ghost that awaits me coming from the window.

The Diary was neglected, under the pressure of work.

Nothing for months. I suppose because I have stifled my private life in work, and disappointment, and work again. A separation from Adam: forgetfulness, then the relentlessness of my memory of him, give way to my work. Letters from him, but I harden my heart against writing. Then it becomes easy not to write, and I take no notice of his ups and downs of feeling, but work until tired out. Now I have come out the other side of tiredness, since he wrote so hopelessly, I have replied. Anyway, being abroad with him spoiled going abroad without him. So the choice is still his. Meanwhile the drudgery of the prison has been almost unbearable. I sit in my blue chair, listening to the endless essays droning on, catching at a word here and there, often a whole sentence; but it conveys nothing.

Anyone would think from this that I was not a good tutor; not so: I will not go into it, but it was not what I would have chosen had I been free. I continued to note down the stories I had little time to write up.

David told me of a friend of his who had been in love with another, a young man killed in the war. The friend could never have had him: he took no notice when alive and, dead, was dust. So the man married the dead boy's sister, because she was like him and had all his ways. In the end he learned to love her for her own sake, not only for his who was dead.

This was like the clue to C. S. Lewis, which Bruce, his colleague, told me. During all his early years at Magdalen Lewis remained a reticent bachelor, whose private life nobody knew. He worked in college in the week, and left at the week-end for a lonely cottage he had up on Shotover. Nobody knew why. Was he living in sin? Did he keep his family there and not want anybody to know? One day a colleague, caught in a heavy shower, entered the cottage – which was empty – and as he thought, the secret: a woman's stockings were drying before a fire. The truth was stranger. Lewis's nearest friend had been killed in the war; his dying request was that he would look after his mother and sister. Lewis faithfully carried this out, though hardly able to bear it; torture to him. He was something of a masochist; he ultimately married, a few years before his death, a woman dying of cancer. Underneath the bluff, blustering personality the public saw was this this self-torturing spirit – hence the streak of genius, no more, which made him remarkable.

Though our personal relations were friendly enough, intellectually we were at opposite poles, and once were called upon to debate publicly in St Mary's. Lewis disapproved of my historicism, I disapproved of his anti-historicism. He disliked my scepticism – which actually had been much influenced by Newman's *Grammar of Assent* – by which I attached more importance to the circumstances which make people think what they think, than what they suppose themselves to think in and for itself. This relativism ate away the certainty of doctrine, the absolute validity of people's convictions – and conviction was the breath of life to Lewis, particularly in the nonsense realm of theology.

He carried this into the field of literature and literary criticism, calling it 'the personal heresy' to attach importance to the biographical circumstances that illuminate a writer's work. He thought that judgments, especially his own, were absolute. In fact, his could hardly be more personal – absurdly so: as in thinking that English poetry reached its terminus with G. K. Chesterton (he could not bear Eliot's, in spite of their being co-believers).

During the Second German War Charles Williams arranged that these two eminences should meet on neutral ground at the 'Mitre'. Eliot, always a little shy, began tentatively: 'You look younger than I thought ... judging from your photographs.' This did not go down well, so Eliot tried again: 'I have been reading your book on Milton; the part about Virgil is very good.' This was worse. As the waters closed over poor Tom's head he was heard to falter, 'Speaking as a publisher ...'

Lewis had not only a powerful *parti-pris* but was obstinately perverse. When his sixteenth-century volume in the *Oxford History of English Literature* came out, I wrote an appreciative review, which pleased him. But he had singled out Cardinal Allen as a significant Elizabethan prose-writer, who wrote only a pamphlet or two, and totally ignored the far more significant Jesuit, Robert Parsons, who, Swift thought, wrote excellent prose. Lewis wouldn't take the point; intellectually conceited, he wouldn't take telling by anybody. Far worse was his prejudice against the early Humanists: he preferred sterile medieval logicians. McFarlane, a true medievalist, regarded the whole argument of *The Allegory of Love* as at variance with the facts of medieval life: Lewis had taken literature for life. All the same, he was an able thinker: his *Experiment in Criticism* exposed the inadequacy of Leavis' criticism, for all its pretentious claims.

Oddly enough, what Lewis had wanted to be was a poet; he had not the temperament, nor the mind of a poet – a clever, ratiocinative intellect, he wrote verse. Something of poetry came through in his children's fables – all of his work that I could take. As for his autobiography, *Surprised by Joy*, I found the arch self-consciousness acutely embarrassing. All the same he was the biggest man, and the best scholar, in the Eng. Lit. School at Oxford. They never would make him a professor, so Cambridge created a chair for him, though he was less at home there.

A more eminent literary figure appeared on the scene: Yeats was given an honorary degree. I had missed him in Dublin and, as usual, made no effort to meet him in Oxford, though Maurice did. I contented myself with describing the proceedings in the Sheldonian.

As he advances up the gangway an expression of confused diffidence mingles with one of ingenuous pleasure. I am surprised to see so large, so noble a figure; the hulking shoulders, well balanced though somewhat rounded by age, and the shock of grey hair, lifted back in two swathes from the wide brow. While the Public Orator's eunuchoid chaffering goes on, the poet looks lost in embarrassment, then advances with slow considered steps up to the Vice-Chancellor and takes his seat as a doctor. I hadn't expected so masculine a figure; yet how feminine is the expression of the face. The eyes are weak behind the huge spectacles, giving the face an owl-like appearance.

At first a bit dazed, he looks uncomprehendingly around. The head settles into its regular habit of repose (or is it the mask long arranged with which to greet the world?). I observe the conflicting characters of the expression: drooping corners of mouth; melancholy and petulance; the thick loose lips, sensual and self-indulgent; a puckered look of a spoiled child; weak eyes, visionary and estranged from the world. All this conflict of expression, simultaneous and not confused, leading up to the wide brow, candid, serene – as if the restlessness had achieved at last calm, above the war of passions, weakness, and the world.

At home that August I went on with my Labour *corvée*: I peddled a dreary propagandist called Winterton around a series of street-corners, St Blazey, a somewhat blighted place, Trethosa, Grampound, lovely Mawnan, worthy of less demotic attentions. I was at pretty Portloe with Tom Bennetto, a worthy old schoolmaster, whom I found sympathetic. The Federation of Cornish Labour parties met at Truro; then a Divisional Council. Down came Dr Marion Phillips again, with whom I perambulated to Bugle and Nanpean – how I grew to grudge against the latter, speaking at the open space on the curve of the steep hill, with the grinding gears of the buses to speak against. However, Transport House was doing its best for me – in 1930 we thought we were on the way up.

One Saturday was given up to a demonstration at Camborne; not my favourite town. That ugly industrial area with its rows and rows of miners' cottages, its graveyard of chimney stacks, and then prevalent Nonconformity, was our nearest thing to South Wales. Its local life was dominated by a friendly figure who was Chairman of the County Education Committee, C. V. Thomas. He belonged to a tin-mining dynasty; his grandfather had been the remarkable Captain of Dolcoath Mine, most famous of Cornish mines. 'C.V.', as we called this ponderous figure, was more of a manipulator, with large interests in Malaya. I got on with him rather well, considering that he was the incarnation of the type I disliked: well-off, self-satisfied Nonconformist, and of course Liberal. He and the County Secretary for Education, F. R. Pascoe – a buccaneer, no humbug – used to take me round in their cars, one an official one, the other a rolling Rolls-Royce, which made me slightly car-sick, along with a fatuous woman-alderman, whom they teased and flirted with alternately. Mounted on my high horse, I took no notice.

Both of these old boys had an eye to the girls. The great 'C.V.' – a dominant figure in his ambience, large fat chapel at command, in which he pontificated – made a point of taking the Scripture classes for the nubile VI th form girls (all very harmless, of course) in Cowper-Temple religion which had emerged from the Nonconformist agitation against the great Education Act of 1902. I recall a ludicrous story, told me in that rolling car, of C.V. undertaking to find a moneyed wife for the impecunious baronet who inherited an enchanting house and estate in lovely Luxulyan Valley. Upon the breakdown of C.V.'s efforts the luckless baronet went to live with attendant housekeeper in a bungalow on Par Sands – portent of the social amenities of today. What a kindly old pomposity C.V. was! One of the Christmas messages to his feudal dependency – Moab is my washpot, over Edom will I cast out my shoe – began with a quotation from John Wesley; next stage up came something from Jesus Christ; last, and most important, the Master, C.V.'s own words.

If only those Cornish Nonconformists could have seen themselves as others saw them!

More to my taste was my first country-house week-end with Charles Henderson at Penmount. This was a Georgian house in a draughty situation on a hill overlooking Truro from the north, the ground falling away to the west into the deep valley of the River Allen; enchanting spots with names like Idless, Killagorden, Bishop's Wood and (Our) Lady's Wood, Treworgan and Ventongimps. Charles undertook my induction to the churches and neighbours around: his own St Clement's at the other end of the parish down by a creek of the river, diminutive hamlet, where I suppose the Saint must have landed and ministered, thatched cottages with rose-gardens – it is only after nearly fifty years that I have written a poem about it in his memory. In the evening we explored Castlean-Dinas, largest of the prehistoric hill-top camps dominating the cross-coast route over Goss Moor. In those days the Moor was less intruded upon: bogs and pools, plenty of snipe, its own flora, bog-cotton and bog-asphodel, whortle-berries for the picking amongst the adders.

Next day, Sunday lunch at Killagorden, sequestered Queen Anne house deep in the valley, crammed with old family china. It was the home of the Tomn family – I was too late to know the formidable heiress, Lilian Knowles, who had taken a

First with Smuts at Cambridge, became a well known economic historian, professor at the London School of Economics and died in early middle age. How I envied her heir, a good sort of yokel, gone back to the soil, as often happens. Tea with the Masefields at Mawnan, where they used to take the rectory, known as 'the Sanctuary', a suitable cover for Mrs Masefield.

Supper at Lis Escop with Bishop Frere, the first time I had met him, though I admired him from afar. He was all that one could wish in a prince of the Church, a bishop rather after the fashion of the French Church, as one sees it depicted in that delicious book – *Au Presbytère*. Frere had been made a bishop to help with the revision of the Prayer Book, rather against his will, for he was a monk who loved the life of the Community of the Resurrection at Mirfield. Q., a man of quality himself, could appreciate another, and said to me, 'Baldwin did better than he knew when he appointed Frere to Truro.'

An outcry followed on the part of black Prots, not mollified by the Bishop living like a monk at Lis Escop, with two or three of the Community for company and to look after the household. Frere was a man of exceptional distinction: historian and liturgiologist, musician and linguist, who spoke Russian and knew the Eastern Orthodox Church well. A man of good family, he was a man of the world, though quite unworldly, for his inner life was dedicated to religion: he was something of a saint, the spiritual quality transparent – if anyone could have pulled one into the Church, he could. Frere was above the realm of understanding of ordinary Cornish folk; his successor, Hunkin, too well within it.

Nothing could have set one more at one's ease than Bishop Frere presiding at Sunday supper; like the gentleman he was, natural and easy with everyone, for all the asceticism of his appearance – the austerity was for himself, the silvery beam for others. A burst of laughter rang from outside – 'rigs of fun in the kitchen', the Bishop said; he had a Father Housekeeper who presided there, and a tall handsome young monk from Mirfield to help. Evelyn Underhill was a guest – a well known writer on religious mysticism at the time. I did not make much of her. My mind was full of Newman, for I had just finished my concentrated attack on *The Grammar of Assent*. It did not seem that anybody else at table had tackled it; few have – but it exerted a lasting influence on me, with its scepticism about ordinary mental processes.

When I got back to Oxford for term my old tutor, E. F. Jacob, invited me to talk to the History Society at Manchester. Like a fool, I chose to talk about Newman and the 'illative sense', the whole apparatus – nobody knew what I was talking about. I hadn't yet learned the art of making myself clear the hard way, by speaking at street-corners: the only thing I did learn from those deplorable experiences.

At Oxford I was bidden to meet all sorts of interesting visitors on their way through: John Livingston Lowes, for example, in the literary news for his book, *The Road to Xanadu*, the reading that fed Coleridge's imagination. R. M. MacIver was similarly to the fore in political theory with *The Modern State*. Later I came to regard the subject as largely chaff; so much of political theories being merely generalisations of party or group interests, or prejudices, or – for one must allow for the irrational – fancies and delusions. What substance remains over may be gathered from the admirable books of Graham Wallas or John Plamenatz – certainly not from Harold Laski, essentially a political journalist, or Brogan, an historical journalist. It is obvious from Laski's successor at the London School of Economics, Michael Oakeshott, how exiguous is the valid thought to emerge on the subject.

Meanwhile I was struggling with it – never have I had such uphill work in writing a book as with *Politics and the Younger Generation*. I do not regard it now as any other than an historical curiosity, or perhaps evidence for the state of mind of my generation. I suppose it served my purpose: I worked out what I thought for myself, Marxist as I was intellectually, without swallowing Communism whole, like the others. The Diary that summer says:

Unhappy days these are: I have been journeying with infinite laboriousness through the ante-penultimate chapter of my book, put off by tutorials, callers, worrying letters from the constituency, and innumerable distractions that take one's mind away from the one thing (at the moment) I care for. So much so that I haven't even regretted Adam much, though it looks as if we have lost each other irrecoverably, partly through my own fault. Sometimes the image of his head turned this way or that, his beautiful melancholy eyes, some charming trait of character, natural and grave, passes across my mind. But I hardly have the energy to visualise him so completely as in the earlier days: perhaps it all goes into my book, leastways it should.

But this afternoon I paid him the tribute of a few moments at Mansfield – nothing vivid about it, just hopeless. A dark day of summer cloud and rain, young men in white playing tennis on the lawn. Charles [Henderson] wanted to go down that road I hardly ever go; we went by, but I came back and stood there remembering. Charles kept saying, 'I don't think very much of the buildings, do you? Who is it? Champneys, I suppose.' Or, 'Have you ever been into the chapel? – such funny windows.' Then at last, 'Did you ever know anybody here?' I heard myself say: 'Yes, I once knew somebody who was here for a short time.'

All the same, I wonder what Adam is doing now, and whether he has got to Göttingen all right? At times I think he may be ill, or settling into a new environment, making friends with his usual facility. It would be comforting to hear happily from him. The last letters he was concerned about falling for a girl, all very unsatisfying, I wasn't clear why. He said she was incapable of understanding him beyond a certain point. I suspect that he never will be happy in these affairs, there are such depths of uncertainty in him. This was what appealed to him in me – that I was so certain myself. For all his attractiveness and sensitiveness he wouldn't make much of a lover for a woman, for what could she rely on? I begin to think of him as a Don Juan of friendship – I wonder the phrase didn't steal into my letters.

Perhaps he may find a woman who will help to develop some certainty and confidence, a sense of security. Then he might marry, have children and be content: the rôle I played in his life will have been useful to his development. We might even meet again – though how altered he would be, not the same Adam I loved. No doubt we should still be friends, we have so much in common to talk about.

At the beginning of the year we had been frequently in touch. On 2 January he was writing to me at midnight after a long walk through the dark from Solz (whence the title came – Trott zu Solz), where his cousins lived. He found the sense of hidden danger at night exciting. In the library there he had found an eighteenth-century edition of Hogarth's etchings with commentary by Lichtenberg, a professor at Göttingen whom some people called the German Swift. 'I have been holding the principle of independency against my brother with all success, but little satisfaction; it is a poisoned air ... How much do I long for a continuous neither too happy nor unhappy state of mind to withstand the ups and downs of one's life.' There we were again. He wondered whether a sudden change might bring the possibility of 'my consoling you, and you being the one who needed a friend to advise'. Immediately on his return to his law-studies in Berlin he wrote, 'I am so thankful to you for your letters and for your faith in the future of our relation.' My letters had reminded him of Fouqué, whom I had not read – they must have been in the vein of German romanticism in which Adam was well soused.

In February, 'my letters must seem to you to be written in an abnormal state of exaltation; yours tell me as vividly as could be what you are doing and occupied with at the time. And what more does one want?' I was trying to prolong the sense of being together by evoking the past. But this was not the 'present' for him. 'I really don't know what upsets me, but what horrid selfishness that all is; perhaps, A.L., you ought to drop me for a time, till I have recovered a normal conception of my duties to my friends ... I hate this anarchy, as the hero of my Jean Paul novel hates all "unfinished" things and has a complex against half-painted pictures, unsettled law-enquiries, etc.' That was the way it was with Adam. 'Perhaps you are right: I ought, and wished, to be your pupil in politics and history and literature, and might be able to give a little in return by friendship – that would turn all to the creative and organic [natural?] way.'

This is what I believed in: a more factual and dependable frame of mind, based on politics, history, literature, instead of endless analysing and doubting and swinging from side to side in the German manner. What did that lead to? (Answer, shortly – Hitler: no doubt or uncertainty in that quarter: he was the answer to it.) Time, however, showed that Adam could not bridge the gap, the German character of his mind was too deep-rooted. The dilemma appeared tragically in the Kaiser's grandson, Prince Frederick William, brought up much in England, who tried to make himself over, married a

Guinness, etc. – but the strain of it all was too much: he drowned himself in the Rhine after the Second War.

Adam left the decision whether we should meet at Easter to me. He hadn't the money to come to England or meet me in Paris. 'It might be better to let it be the Rhineland.' By that time I was too much occupied with the book to move away from it.

His next letter continued the Anglo-German argument – I was continually sending him books and articles, poetry and politics, to anglicise him. He was finding his law studies

unbearably dull and dry ... But indeed have you not got your path on which you can rely and advance – and which must somehow furnish an unchangeable perspective in matters of the heart also? And am I not on the other side the slave of ever-changing experiences and sentiments? ... Perhaps I am arguing subconsciously against the 'Cornish element' which may resent emotion as a motor of life[?] I so much like reading your articles and reviews, and was specially interested in your argument on historical materialism and its relation to individual motives. It is striking how one's stand, and how a whole argument, must change according to the political and dialectical situation of a particular time or country ... When you seem to be fighting for a new and truer conception of historical and social reality and its rational structure, it is here the power of the irrational which seems decidedly undervalued. Every movement derives a considerable part of its significance and nature by the thing opposed.

True or not, here was the cloven hoof of Hegelianism. This remarkable young man had, however, put his finger on the appalling fatuity of the bogus 'rationalism' of Leftist thought under the Weimar Republic. I used to take its intellectual organ, the periodical *Unter dem Banner des Marxismus*. It was unreadable; worse than the most fatuous contemporary sociology, it lives in a fantasy world of its own abstractions bearing no relation whatever to concrete events, commonsense or even sense. Such fatuity was enough to drive one mad – or to sympathise with Hitler's blistering contempt for such thinking and such fools. He was well aware that, once given the chance – as the German upper classes gave him his chance – he would knock down these card-castles in a moment. As he did: and it took the whole world to overthrow him.

It is bitterly ironical that I had such certainty then; it was indeed largely a reflection of the security of my background and of Britain's place in the world, won by generations of a valiant and tough, far-seeing governing class. Thrown away by their successors in our time, their place taken by my own working class, incapable of running anything efficiently, bent on wrecking what is, after all, their own show. A contemptible society exists today, visibly breaking apart; but when young, what could one do but hope against hope? Perhaps the hope was mainly a reflection of the vitality of youth – and yet, things need not have gone so disastrously. Now that Adam is long dead, and I old, wholly withdrawn from any hope, it looks as if he were more right than I in his uncertainty, his endemic insecurity.

'Today we passed Walter Rathenau's house and the place where he was killed [murdered by Right Wing Frei Korps thugs]: my thoughts, as they often do, went to you: I thought of the hard and political life you are going in for, and of what we both know and felt about the life of a man like Rathenau.' In those years I had a cult of this Jewish industrialist of genius, creator of the AEG, the enormous German electrical combine, who was yet half-way to Socialism. A man of culture with an international outlook, his writings appealed to me. He made the Treaty of Rapallo with Chicherin – both ambivalent types, they must have understood each other – which ended Bolshevik Russia's quarantine and made an opening for Germany once more to the East. This put paid to Lloyd George's hopes of reconstruction in Europe at the Genoa Conference. Rathenau's genius at reorganising Germany's economy enabled her to fight the 1914 war, when she might have foundered internally. For these services to Germany he was murdered by the thugs who were wrecking the Weimar Republic – aided by the paralytic ineffectiveness of its liberal-minded supporters. It was the thugs who should have been shot.

Adam had been walking round Berlin with a young South African who was coming to stay at All Souls. He was seeing von Seebach, too, who was Maurice Bowra's young friend. One way and another there were a good many *Verbindungen* between Oxford and Weimar. After the Second War Maurice received his reward, the Order *pour le Mérite* – he had not expressed in print what he thought of the Germans.

Adam's next letter, in March, was full of reproach. I was drifting away: I really could not stand his perpetual *Verwirrung* of mind. There came a limit to sympathising with a state of mind that seemed bottomless. I could appreciate the selfish realism of the French mind, but I could not grasp the formlessness of the German – and yet Adam had that irresistible intuitive sympathy. He was sitting on a grey March evening in his uncle's room at the Schloss, 'trying to imagine you sitting with me here where we once were together in sympathy and content.' He felt that I was failing him. 'If you despise my life as not being devoted to definite purposes, and my intellectual life as being dominated by emotion – was it right ever to allow me to play such a rôle in your life?'

He was well capable of speaking up for himself. The simple fact was that I could have too much of his state of mind – and he was very demanding – like the Germans. What was the essence of the situation? Was it that the Englishman wanted to be on top, and so did the German? No: I could not conceive of not being on top and giving way to that state of mind, which did not know for certain what it did want. Just like England and Germany.

I relapsed into silence and getting on with my work. Again symptomatically, he thought that I wanted to throw him over. But 'this was not it, not it at all', in Eliot's phrase. Perhaps I thought I was 'bringing him to his senses'; I certainly was tired out by his uncertainties – only a woman would have had the patience to put up with them, and they didn't seem to fill the bill. 'Is it that you don't approve of that adventurous conduct of life, and its changeable influence on my intellectual existence? Then you ought not to let this fact disturb our intellectual communion.' Then he intuited 'the overstrain of work' which was a real factor in my life. 'Whatever happens I do not want to part from you! And above all see you again as soon as possible!'

What could one do but go on, doing one's best for him – but within limits? The idea of limitation is rather English; the trouble with the German mind is that it has no limits – look at the intellectual megalomania of Hegel, or the illimitable ambition of Hitler. Stalin one day said to Anthony Eden: 'Hitler was a very remarkable man – only he had no sense of moderation.' He saw the look on Eden's face, and then said: 'I see that you think I have no sense of moderation. That's where you are wrong.' This was the fact: Stalin would take everything he could, until he came up against hard-line resistance, as over the Berlin Air-Lift.

In March Adam was having more trouble with a girl – a region in which I could not be expected to help. 'Where the whole matter breathes resignation you cannot help it through a definite act of renunciation – deliberately not seeing her has made me all the more miserable.' Why was he not more successful with his girl-friends – and with such looks? Here was another thing that I could not understand, and I was certainly not going to enter that region. Against this was the tantalising assurance, 'I on my side have never ceased to believe in you as I do in nobody else. If this gives me the position of somebody who admires you, it was a dour superstition of mine to believe that all that belonged to me too to some extent. There is no reward for that from my side ... I have an intense feeling of my inadequacy in our relation.'

How German it was! What did he want? Evidently to have his cake and eat it; and then the inferiority complex. I simply didn't bother with such considerations; I went straight ahead. But I always kept a weather eye open for the weather. 'There was perhaps no time when I realised deeper and with more gratitude what you and your existence mean to me and how it has entered into my life. Nothing like has ever happened to me since, and all hopes and possibilities for the future I often rest on this communion.' I suppose I should accept that generous statement of faith. Poor Adam; I think it was true, from what I have been told after the war, that this early experience of ours made a profound impression on him – as it did on me, profound and undying.

His extraordinarily sensitive antennae caught at once my suspension of judgment as to what would come of it all. 'I respect the hesitation that is manifest in your last letters, as it answers to a definite feeling I have about myself. But I am afraid you must accept me with it or reject me altogether.' Again it was rather English of me neither wholly to accept or ever wholly reject – everything would depend ... 'Does not true unity rest on complementary difference rather than agreement?' Here he was right, and I must plead guilty, in those fanatic days, of wishing to impose my will on circumstances as I had imposed it on myself – until circumstances eluded me to my anger and resentment, and the body revolted against the inhuman control by the will.

Once more Adam's intuition put his finger on the spot. 'One wishes not to lose something that one considers a most precious part of one's inner life. This, I believe, is an irrational motive into which one ought not to introduce the sense of purpose and design. Yet I am not sure whether you think the same.' At that time, I was all purpose and design – indeed, had had to be so from boyhood, or where should I have been? 'I observe how the tone of your writing in the last letter too has changed, and everything seems to have become relative – but I wonder whether the matters of the heart can become relative after all.'

In this intense correspondence Adam kept his end up. 'Relative', however, was not quite the word: 'contingent' described my attitude, i.e. that it depended on him: it was not going to be all take on his side, and all give on mine (cf. England v. Germany). He expected me, for example, to enter into the perplexities of his affair with his girl. 'You need not be ashamed of my being caught by her. The nature of her affection for me I do not fully see – the fact of its being limited makes it eternally unsatisfying.' Here was the German desire for the illimitable again. The English mind has a definite sense of limits. 'To prove the intimacy of telling you about all this I should love to spend a week of rest and peace with you. I feel that it would be the best thing in the world. I think you ought not to go abroad these vacations, and waste no time. So my coming would be the best after all.'

I did not cast myself for the rôle of father-confessor in this relationship; I would not interfere in his affairs with his girls – though earlier he had offered to give up one if I wished it! I wished him to be perfectly free to follow his own inclinations, but to be involved myself was something at which I drew the line. I did not encourage a visit; correspondence was dropped for a time: I plunged deeper into my work, he plunged deeper into the morass of personal relations, for which he had such a despairing gift.

We did not resume till the summer vacation, when he had 'got over a rather miserable period' and achieved his 'own victory' – over the girl or himself, I do not know which. 'It gave me a warm feeling of joy when I realised that you were sorry to have thought and intended to forget me.' Here he was mistaken – as others have been subsequently: a break was not what I intended, but suspense, a watchful suspense, contingent upon developments. And now the promising affair with *that* girl was over. 'I cannot blame you for getting doubtful about the use of carrying on these sometimes painful relations ... That last time in Berlin I was most miserably involved in every kind of disaster, starting from that very unhappy relation to that girl.' I knew that he had been preoccupied, and sensed what was the matter – but did not wish to impinge upon his confidence: a combination of sensitiveness and self-protection precluded me. The result was that a number of English acquaintances knew more about Adam's external life than did his 'dearest friend', who refused to know more. The result was to keep our relationship intensely pure – I do not mean in the ordinary physical sense, which it was, but aesthetically, almost spiritually, since the world of beauty was the life of the spirit to me.

During this period his confidence had sunk to 'the lowest possible point', he was possessed by 'utter hopelessness'. It was this in him that I did not like, the alternations, the plunges into despair – when my own gospel had always been 'Never give in, never give up.' 'You will probably have never lived through a time like that with your self-confidence and fighting powers.' However that might be, I was learning about life – through him. Paradoxically, egoist as I was, I was not given to analysing myself, pulling myself up by the roots to see how the roots were getting on. Proletarian commonsense kept me from that futility: my intimate Note Books and Diary are evidence that I was passionately engaged in observing the beauty of the world, significant external experiences, and try-ing to render *them* in words.

'The idea of your eventually giving me up weighed heavy upon my mind, especially because there seemed no means of holding you back.' Yet during all that time of misery there was no time 'when I had not stood loyal with all my heart to you and our friendship.' Again, no doubt he was right. And yet to what point was it? It did not prevent him from plunging into these affairs which promised ecstasy and ended in misery. His marvellous intuition told him what I thought about all that – I cannot think that I did, though my side to the correspondence was destroyed in the subsequent disaster. 'Nothing pained me more than the idea of being a fool in your eyes.' Well, wasn't he being one in these swinging alternations? Or perhaps he was just being German?

These swings from one side to the other related not only to girl-friends. 'Did you meet Richard Hare [a Balliol friend we had in common] after his being in Berlin? We had two rather terrible times with each other, and I felt very much ashamed of myself about it – as I hated very much his presuming, with his well known smile, that he was on as intimate terms with you as I am.' Though jealousy was a positive disease with the Germans, it was not, to my knowledge, characteristic of Adam. 'At the same time I had a series of misunderstandings and trouble with the nice British-Embassy secretary I told you about.' What was this all about? I think I can guess. Adam had now moved on to Göttingen university: 'Göttingen is lovely, and I wish we had spent our German fortnight together there.'

Well, I had made no complaints about our time together in Berlin, though the groundswell for me was of overwhelming happiness in unhappiness. I had learned from my life to put up with what one could not help – and yet, is that precisely true? How subtle life is, and how difficult to render it in words – Eliot constantly complained of the difficulty. One must distinguish. I was certainly not one for accepting things as they were – everything shows that I was not an accepter; it was that I was willing to put up stoically with what came, until such time as I could alter it. I expected nothing from the outside world; I expected, and exacted, everything from myself and I was maddened by defeat from the outside, especially from the inferior.

In Göttingen he was happier than in Berlin, where the political situation depressed him, and might well have depressed anyone. The idiotic Communists were making the paralytic Social Democrats the main target of their attack.

Next year, in the Berlin tram-strike the Communists actually collaborated with the Nazis to defeat the Social Democratic workers. Couldn't they see that, by undermining Social Democracy, they wouldn't win? It would be the Nazis who would. I kept arguing this with Ralph Fox, who would merely trot out the Stalin jargon calling Social Democrats Social-Fascists. Hitler – quite apart from his dynamism – had immeasurably more sense of power, which is what politics is about. Lunatic liberal-mindedness added another obstacle to any effectiveness, with its fatuous campaign against 'power-politics'. Pure cliché! What is the alternative? Weakness-politics? Futility politics? Nothing could exceed Hitler's contempt for their spineless futility – and I came, through bitter experience, to share it.

In Göttingen, 'dearest A.L., I will confess the personal side occupied my thinking of you lately more than the academic, in spite of the real helpfulness of the latter, and the expectation of future exchange that seemed to open up.' I had sent him an article on International Law by J. L. Brierley, Professor of the subject at All Souls, admirable man, with the mind of the best kind of jurist (in total contrast to Zulueta, whose Basque mind had nothing judicial, or even judicious, about it: just a good Latinist, ultra-montane Catholic, who regarded us all as 'heretics'. Mean too, where Brierley was philanthropic, public-spirited and generous). Adam was more concerned with the personal: 'I know that it is your idea to achieve what one can, and remain faithful to the fixed destination. But what for you is a constant and firm source of self-readjustment seems in my situation a continuous process of self-questioning.'

Damn self-questioning! This was what was getting me down, not in myself but in my relation to him. 'There is no guarantee in my present intellectual set-up that it will be the lasting foundation of my doings. You know the chaotic political situation in this country and can measure the strain of holding a true course against it.' I could sympathise with that. I thought Social Democracy the best hope, if only it could be rejuvenated, revivified and delivered from its paralysis by an infusion of youth. And this was the rôle in which I had cast Adam. In regard to politics, 'I see theoretically my standpoint in relation to it; but I need an inner distance and chance of

acquiring strength and knowledge that I don't find in pursuing
legal training.' I didn't wonder at that, but – oh dear! – 'inner
distance' and 'acquiring strength'. To this end he kept going
the idea of coming to Oxford. 'And then we might renew and
build stronger the foundations of future companionship.' He
certainly was not letting go of me.

In November he was stopping at Celle for his examination,
this 'nice old Hanoverian town' full of castles and alleys and
gardens, ponds with swans and ducks. 'I remembered your
stay in that small Westphalian town, and your poem on the
grey geese flying over: a vivid vision.' He goes on to what I
had evidently hinted about his vagueness – I preferred concrete
description to abstract analysis. More about his 'hopeless futility' – silly as I thought that: 'somehow I think that this lack of
balance hurts my pride.' If so, couldn't he shut up about it and
get on with the next thing to hand?

Not at all: everything was in question. 'I have been terribly
inadequate in one of the most important sides of our relationship: i.e. to be your follower and pupil, and at the same time
not to lose the value of being your friend. This, I think, is why
my admiration and objective belief in you could never exist as
an important issue in your opinion.' Behind this was the
German concern with *Gleichberechtigung*, equality of treatment. He was concerned to assert his value for me, but why
assert it? He could assume it. On the other hand, it was
inconceivable that such doubts and questionings, such
alterations of mood, such a German outlook, could influence
me in any way, except to increase my distaste for it. Adam
once thought he had found in me the one Englishman to
appreciate Hegelianism! I think I understood it, and its deplorable influence, only too well. He concluded: 'Don't forget that
I am so much your follower in many ways that it would be
strange if I did not need you.'

In December he was worried about his father, who had had a
bad fall at the age of seventy-six. Meanwhile he had acted on an
earlier suggestion of mine – something that I had thought then
too good to be true (I never expected any bonus from the
outside world: I had only to wish for something for it to be
denied, unless I wrested it from circumstances by the sweat of
my brow; to others things *came*) – and put in for a Rhodes

Scholarship at Oxford, giving my name and reference. 'I made the study of international law, and social and political subjects, the ground of the application.' I wrote enthusiastically in his support. At the end of the year, he had done well in his law examinations – he was a serious student – and was grateful for my support: 'I feel that you always act with a whole heart.' As soon as he heard the result 'I want to make plans about our seeing each other again – I so much want to.'

With so much on my mind, there was less time to record the inner life in the Diary. But one summer night at Oxford,

my mind is haunted by the images of the two people I love. An ordinary enough day, up early to lecture, much spiritless reading and some talk. Suddenly I stop and look across at the blue chair: I have a vivid sense of Adam sitting there, leaning forward in front of the bookcase, but I see the books through him. Still he was there very plain, the light on his hair shining fair and golden. The attitude the one I know so well, so appealing, like all his movements, leaning forward with elbows on knees, face in his hands. That's how he used to sit, thinking things out. I say out loud, to myself alone: 'Oh, that's all right now, my dear. That's all right' – consolingly, quite naturally, as if he is there. So vivid a sense of him, I wonder if he is thinking of me just at that moment?

This was quite likely, I realise after a lifetime of telepathic experiences; to correlate with Adam's extreme intuitiveness, I was myself, and always have been, psychically responsive.

My mind wandered off to what a gift love is: if one is inconsiderate, it makes one consider the other; if selfish, unselfish; where one was ungenerous and calculating, one becomes more free, prepared to take risks. In the end the physical doesn't matter, each has the sense of the other's presence, a thing of the mind.

Then my mother was there in his place: not at first clearly, I had some difficulty in imagining her face. That made me think of her as dead, and all I should have would be her image to remember – and I might not be able to call it up clearly in my mind. That brought her countenance instantly into the room: so lovely, pale ivory, sad, with the resigned expression of the mouth, the delicate shell-like ears, the wavy hair drawn back. She is very beautiful. This unpredictable moment caught me off guard. When I am home again all will be as usual: I should never be able to let her know how much she means to me, but perhaps I don't need to say it.

At any rate, I never did. How devoted I was, and how sadly it all ended! One night I was alone in College – very few lived in All Souls during the week – when all the lights went out.

The Manciple has set a candle at the head of the staircase for me, and a candlestick to take up to my ghostly bedroom, 'as in the good old days', said he. I sit at my desk with three tall candles flickering by the open window. It gives an eerie appearance to the room. But it looks *right*, as it was known to how many previous occupants. I can well understand W. P. Ker refusing to have electric light brought into his rooms.

While the lights were off I went for a walk over Magdalen Bridge, into squalid St Clement's along the fouled pavements, pubs every few steps. Sordid types outside the doors, a tart back to the wall having her cigarette lit by a young man. Twisted types limp along, harsh ugly women. And these are the people for whom my scheming and planning, my New Jerusalem is intended. They'd foul the door-step before they got into it.

Along the Marston Road was the place where I saw a woman scrubbing and washing a child's headstone, bending over it as if over a sick-bed, putting a long arum lily far down into the grave as if to reach her child. This was the place: now it is night. I do not know what has drawn me forth, my footsteps stumbling along the bitter pavements of the city. Then it was spring-sweet afternoon; rain and sun, battering the meadows, drove me to take shelter under the copper-beech, whence I watched the three silent figures by the grave, oblivious of rain and sun. Farther on, unable to keep to the kerb, empty stomach, light-headed, steering uneasily, I put the question: 'Shall I go mad?' The long acre rights me: scent of evening and dew and summer mists, through which the trees loom dark and soft. But a couple is up against the paling, with a dog to defend them – superfluously, they are so inseparably stuck together. Animals: the play of a middle-aged woman with a middle-aged man makes one sick of one's kind.

On my way back the place is full of couples, two couples companionably sharing the bench at the top. Policemen are about on bicycles, the streets even more sordid, pubs still more in evidence with their cheap glitter. [I was a tee-totaller and had never entered one – how well geared to demotic life!] In an interval two young whores with gay caps cross my path, trailing a cheap scent in the fragrant air of St Clement's, stinking of piss and stale fruit. They pass into a dark doorway near the corner-house, neon lighting 'Chips' and 'Beds'. Not for anything in the world.

This might be my friend Graham Greene's world – the squalid released the springs of his imagination – it certainly was not mine. I had seen enough of it, close at hand, in my early life in the village. I preferred the life of a country-house. Unattainable. Next day I was

working feverishly at the Concept of Class section of my book. This evening, some consolation (in vain) in hearing the cars and buses go by, the soft horn that reminded me of the Munich taxis. I wish there had been tram-bells: it would have completed the illusion of my time in Berlin, and my room in the Uhland Strasse at night as I lay in bed reading *War and Peace* under the green lamp. Today, getting up, I recaptured the thought I had lost, directed against the lovers on the bench. A street-lamp nearby was besieged by moths, enjoying themselves frantically before they got burnt. In the end, the lamp shall eat them up too.

I thought of someone revisiting Adam's rooms, perhaps when he has died or forgotten the past. The other goes back to live in those rooms, to recapture and relive his memory [as I am doing fifty years after]. The family there can tell him of a side of Adam he never knew [as a woman still alive in London can].

Perhaps these jottings may be of interest to the psychologist for what they were – evidences of repression, too rigorous discipline, overstrain.

I was engaged in a cult of sensations on the margins of experience, straining myself to the limit. This had its strange rewards, some of them psychic. That summer D. H. Lawrence, who meant so much to me, was dying; after his death it transpired that in his last months he had been haunted by the image of a Ship of Death, about which he wrote a poem, unfinished when he died. One summer evening I saw

a phantom ship in the bay, a strong breeze and wearing full sail. First seen from the headland, stern-on going east, a tall straight line a bit thicker at the spars and leaning a little away from land, whence the wind was blowing. Later, wind increased, ship coming due opposite making for the headland, then sheered off to make the bay again. She seemed to be going in circles: a beautiful spectacle from the cornfield where I usually halt to write: the ship with dun brown tattered sails between the steep V-sides of the coombe, skimming swiftly by, the water nostrilling from her prow and alongside.

But suppose if no-one else could see her?

Shortly after I learned that Lawrence had died about that time, and I believed that I had seen his Ship of Death.

I often have the sense of nostalgia for the past. It came to me this evening as I stood over my supper in the kitchen, bread and butter and buns on the table, the dreary soaped-in clothes waiting for the morning, washing-day. I was in an eighteenth-century country house; it was Pope's, and he was standing up reading from a calfskin-bound volume. Hardly any scene, only a tall window of the time looking on to a border of flowers. A hot summer day, full of country sounds, hum of bees and flowers: I could almost feel the heat in the room. Everything was of the period, and I so much of it that I became unsure whether it was Pope or me. I was living the life of those high rooms, rather bare, books in brown leather bindings, and the sense of comfort in discomfort. I thought too of Sans Souci, perhaps the high windows brought it back: I imagined the palace peopled again, a few figures in wigs and full skirted coats down the length of the corridor; Frederick in the background, his room light and airy. From an angle of the colonnade at the back, some bustle in the red courtyard; hum of summer, country smells, but unmistakably also of ordure and open drains mingling with the delicate and fine in my eighteenth century day.

Towards the end of the year, in Oxford:

I come out from the lighted room into the night full of rain-wind from the south; bells beyond the walls out in the city. A flag of smoke flies over rain-washed roof; domestic lights lit in winter windows. Oh sanguine bells, ringing as if to call the heart home. Come you home then, come home! I try to find where they are; bewildered I pursue through courts and quadrangles. The wind takes them up and flings them down out of the four corners of the sky. They speak to the heart of what has been: the aldermen step bravely out, gowns bellying in the wind, the street alive with sound and movement – but they are the gestures of the dead, the voices of the centuries gone by. Now the bells are faint in the distance, I can hardly hear them, or the footsteps of those who went away in the blue of summer morning to foreign fields. When the bells are ringing and the wind sits south, they come home again. Come you home then, come home!

6
Politics and Poetry

With my constituency, Penryn and Falmouth, to nurse I was now frequently up and down between Oxford and Cornwall by train – a waste of time and money. In Cornwall I spent some of the money I earned the hard way, by teaching and examining, on supporting my parents, while I contributed to Party funds according to my small means. I was not to make a fortune out of politics, like our unambitious Knight of the Garter, or other Labour politicians with their farms and swimming pools in Sussex. And where Tory opponents made their money out of Cornwall, I spent mine there.

Journeying back from St Austell in the New Year I had one of those odd experiences for which I was constantly on the look-out. The Sunday train was occupied by a group of odd people, all the men wearing beards, an oddity then.

A young man had a flaming beard, golden and ginger, bright and aggressive; a middle-aged man had an iron-grey beard, and looked a foreigner. Why were these people so distinctive, in dress too? One ungainly man in heavy clothing might have been an Irish peer. I kept hovering on the edge of knowing who he was and then I saw he was the spit of Charles James Fox, beetling, highly arched eyebrows, black hair turning grey brushed back from the broad brow, the lumbering figure. The face was recognisably pursy, with broad jowls; the tunbelly even more recognisable, covered with thick broadcloth, innumerable small buttons down the front.

They behaved oddly too. The man opposite me propped elbow on window ledge and read the *Observer* sideways, out of one eye, the other fixed on me. He had gentle celibate manners, spoke in low tones to the waiters and waited patiently for his China tea. Nobody would share a teapot in this eccentric car. One man was hideous, goggle-eyed, enormous nose, no chin; pasty coloured, sloping forehead, cockney voice. I detested him for his bad manners to the attendants. Odd man out in this *galère* was a market-gardener from St Ives, who spoke with sing-song West Cornish intonation, and drank cups of tea from the station wagon wherever we stopped.

Who were they, Charles James Fox and all? Had I had an optical illusion? Or a visitation from the past, like Miss Mober-ley and Miss Jourdain at Versailles, whom Geoffrey Faber of All Souls was then republishing?...

Shortly followed my first week-end at Easton Lodge. This was the home of Lady Warwick, famous mistress of Edward VII, who had become converted to socialism and remained constant to it – one more of her extravagances. I recruited Richard Pares to this venture of G. D. H. Cole, who was now endeavouring, by founding the Society for Socialist Inquiry and Propaganda (SSIP), to repair some of the damage he had earlier done to the Fabian Society. What gave Cole's new venture some hope was that it had Ernest Bevin with it. Bevin had not only vision and character but, the leading Trade Unionist, he had the big battalions. It was imaginative of him to give us younger intellectuals our chance. And he was willing to help us in other ways too: he provided the support for the *New Clarion*, for which I was recruited as a regular contributor and wrote many articles. This was specifically designed to appeal to the younger generation; here I could put forward the conclusions I was painfully working out in my politics book – more theoretical than practical, Marxist but not Communist.

Cole should have kept contact with Bevin at all costs. In the event he lost it. After no long interval the propaganda sprang up for a Popular Front with people further to the Left, notably Stafford Cripps and his following, and even fellow-travellers with Communism. Bevin would not have this at any price; he had a life-long experience of dealing with Communists. He knew that they would use the opportunity to break up any organisation that was non-Communist from within.

The original aim of SSIP was a rejuvenation of the Fabian Society for us young people. After the appalling catastrophe of 1931 and the set of the 'National' government, the Popular Front idea had an obvious appeal. A violent tug-of-war took place within SSIP, poor Cole pulled this way and that – as usual by the impossible Postgates, near-Communists. This meant a breach with Bevin. ssip broke up – fragmented itself to join up with Cripps and form the Socialist League.

I took the wrong line about this, following Cole and the ssip executive – I remember receiving a letter of approval from Margaret Cole for my 'loyalty' to the executive. I was not one for taking a minority line and making a nuisance of myself, but it was fatal to get out of step with Bevin and confirm his distrust of the intellectuals. The Socialist League came to nothing, and Cole retreated into the broad Fabian bosom he should never have left. Here Hugh Gaitskell came in, for whom Cole professed a platonic love. Hugh as a young Public School man, and a more integrated nature than I – for he had had nothing of my struggle behind him – had none of my inhibitions.

However, I had learned my lesson as to Cole's capacity for leadership and took no part in the Socialist League. I became a *New Clarion* man, while it lasted. Bevin was a West Country man himself, with a sizeable Transport Union membership in Cornwall, while my china-clay working father was a member of the General Workers' Union which Bevin amalgamated with his own. The big man not infrequently came to speak in my constituency; I have gone up into the clay-area with him for meetings when only a handful of men turned up. I often thought of it subsequently when he became a world figure. They wouldn't listen to him when they had the chance; nor would the country listen to Churchill's warnings.

I can see Bevin now at Easton Lodge, sitting beside Lady Warwick in their arm-chairs, each of them so fat that they welled out over the arms. She was still beautiful, deep violet eyes, with the amplest velvety bosom. I used to think of Albert Edward pillowed there – she had in the grounds a Temple of Friendship dedicated to her memories, with many photographs of him. I never penetrated that sacred preserve. After my last week-end at Easton Lodge I sent her as a memento a little book I much treasured, François Mauriac's *La Province*. Shortly after, Richard Pares drew my attention to an item in a Bournemouth bookseller's catalogue: some cheap French novel, by Paul de Kock, beautifully bound and inscribed, 'For lovely Warwick, Albert Edward, Christmas 1894.' Probably more in her line than my chaste offering. Bevin, no Celt like

MacDonald, had not the slightest tinge of inferiority-complex, nor the susceptibilities and sensibilities.

Lady Warwick's estate at Easton, her own Maynard inheritance, was a centre of free thought and conduct in those days; on the edge of it was Dunmow rectory, the home base of H. G. Wells's variegated domestic life. Though I recall within doors the pots with palms, the background to Bevin and Lady Warwick, I can remember nothing of the discussions – mere chaff. All that the Book of Life records was 'the melancholy cry of peacocks, the incessant chatter of the room.' But I did note down people's verbal characteristics: Cole's regular cliché, 'What I'm thinking in terms of': Trade Unionist Pugh's, 'It's all a question of ta-ime'; and W. A. Robson, of the L.S.E., ending his sentences with, 'And so forth and so on'. In fact, we never got anywhere, though we returned to the entertainment for further week-ends in March and June. I recall Cole's joking condescension to a beautiful Oxford girl anxious to take part, that – 'if she were very, very good, she might be allowed to come.' This was Elizabeth Harman, a cousin of Neville Chamberlain, now Lady Longford. She certainly stayed the pace better than I did – and brought Frank along with her, now another Knight of the Garter.

I was merely struggling to work out what I *thought* about politics, as I had done earlier with my little book *On History*, which has served much better as a programme for work in that field.

11 February: 'Midnight and I have just finished rewriting my first chapter, the third draft! Wild horses wouldn't drag me to do it over again.' In May: 'Nothing is ever done easily; I have had trouble enough with my book for the last two years for it to be a work of value – I wonder if it is going to be?' I do not now think that it had any objective value – it is a mistake to write a book on politics when one is young: one needs maturity, experience. When it came out, R. C. K. Ensor compared it unfavourably with Cole's *World of Labour*. But there was no comparison: Cole's was a book of factual description, mine was trying to work out a theoretical standpoint covering not only politics but economics, history and even literature. Such value as it had was subjective: it provided a firm enough

intellectual base from which to confront that evil decade, I knew at least where I stood, without committing the follies of my contemporary intellectuals in throwing in their lot with Communism, or the Left Book Club, or – like John Strachey, Harold Nicolson, Catlin – with Mosley.

Even with regard to economics I had a line of my own. I was acutely anxious about the increasing deficit in the country's balance of payments long before professional economists seemed to think it important or to be worried about it. Except for Keynes they were all immersed in their Free Trade – Free Enterprise dogma, by which the economic mechanism automatically righted itself. In my anxious view of life, and with my experience, nothing automatically righted itself: intervention was necessary. How could the deficit in our balance of payments (not trade only) be corrected? Obviously by scaling down luxury imports, what the country did not need, or needed less than other things, concentrating on the productive as against the less productive or non-productive (let alone the counter-productive, e.g. drink, tobacco, drugs). I considered that the country's economy within should be regulated in accordance with some scale of what was productive downwards to the non-productive, the superfluous and unnecessary; what could be dispensed with.

I was no economist; it was not my business to define this concept of productive v. non-productive, though it clearly related to what was of more or less utility to subsistence. Some idea of that sort had been at the back of Mercantilism, as it was called by orthodox Free Traders: it was what the ablest minds of statesmen and economists before Adam Smith had considered in the best interests of their country. Keynes was at last realising that these men had been no fools; however, the Free Trade – Free Enterprise orthodoxy of the profession held them in a vice: they could see no other. I put my difficulty to Roy Harrod in a letter, to which he replied, explaining the orthodox view that the mechanism righted itself: which ever way you spent available resources, it gave rise, indirectly, if not directly, to the same amount of employment. I simply could not believe this. If you spent £100 on imported wine, which mostly went down the drain – no doubt giving rise to *some* demand for our goods in exchange – it clearly did not create the same amount of employment as if you spent £100 on boots and shoes for a number of people. The implications of this for Labour policy were obvious.

Meanwhile the heavy balance of imports against our exports was increasing and in the course of this year was to produce an almost fatal crisis for Labour, wreck its government and put back the Movement for more than a decade. Why would not people look ahead? (They never will, until too late. But then, intelligent people do not wish to be caught in the consequences of the folly of the unintelligent. I have come to see now, at the end of my life, that my revolt was, like Swift's, against *la condition humaine*, the way humans are. No point in it. In the end, since 1939 I have come to act on that principle: it means, in practice, withdrawal; if they like to be such idiots, let them take the consequences.)

In the economic crisis of 1931 the professional economists were paralysed by their abracadabra; I have never had much respect for them since. Even Lionel Robbins, high priest of orthodoxy, now admits in his autobiography that he was too rigid on the matter, so impressed was his purism by the possibilities of corruption, tariff lobbies, etc. against any form of protection. Nor do I think that the 'expert' advice of the economists since the Second War has done anything but hamstring the country's economy and kill incentive and efficiency. Once Keynesianism had become orthodoxy – spend, spend, spend – they adhered to that in the wrong circumstances, encouraging every kind of waste, piling up excess government expenditure at every level, encouraging the Trade Unions in impossible wage-demands while working and producing less and less. The upshot is a stricken economy, a slack, inefficient, contemptible society, visibly breaking down under the burdens placed upon it.

The economists put forward as absolute truth, as if it were mathematics, what is relative to circumstances and contingent upon them. Robbins disapproved of Beveridge's distrust of economic theory at the London School of Economics. My sympathies are with Beveridge over this: economics is not a pure science like mathematics, i.e. it deals with the actual, factual world. Beveridge's preference for the description of economic facts illuminated by common sense deduction is more trustworthy than the abstractions of theorists like Kaldor, with their crazy obsession for taxing productive enterprise out of existence. (I believe the name is Hungarian, and that he is a passionate Social Democrat; he should try his Social Democracy on Hungary.)

Keynes, however, encouraged me. He recruited me as a reviewer to the *Economic Journal*, which gave me the chance to review Tawney's *Equality* sympathetically. Not that I thought that people were equal in strength, gifts, ability, etc. but that society should be directed towards making up for inequalities. I still am – no reactionary – in favour of that, though not for levelling people down to a dreary sameness, on the mistaken assumption that they are equal in aptitudes, tastes, equipment. Keynes welcomed also my reviews of Russell's book on *Power*, etc., and my first modest contribution to historical research: 'The Dispute concerning the Plymouth Pilchard Fishery, 1584–91.'

That term I was entertaining as widely as ever: the Comte and Comtesse de Luppé, I don't remember who they were or why; to meet them I invited Miss Starkie, as I called her impersonally, and Woodward, who had had his Paris period, though he didn't speak French. Another day I entertained Jimmy Maxton, celebrated then as the reddest Clydeside MP. Rather than an *enfant terrible* of the House of Commons he was their favourite bush-baby, whose measure they had taken. With the long locks he cultivated for the sake of publicity, he looked like a witch, but was a harmless sentimentalist, for ever breaking the rules of debate (which paid publicity-wise) and then making abject apologies, which won people's 'hearts'.

The ILP (Independent Labour Party), which had played an historic rôle under Keir Hardie and Ramsay MacDonald in creating the Labour Party, fell to pieces in Maxton's nerveless hands. Like so many Leftists he had no sense of practical reality, let alone political power, and like them was always 'up agin' the government, even of his own party. This made him what Churchill described Aneurin Bevan as being, a nuisance, though not a squalid one. Both Maxton and Bevan had charm – but what is the use of that without common sense or loyalty? In the hands of such people the ILP became just a fragment of the Lunatic Fringe – and MacDonald and Snowden gave it up long before the end. As the organisation frittered its life away in internal disputes Maxton would say, 'Tell me what I am to do. Only tell me what you want me to do.' Imagine it in a leader! Contemptible. Contrast Hitler, who knew all too well what leadership meant.

It was heart-breaking to be involved with such people, and bit by bit it disillusioned me with the Left. The Tories, Baldwin and Chamberlain, knew well enough what politics was about and how to take advantage of our fatuity. In utter contrast with our lunatic fringe stood Bevin, who knew instinctively all about political power and how to attain and exercise it. *They* hated his guts for it – and didn't much like me. I held them in contempt; but Bevin trampled on them, quite rightly, and wouldn't have them in his government when Labour at last came to power in 1945.

I kept contact with my Canadian friend, Eugene Forsey, of the CCF (Canadian Commonwealth Federation), which hoped to become a Labour Party over there, and added a new one, Lionel Gelber, of whom I saw more later. Somerset de Chair appears among my guests, somewhat improbably; he had won attention as an undergraduate for his book, *The Impending Storm*. A promising young man, he got into Parliament at twenty-four, since he was a Tory; but somehow a precociously promising career petered out somewhere along the line. Douglas Woodruff turned up occasionally, still hanging round Oxford nostalgically – he had sat for the All Souls Fellowship without making it; achieving nothing of any permanence, he finally settled for a place in Catholic journalism.

Powicke had now arrived as Regius Professor of Modern History. I recall the consultations before his appointment, which were in Cruttwell's hands as a leading figure in the History School. I was in favour of A. F. Pollard, the most eminent Oxford historian at the time; in addition to his important Tudor books he had created the History School in the University of London and dominated the Institute of Historical Research. Precisely because of his forceful personality they would not have him – and no-one would hear of Namier. Great men may be great bores, and in course of time Namier showed that he had a touch of greatness. Later we came together over our campaign against appeasement.

So Powicke got the job, though a medievalist, as a safe appointment. I was never wholly at ease with him, though he became the father-in-law of my dear friend, Richard Pares. Powicke had a Nonconformist and Balliol background, which doubled his moral approach to everything, not only history but even historical research. Nor was he at ease as Regius Professor – he was more at home in Manchester – or at All Souls, which aroused his inferiority-complex: I think he was one of the many who had sat for the Fellowship without winning it, like his successors Galbraith and Trevor-Roper, with similar consequences. Powicke, a finer historian, gave himself to the job and made Oxford, during his time, the leading centre of medieval historical scholarship in Europe. He was a man of tremulous sensibility, who wrote like an angel; as some-one said, he had a touch of genius without first-rate ability. One saw that in the inadequate structure of his books; moments of illumination, but absence of vertebrate structure. He had never made any money out of his admirable works. Later on I put together a collection of his essays, which made several hundred pounds for him. He then thought he could make a second selection on his own – which he did – arranged fore part behind: the specialist, technical essays in front, those of general interest in the background. The book was a failure. (Just like an academic, I registered.)

Though Powicke became rather affectionate, as I lovingly looked after Richard, helplessly paralysed, I never felt at ease in the household. Powicke's wife was the sister of A. D. Lindsay, the Master of Balliol: all too much Balliol highmindedness and moralism for me. And I had my own reservations. Among us younger people on the Left, A. D. Lindsay was a figure on a pedestal. But he was already on a pedestal in his own view; Richard once described him to me as a very vain man. He thought that, as Master of Balliol, he had only to make pronouncement on public policy *ex cathedra* for people to sit up and take notice. Mrs Lindsay, a twittering little woman, wrote a book on Birth Control, to which the Master wrote a Foreword; but it appeared that husband and wife did not agree on the subject, nor did it seem that Lindsay had even read it. With no human touch, he made a poor head of a college, though an able Vice-Chancellor. He should have been Vice-Chancellor of some new university big enough to carry him on its conveyor-belt. In the end he created a university to suit himself at Keele, of which he became the head, a snug berth for retirement.

Meanwhile, the Buchans regularly asked me up to Elsfield to dinner, each term, until John went off, by MacDonald's appointment, as Governor General of Canada. I went to tea as usual with the Bridges's on Boars Hill. The old poet had independent means, without being well off; he lived in surroundings of careful distinction and beauty, with a big bookroom into which no-one was invited. He was rather spoiled by rich American Mrs Pearce, who supplied him with his cigars and Boars Hill with music in the large music-room she built on to her ample house. Those were the days!

Easter was given up to constituency chores: a League of Nations meeting at Truro, an open-air performance at another exposed spot I grew to dislike, Victoria Square, surrounded by pubs. I recall a drunk who made nonsense of my attempt to induce sense into the heads of the crowd. More congenial was an excursion into West Cornwall, preparation for *Tudor Cornwall* years later, for I was spying out the lie of the land I was to write about – my involuntary preparation bore fruit where my willed endeavour did not. Antron, on the way to Helston, was where a leader of the 1497 Rebellion came from – hence the family was extinguished, I reflected passing by. Pengersick Castle was in a then romantic situation on Praa Sands, sequestered and unspoiled: today ruined by squalid bungalows and caravans. Pengersick had its haunted story of the Milliton, who having committed a murder and escaped from the Tower of London, lay hidden there for years. All that remains of the castle is its peel-tower, the hall and other buildings, visible in an old print I possess, having vanished. Q., who knew so much of the folklore of Cornwall, wrote a short story based on another tradition of that once unfrequented place.

Thence to Wendron to make the acquaintance of the learned eccentric, Canon Doble. His passion was the lives of the Cornish Saints, whom he pursued not only in English libraries but into Wales and Brittany, where he had friends among the clergy. He was the unique master of this idiosyncratic subject.

Years later I was to make a contribution to it with my study of Nicholas Roscarrock's *Lives of the Cornish Saints** – a manuscript which Cambridge University Library deposited for me at the Bodleian, just across the street from All Souls.

Vacation wound up with dinner at Penair, the country house above Victorian Pencalenick to the east of Truro overlooking Fal country. The estate was one of several purchased by the Williams family, the industrial magnates who had made a vast fortune in mining in Cornwall and, on recruiting themselves to the ranks of the country gentry, became marvellous gardeners. John Charles Williams of Caerhays was rich enough, in those happy days, to finance expeditions to bring back rhododendrons from the Himalayas. Penair was then occupied by the widow of Harcourt Williams: she was a Trelawny, with the glittering dark looks of that family, subsequently to become a good friend. She was the only person to warn me, in my ingenuous youth, that to have a constituency on one's own doorstep was not a good idea. For one thing, one never had a proper holiday at home – though that was the least of its disutilities.

I kept going my habit of taking notes wherever I was. On the way home in the train 'an old man was sitting on his bag in the corridor reading a book: rusty black leather binding, it must be the Holy Bible, and he a Nonconformist minister, the sort of gold-rimmed spectacles, the right kind of moustache. Whatever was he reading so intently? I got him a seat in my compartment: the book turned out to be *The Puzzle Book*.' 'A Cornish wood has a peculiar intimacy. As you go further west the trees are smaller and on more friendly terms – sometimes a copse of diminutive oaks clinging to the hollow in a valley fold – a glimpse of water in the sun through trees.' West Penwith is almost treeless; a little estate like Boskenna of the Paynters, or lovely Lamorna before it was ruined, had trees so small that the second storey of a house peered above them.

> 'In the field sloping to the sun,
>   the earth heeling over,
> The seagulls turn white breasts to the sun,

* In *Studies in Social History, A Tribute to G. M. Trevelyan*. Ed. J. H. Plumb.

The lambs cry with seagull bleat,
The blue tide running in.'

Such was Cornwall in early Spring.

And here was my mother in the kitchen: 'Look at it! The sea is mountains 'igh – g'eat white 'orses turnin' up. Black east wind. 'Tes terrible, 'is my dear life.' It was cold, and she was 'shivering like a toad in stays.' Then, 'I can't spell nothin'. I'm the wishtest poor speller that ever was creaated.' She had hardly ever had any schooling: grandmother and grandfather Vanson could not afford tuppence a week to send their children to school very often. To the cat – we always had a cat, though my father fancied a dog – 'Ee's mother's l'il sweet-'eart stuffed with treacle.' I could never take down enough of these sayings, which alternately charmed and irritated me: she was incapable of speaking correct English, or even aspirating an 'h', while I had set myself from the age of nine to speak the best English I could. This was laughed at by the other village boys, but I paid no attention: I knew that one day I'd have the laugh on them.

Even from our horrid little council-house I could see, between the roofs of other people's houses, the bay and the headland: 'the blue Gribben plumed with feathery rain-clouds, the snail tracks on the level sea; massed clouds rolling back from the sea along the coast inland, gulls crying in the near coves. New ploughed earth falls in furrow, a fine pattern where the harrow has turned. The enchantment spoiled by a pushing woman with a pram.'

Back at Oxford my own room was there to welcome me, secure from demotic life, from which to watch and record the beauty of the world. I had not heard of Berenson then: it is only in later years that I have come to see that this perpetual watching, waiting on the moods and appearances of the external world, then registering the experience, the moment of illumination as the most precious thing in life, was akin to his. Berenson's biographer quotes Henry James in point: 'Words seldom catch the excitement, the promise and the despair of it, because the young are too busy living it to write it down.' I was so eager to lose nothing of it that I neglected one side of living, the side that absorbed most people's energies. The sentence quoted referred to travel abroad: 'the secret is to be alone, or often alone.'

Hardy, always a loved influence, has a virtuoso passage at the beginning of *Under the Greenwood Tree* of the different sounds the wind makes in various trees. Here I was noting the noises it made in my creaking panelled room, full of fears.

A charming windy evening: leastways it promised so when warm and firelit and laughing, now it is cold and late. While the wind was getting up there were such nice noises: first, an unexpected rush at the window, lifting it on its hinges; then on the other side of the room at the shutters, which just creaked and shut it out. Next, it got behind the panelling on all sides at once, straining at it, like a ship straining around me. The roar in the chimney ended that illusion. Now the big door into the Hall is banging, with a high note, not deep but protesting. A light over in Queen's wavers to and fro as the branches of the trees cross and recross it. It's nice to be alive when the work is finished and done with for the night.

From my window: three shades of green in the garden: fresh spring green of the Siberian crab-apple, light and dainty, a misty veil thrown over crumpled shoulders; darker green with a touch of gold of the chestnut shooting into leaf; rare whitish green of the copper dome of Queen's behind the foliage, whence the bell strikes four, scattering the notes into the garden. The arched sky is thunder-blue, threatening. Roofs are grey-blue, alternating with purple or ochre stains. The Library windows in line are darkened to sepia-green, deep as woodland pools. How endearing the scene is, from the gathered chimneys that fixed my mind, so statuesque they were that early dawn of pain, to the Japanese cherry on the curve of wall, white and pink clusters. I note every brick of the chimney, every baluster along Queen's roof, almost every stone and line of mortar so lovingly, that my mind shall not forget when the time comes to leave, when it is only a memory and my life has passed from it.

When that time came, in 1974, though I had long moved from those early rooms, I revisited them and went back over them, my mind full of those years and days.

The Book of Life existed to record such moments, like Berenson's Note-Books. The Smoking Room had its own feeling for me, a different inflexion, hardly less beloved.

I look up from the remains of tea, the plates in disorder, the sheen upon silver tea-pot that mirrors the high garden wall shutting out the outer world, tops of poplars and chestnut above, the fleecy summer sky, sugar-basin with tongs of the time of Pitt. Turning, I find the garden strange with an unknown awareness: a tiny fern ensconced in the elbow of a planted cusp nods to me across the lawn. The irises put off their reserve, stretching out their tattered blooms to the bells that fill the outer air. The tulips reach out in open desire. The garden no longer withholds its secret. It bares itself to the responsive intruder.

Not only visual sensations opened the doors of the mystery for me, but aural experiences too, especially bells, which held a spell for me all my life.

From eight to nine the city is full of their sound. Peal after peal rings from the towers, I cannot tell from where; they come from all corners of the skies, reaching to the depths of one's being. They open windows into an unseen world. Suddenly they cease, and the world is empty again. Only the usual noises of summer night for comfort: a breath of traffic, a stray bell chiming a quarter, the rush of a car, footsteps on the pavement; stillness.

Afternoons I went for walks, in those days with my friends, Richard, Charles, Bruce; but I grew to prefer them solitary, one could take in so much more of the world.

5 May: afternoon walk down to Sandford with a stiff wind blowing up the river, ruffling it into waves. I wondered if the two crews going down would manage the passage; they did, the first with elegant rhythm, so spare, in perspective the boat flew like a bird over the bottle-green water. Coming back, I registered that the Catholics are making ostentatious return to Oxford, building now a chapel on to Bishop King's Old Palace, a Counter-Reformation plaster mould on the wall, a modernist negro above the escutcheon. In Christ Church Meadows, a sudden glimpse of Magdalen Tower, grey in passing cloud, then quick sun, then grey again: wave after wave passing over rock. As if the waves of the centuries had never gone by, and this were the first May risen above the trees.

Here is a note about history, the kind of thing I kept usually for academic note-books.

One has become so used to looking at England of the past, or the history of any county, as through a telescope, as if it all happened on so small a scale, a confined field easy to comprehend. Then all was simple – so few people – everybody, one would have thought, knew everybody who was anybody in the London of Queen Elizabeth I, or of Queen Anne. Hence one thinks of everything happening on a small scale. It is hard to think that the Oxford of Newman was much like the Oxford we know [only the inner core today]. The Oxford of the Civil War occupied the same ground, a bit more cramped within the walls, elbowy, airless, but with open country coming up to them. When Hawkins and Ralegh went up and down to Plymouth, or the Queen visited Oxford and Cambridge, or Kenilworth, they covered the same ground as we do. But in their experience the country must have been far larger, the distances to travel slowly on horse-back much greater; so few people, large tracks sparsely occupied. It took a week or ten days to get to Edinburgh; going down to the West Country took four days. A man could easily disappear. Our simplified view of the past imposes a restriction upon it. Today the whole world is more unified: hardly a corner in which there isn't some one one knows.

This insight into the past I saved up, until it appears decades later in *The England of Elizabeth*.

Whit Sunday. A gust of wind struck the chestnut trees broadside on. Yet the word 'struck' is not right for so complex a motion as the wind has set up. The trees are in full flourish, like mountainous flowers; the wind ruffles the surface, then penetrates the foliage, splits up the mass into innumerable bunches of swaying leaf and flower, all swirling in subtle contrary movements, now here, now there – a crest of white blossom uppermost – then a chasm of greenery opens up the bare structure of the riven tree. It is like watching a seething mass of green water swirling in complicated movement, inshore green driven on the rocks, split into a thousand crests of laced ridges of foam.

In those days we mostly attended chapel, where the services had remained unchanged since before the Oxford Movement; our old Prayer Books called upon us to pray for Queen Adelaide, the Queen Dowager. I longed to see a high Mass celebrated in that noble building, and sometimes there on my own would intone the beginning of the Latin 'Credo' in plainsong. Listening to prosy sermons was another matter: my attention wandered to the inscription on the frontal, *Justorum animi in manu Dei sunt*, or to 'the shadow of a small bird crossing the pictured window.'

Out! – out, like a schoolboy let out of school, into the Meadows or through the Parks to my favourite spot then in Mesopotamia:

The lovely waterlight under the leaves
That catches at the heart
And fills the eyes with tears...
A silent rat slips obscenely by,
Fat belly dragging on the refuse bank.

My world had its fauna too, one of the oddest being C. R. M.
F. Cruttwell, with his copper nose and idiosyncratic language.
Richard use to call him 'the Dong with the luminous nose' and
collected his verbal expressions. I have already defended him
from his pupil Evelyn Waugh's aspersions: though Cruttwell
had a tongue like a rasp, he had a good heart; his wicked
phrases were a form of art, which one did not take seriously.
The successful cleric, Nippy Williams, whom nobody loved,
glistened with sleekness and prosperity. Canon of Christ
Church, he married a large, voracious-looking woman; as he
paced out ecclesiastically in the Meadows, face shining with
complacency, Cruttwell would say: 'There goes Mr Worldly
Wise-man, with his wife, Mistress Carnality'; and add, 'exud-
ing not the grace but the grease of God'. Or, 'looking like a
Roman emperor who took to debauchery in the intervals of his
intellectual exercises: I don't doubt his ability, but he has an
unfortunate Christian appearance.' Cruttwell himself was a
practising Christian, charitable with money, but not verbally.
Richard would lead him on to ever more extravagant flights,
but did not preserve his Cruttwellisms. I cannot now
remember all his terms of art: academic males were 'hacks',
females 'drabs', unless they were emotional, when they
became 'breast-heavers'.

At bottom he was a kind man, a repressed sentimentalist.
Elderly General Swinton, who had been forked by the War
Office into the chair of Military History, was terrified
of Cruttwell's tongue. He knew that Cruttwell was a far
better military historian, and that Cruttwell thought him idle.
Which he was; also talented, and rather a dear. He presented
me with a dashing red tie, *très sportif*, of which I wear a
replica today. Swinton had a house up the Woodstock Road,
complete with Raeburn portrait of an ancestor; himself had
an artistic, inventive streak. He had much to do with the
invention of tanks; (and made H. G. Wells cough up £500 for
saying he hadn't). Ironically, during the next German war

his daughter was killed by an oncoming tank just outside the house.

In April I was entertaining a group from the Russian Polytechnics, some ten of them to tea; at another time one of my pupils, Devlin, with a powerful booming voice. Some years later, attending a performance of *King Lear* by chance, I wondered where I had heard that opulent voice before, and found, looking at the programme that it was my pupil, become an actor. Sooner or later, everybody turned up at All Souls. Now it was Wallace Notestein from Yale, who was to become an Associate Member. He professed being an Anglophile, and made a good thing of it; for he built up at Yale a remarkable department of scholars in English history, *protégés* of his. Notestein wrote one or two discriminating books, but devoted himself mainly to editing seventeenth century parliamentary diaries. Friendly as he was to all, and friendly enough as our relations were, I was not quite his cup of tea. He preferred purer academics like Pares; and events and personalities at Oxford were reported to him by an unfriendly pen.

This summer I met Matthew Arnold's grandson, Arnold Whitridge, very like his grandfather to look at: not at all the broad English face of Dr Arnold, but the refined bone-structure of the Celtic side of the family, the Penroses. * Arnold Whitridge continued the literary inflexion of the family, writing a book on Arnold of Rugby. This brief encounter bore fruit forty years later, when I was writing my biography of the poet, with its emphasis on the Celtic side. In Cornwall I became a friend of Will Arnold-Forster, great-nephew of the poet, grandson of William Delafield Arnold, who died on his way home from India, for whom the beautiful memorial poems were written, 'A Southern Night' and 'Stanzas at Carnac'.

Will Arnold-Forster was a man of distinction, a bit of a doctrinaire, who had made sacrifices for his convictions. The heir to beautiful Basset Down of the Story-Maskelynes, he handed the inheritance to a younger brother, to concentrate on an independent career. He was a talented painter, who gave up painting for a spell in the International Labour Office at

* See my *Matthew Arnold: Poet and Prophet.*

Geneva and public service. He had indeed 'gone to the good', in Charles Henderson's phrase, and I wasn't much in favour of that. He was married – hardly a marrying type, one would have thought – to Ka Cox, celebrated in her day at Cambridge as the girl to whom Rupert Brooke wrote the love-letters many people wanted to see. Though I had no difficulty in getting on with people at All Souls or with my varied acquaintances in Oxford, I could never make the grade with the Arnold-Forsters, benevolent as they were.

Too sophisticated and precious for my taste; Ka was human, but to me rather aunt-like; I coined the expression 'tantular' for her. Will was not very human: no free flow between him and me, a series of brittle contacts in staccato utterances from him. He was like a faun leaping about the boulders and crevices of the fantastic garden he created at the Eagle's Nest above the cliffs of Zennor. The place itself was spectacularly beautiful – one could not come to terms with it. The house crouched among giant rocks high above the coastal plateau, with a further drop of several hundred feet to the sea. A pure wind, in every sense, was always blowing up there. The house looked down upon Higher Tregerthen, the cottage where Lawrence had lived during the war: it appears in his letters. In the big Morris-papered sitting room a pane of glass had been set in the wall by the fireplace to let in a view of the sea. One was up among the clouds: one could hardly breathe in so rarefied an atmosphere.

Will once conducted me round his fabulous garden, rare scented flowers in arbours contrived out of the rocks and such stunted trees as would grow at that altitude. With my working-class background I knew nothing about gardening: Will must have found me a fearful bore [I don't suppose they knew what I was thinking of them – years later I put them into a story]. However, we were in the boat together: for a time he was Labour candidate for the St Ives division – a hopeless area; mine was promising – after a decade of effort, Penryn and Falmouth went Labour in 1945. So occasionally we collaborated – we were in similar situations in our respective constituencies – two intellectuals in backward areas, though my contact with the people was much closer.

More congenial, spontaneous and free, were my nonpolitical contacts at home. I had had to dash down to give a lecture at Lis Escop, in that large bare room with creaking chairs. The Bishop lived ascetically, the carpets in the drawing-room rolled up; it was said that he blacked the boots of his guests, out of monastic humility. I can see him now arriving for another occasion at the Church's Teachers' Training College – the tall cassocked figure, episcopal hat with purple ribbons; he looked like a French bishop – being cheerfully greeted by Maisie Pedder, the Principal. She was another whose friendship I made through my incursion into Cornish public life. A character in her own right, she had had an interesting time as secretary to G. K. Chesterton. This had its influence in a blue tip to her nose, and she was good fun. Later on I did my best to help to save her College, which was to be closed by the Church, and amalgamated with Fishponds at Bristol. This was an early problem which Joe Hunkin had to confront on succeeding Frere, and in spite of our efforts, he gave way and sold the pass. This was subsequently found to have been a mistake, when the need for more teachers was felt.

At the end of that summer term I learned from experience how easily Lionel Curtis could get anyone to do anything. A Historical Pageant was being organised at Shipton Manor, an Elizabethan house near Kidlington lived in by Frank Gray, the rich and therefore popular Liberal candidate for Oxford. (The city had a ripe record for bribery and corruption, and Frank Gray, who held the seat for a time, was unseated for the usual reason.) Various scenes were being written by John Buchan and his daughter, Alice, by E. V. Knox and A. E. Coppard. Lionel was deputed to get me to write one; I was quite clear that I would not. Arthur Salter's brother, who had been badly wounded in the war, was mobilised and brought in; I couldn't resist that. I duly wrote my Elizabethan scene.

Term ended with the usual summer chores: lecturing to a WEA school, showing Trade Union students around All Souls, a University extension lecture on Swift, and a bale of School Certificate papers. My homeward journey offered promise of better things: a West Country historical tour was a preparation for later historical writing. As Cruttwell said, I had never been anywhere or seen anything in England; after getting to All Souls I was better travelled abroad. Now I set off happily by bus for Salisbury, which I had never seen. A pocket-book is full of notes of chantries and tombs; I can retrace my steps, 'sitting under the elms in the Close; the sound of "Come to the cook-house door, boys" comes on bugles from a camp outside the city.' I find a full description of the city church of St Thomas, with painted roof and crowded Doom over chancel-arch. This would bear fruit in the far future with *Simon Forman*, whose haunts these were in his early years.

8 August: I noted as 'a lucky day', so simple were my expectations.

At breakfast, unexpectedly, five guineas for my lecture at Oxford, with an encouraging letter from the Delegacy of Extra-Mural Studies; four shillings and sixpence repayment which I never looked to see again, for a telegram chasing David Cecil around the country; sixpence conscience money from somebody anonymous in Oxford, for I can't think what; and a trip to Wilton memorable for honeysuckle on grey walls and sweet-toned bells; to Ringwood in the afternoon and for the music of wind in pines, like the high woods above Hagen in Westfalen. Back by bus with a sprig of light heather; catching the train as it comes in, a Saturday night crowd of jolly men and marketing women; a hasty snatch for a *New Statesman*, opening it to find unexpectedly a poem of mine. What more could one want? Now for disaster.

Passing through Breamore, between Salisbury and Fording-bridge, I remembered Henry VIII's grant of the monastery to his cousin, the Marquis of Exeter, whom he shortly after executed. Between Salisbury and Romsey I was taken by the signpost 'To Winterslow' – was this Hazlitt's Winterslow, to whom I had been devoted from schooldays? I was on my way to Wardour Castle in pursuit of the Cornish Arundells. Little did I know then that the last of them, John, the last Lord Arundell, who died after years of prison-camp in Germany, would become a friend.

My introduction to Wardour I owed to Doran Webb, the architect of Blackfriars at Oxford. The vast Palladian mansion, by Paine, was inhabited by the formidable dowager, Anne Lucy, heiress of the Catholic Erringtons, who terrorised her chaplains and tyrannised over her successors at that time rele-gated to a wing. (Later, I wrote her story up in 'All Souls

Night', a favourite with Halifax, connoisseur of ghost-stories.) This venerable figure made no appearance, so I was able to see the place in peace. In order to build the palace, the Arundells had sold Wardour Street! The founder of this branch, Sir Thomas Arundell, was a younger son of the house of Lanherne in Cornwall, who got the estates of Shaftesbury abbey at the Dissolution. Protestants under Elizabeth, they lapsed back under James; late that century their heir married the heiress of the old line at Lanherne, which had never conformed, reuniting family and fortune.

Since the historic house was emptied after the war and my friend's death, I transcribe a note as to the pictures, dispersed like so much of what an historian values. Here in the large state-room was Sir Thomas, seated writing at a table, leaning forward, brow on hand. He had made his way up as a servant of Wolsey; under Edward vi he lost his head as a follower of Protector Somerset. A Jacobean portrait showed the first peer, made Count of the Holy Roman Empire; a step which enraged Elizabeth i. A third was of Charles i's peer, a rough red-faced man, whose wife defended the Castle against the rebels in the Civil War; then blew it up, rather than let the Puritans have it – one of the innumerable losses of that piece of political lunacy: a late medieval house with Renaissance chimney pieces and sculpture. A daughter became a nun at Rouen: here she was kneeling in Counter-Reformation devotion. A large picture of her parents showed them on their knees, looking up at a Crucifixion, full of religious sentimentalism, gesturing, holding up hands, black clouds scudding across the landscape. (Where is the picture now?) The story was painted to accompany the daughter's exile. This was my first acquaintance with the foreign inflexion that distinguished old Catholic houses I came to know well; Stonor, Coughton and others: instead of portraits by Kneller or Reynolds, they were apt to be by Largillière or Battoni. 'From the railway I got my last glimpse of the woods of Wardour, evening sun on glistening raininess, blue mist enveloping farthest ridges and crested trees.'

On to Sherborne, first of many visits to that unspoiled town, outcrop of grey and honey-coloured stone in the chalk landscape of Dorset, cathedral-like abbey, ruined castle, and grand Elizabethan house of Ralegh and the Digbys. (More unconscious preparation: I was to write later on about Ralegh.) Of the Digbys I transcribe the characteristic inscription on a vast baroque monument – one specimen of such things, of which the Notebooks are full – to the glory of John, Lord Digby and Earl of Bristol, who died in 1698:

Titles to which the merit of his grandfather first gave lustre and which he himself laid down unsullied. He was naturally inclined to avoid the Hurry of a publick life, yet careful to keep up the port of his quality, was willing to be at ease but scorned obscurity, and therefore never made his retirement a pretence to draw himself within a narrower compass, or to shun such expense as charity, hospitality and his Honour called for. His religion was that which by law is established, and the conduct of his life showed the power of it in his heart. His distinction from others never made him forget himself or them. He was kind and obliging to his neighbours and condescending to his inferiors. Nor had the temptations of honour and pleasure in this world strength enough to withdraw his eyes from that great Object of his hope which we reasonably assure ourselves he now enjoys.

The young historian, preparing himself for his vocation, concluded that there was really nothing to say about John, Lord Digby, Earl of Bristol, unlike his grandfather: a pompous mediocrity. Here was the living scene.

The Lady Chapel, formerly part of the Headmaster's house, was now being restored. Old men and women of the almshouses, decrepit and servitor-like, were coming in twos into the ark of the church: the women in scarlet cloaks and black bonnets, the men in blue serge, brass buttons, and shovel hats. As I was looking up at the church a beautiful woman in green arrived with her father, venerable with pointed white beard and spats. She – fair, face powdered white as I like it, green eyes – gave me a cool, unabashed moment's contemplation, then dismissing me went on into the abbey.

On I went to Exeter; since it was grievously damaged in Hitler's Baedeker Raids and its character much detracted from, churches and terraces lost, a large area rebuilt – here it is as it was. 'Many little red sandstone churches in the High Street give it its distinctive appearance.' I had not then seen Norwich or York, but their even more numerous churches were grander: those of Exeter were diminutive, odd-shaped, squeezed in between houses and shops.

St Stephen's Bow is very old: a Charles II church with an altar elevated over an arch, with a passage underneath outside. St Petrock's has another odd shape. St Mary Arches was a specially civic church, with many mayors' memorials on the walls. One early Tudor one, to Master Thomas Andrew, sports a realistic figure with slanting eyes beneath a canopy. The churches push up with the houses enclosing them, scarcely room to breathe: it brings home the time when the merchants and tradesmen lived cheek by jowl in the city, geared to their own particular parish.

One afternoon I spent in Commin's haven of a bookshop, then full of antiquarian books I could not afford to buy. Today the second-hand bookshops, which were such an attraction in English provincial towns, their differing inflexion and character, have almost all gone, the books dried up. My eyes were glued to James Thomson's *City of Dreadful Night*, 'which I have long wanted to read. A terrible poem, which communicated its terror even to the books, the musty room, the noise of traffic outside.'

I was now going over the ground of the Prayer Book Rebellion of 1549 – grist to the mill for *Tudor Cornwall* a decade later. Clyst St Mary was fired in 1549, the bridge-head held. 'The village sprawls down the hill, at foot the river Clyst spreads out, breaks into branches and a stretch of marsh, with raised causeway across. A defensible place.' I was taking a leaf out of Macaulay's notebook, and noting exactly how places, portraits of people and the effigies on their tombs looked as one had them under one's eye.

The medieval bishops of Exeter, Grandisson and his successors, favoured Clyst for their residence:

now Bishop's Court, above the valley on the old road to Honiton, a Colonel lives here and owns the broad acres of the bishops. An old wall enclosing a fruit garden the only vestige of theirs that I can descry – yet the bishop was there longer than these later owners in all the years since the Reformation. Perhaps some of the oaks go back to them, the park well kept by the Colonel. Going down the ancient road cut in the red soil that carried the bishop to his cathedral, a luxurious purring car fills the road; back seat similarly filled by two military figures bolt upright, square khaki busts, a line of ribbons, neat red face grizzled at the temples, a briar pipe. The car was flying a red flag, fluttering in the breeze that for me remembered the bishop.

The past was more living to my mind and in my imagination – evidently I was meant for an historian – for me the place was filled with those shadows.

Suddenly I was seized by the thought – suppose if, after another Dark Age, the world should come back to be civilised again by the Church? And the bishop return to park and chapel waiting for him, as in the days of Walter Bronescombe, Stapledon and Grandisson; Stafford, Courtenay and Arundell; Oldham and Veysey, the last of them to inhabit here before the cataclysm overwhelmed them and confiscated their lands.

I was possessed by the dream as I sat there: 'in the gate, the road winding round before mounting the hill to the park. Summer wind fills the cawing trees, the turning road a plot of alternate leafy light and shadow.'

Tawney held that the first requirement for the study of economic history was a pair of stout walking boots. I did a lot of walking on this probationary trip; I wrote a series of articles for the local paper, the *Cornish Guardian*, to earn a few pounds. At Tiverton: 'in the vestry a collection of old books in dreadful condition, so high up as not to be looked at. Four portraits, Laud, Strafford, Montrose and the donor, John Newte, evidently a Royalist.' Crediton church had a library too, with rare books: an early edition of Donne's *Poems and Letters;* Lancelot Andrewes' XCVI *Sermons*; George Herbert's *Divine Poems*; a Chaucer, a Vinegar Bible, along with Ralegh's *History of the World* and Swift's *Tale of a Tub*. The Governors' Room had seventeenth-century table and chairs, Civil War buff-coat and breast plates, riding boots and dispatch-box.

The Devon landscape, near as it was to home, was all new to me. Newton St Cyres was 'mostly white-washed thatched cottages, with green shutters; on one the thatch so smooth and clipped – like a tawny cat.' Evidently a good craftsman at work, the craft now largely lost. Bradninch country, high up between the valleys of Exe and Culme, was a country of its own and owned by the Duchy of Cornwall. Immensely steep hills to get up there:

but having toiled and sweltered up, pursued by a horde of flies, one has for compensation long views back over the Exe and beyond to Haldon and the rim of Dartmoor, forward to the Culme Valley and upwards to the Blackdown Hills and Exmoor. Everything is so untouched, the way stony, unused by cars; meadowsweet growing in clumps, filling the afternoon with scent. A fine beechwood you go through: the haymaker who directed me called it a copse; but it's a noble wood, the tree-trunks like pillars in a cathedral, making the way cool as a well.

Before my ascent from the medieval bridge, I looked at what remained of the Carew house at Bickleigh, and on the way up at their monuments in the church. Humphrey Carew, who died in 1616, looked rather absurd in Jacobean bloomers and painted face. A Restoration lady was Elizabeth, daughter of Sir Reginald Mohun of Boconnoc, loveliest of Cornish parks. A touching monument was of a girl who died in childbirth, with her baby: an Erisey, from that enchanting old house, lost in the lanes of the Lizard peninsula.

People and places were coming together in the mind of the young historian – something to feed on, not like the profitless chaff of politics.

Back in Exeter I called in at a tiny church, St Pancras, with a monument to Loveday Bellott of Bochym, another old house by the road to the Lizard. This girl died, in Queen Anne's reign, 'of the smallpox, a distemper so remarkably fatal to her family that no less than four of her sisters died of it in the months of February and March 1717, in the boroughs of Penryn and Fowey'.

Out at Chagford I looked into the porch of the 'Three Crowns', a stone bench on either side; here it was that Sidney Godolphin, Cavalier and poet, died in 1643, having been mortally wounded in a skirmish nearby. 'The road to Okehampton skirts the edge of Dartmoor, with a high tor always in view, patchwork fields creeping up the breast of the hill. Over the moor white clouds go gallantly by in full sail over the ridge, their shadows gliding over open spaces laced with the sun.' At Okehampton I chummed up with a gipsy parson in a caravan, who showed me its interior. An Anglican, his view was that the Church might break up; he didn't hold with the Virgin Birth (which clerics at that time were supposed to do). Going about on my own as usual, I could observe the way people's manners varied according to class. An upper middle-class person entered the bus and simply took the best place, without fuss or bother. A lower middle-class woman insisted on another taking the better seat; the second then caused a general commotion, by rising again to move the first into her seat, assuring her that it was much the nicest. A lower-class fellow entered and took naturally the last place, as if it was his. I watched, my sympathies being with the last, while I respected the first: none for the fussers.

So I crossed the border into Cornwall, stopping at Callington to view the Renaissance tomb of Willoughby de Broke (much mutilated): Henry vii's Steward of the Duchy, in mantle of the Garter, chain and George; at the soles of his feet a grotesque of a monk, telling his beads. 'Why should Willoughby de Broke have chosen Callington for his burying-place?' I asked – a question which today I could answer.

Arrived home, two experiences marked the contrasting sides of my life. Passing through the old mining village of Mount Charles, I was called in to an old man who wanted to see me: altogether pathetic, he was dying of cancer of the throat. The pride of his life had been his aviary: for years he had kept canaries, now he could no longer look after them.

He had known my father and worked with him for years. I told him that Father wasn't very well either. A little frail old man, Billy Morshead by name. Yellow and parchmenty, almost Chinese, he got up from the chair to receive me, eyes frantic and appealing, the terror always before them: nothing to be done. He had twice been to Plymouth for treatment. 'You see this lump here has got to go,' frail finger pointing. It seemed a hopeful phrase, then I realised that it was a form of words he repeated without belief. 'Where 'twas, when I went up the second time it was going on all right; then I had radium on the old wound' – he pronounced it 'wownd'. A stale smell in the room: was it old age, an old lone man unable to look after himself, or cancer? I was afraid to be too near him; yet I had held his hand on entering; it was more than I could bear, to witness his hopelessness, visibly waiting for death. I wanted to rush out, from this third presence; yet I was determined to do my best and get his attention away for a moment.

'You know I've been away a good many years,' he said; 'I've been in a good many countries, Canada, America, Australia.' I thought of the forlorn birds out there in the hut, and told him how beautiful I thought them. He was sad about them. 'You see, I used to show

them. It's nothing to what I used to have; I've had a hundred and fifty
of them before now.' This was the old man's love, breeding his birds,
watching over them and caring for them: the clue to him lay somewhere here: it answered to his need for love. I would have stayed, but
I couldn't: it was too hopeless. I said that I would tell Father I had
been to see him, and went sadly on my errand.

Then on to the coast, the sea calm and pure, colours clear and
rain-washed. I stopped at a favourite spot on the cliff-path and
looked up at Duporth House – so longed for and for so long, now to
be sold again. But, oh, so unattainable, the lights in all the front
looking cosy and warm. In the bay a small ship waiting to come into
Charlestown, a light at her prow and mast-light rocking to and fro,
casting a clear beam on the water. On the beach below:

> The forlorn and lonely tree
> Beacons out to sea.

A line came into my head:

> the lonely lighter on the hispid sea.

The wood clustered darkly round Duporth, in the sky behind a bank
of cloud mounted precipitously. I thought of my long-intended
poem, that comes again and again into my mind, about the End of
the World... Coming down hill to the basin, I watched a ship going
out in the darkness: a three-masted schooner, with an oil-lamp at
mast that left a pinkish patch of light on the water. Perhaps I would
use this image of the ship going out into darkness and the unknown
... The poem could end:

> There shall remain
> Only this hope,
> Only this star.

Coming through the copse at the top of the cliff in the dark I had been
terrified: I kept thinking there were hoofs following me, a horse
tracking me down. Perhaps the end would be like that: hundreds of
horses, the horses of the Apocalypse, thundering upon the earth.

After that, the ship's going out was comforting, soft voices of the
men calling out from the quay-side to the vessel: 'Easy!', 'Easier!',
'All right.' Then, 'All right now' ... 'So long!', as the ship
manoeuvred out of the narrow mouth into the night.

The *culte de sensations*, as I called it, exacted its price in frequent
terrors, especially in my haunted bedroom at All Souls, which
I would not, however, give up.

Doran Webb had arranged for me a private visit to the original home of the Arundells at Lanherne, which, after the French Revolution, had been turned into a convent for an enclosed order of Carmelites. Dr Stephens, my antiquarian friend, told me that when he had to visit a sick nun, one would precede him ringing a bell, to warn the inmates of the baleful presence. (Would they know the anthropological significance of the ringing of bells, i.e. to keep evil spirits away?) I met Doran Webb at St Mawgan with expectancy, for we were to have an interview with the Mother Superior. We were given tea in a panelled parlour by the chaplain, an Irish priest who had spent some years in Mauritius, and then shown up into a bare room, with two chairs set before an iron grille with black muslin drawn across. One could see nothing of one's *vis-à-vis*. It was odd conducting a conversation in such circumstances. Webb explained that I was interested in the Arundells.

'Oh', said the voice behind the veil, 'then he's interested in Lanherne . . . Have you seen the chapel yet?' They thought that it had been the ball-room, the sacristy a banqueting room, (more likely the chapel was the original hall, the sacristy the withdrawing parlour at the dais end). Had the house had a chapel? *'Yes'*, two voices chimed. 'We call it now the Chapel Cells: we had it made into cells for the sisters, but you can see the roof decoration and the plaster work still.'

Webb prompted with, 'Mr Rowse knows Father D'Arcy at Oxford.' 'Oh', with eager interest. They launched forth about his new book, *The Nature of Faith*. I teased them with how much it was praised by Dean Inge. This gave them their opening: 'Are you a Catholic?' Candour compelled me to disappoint them, politeness to tell them how many Catholic friends I had at Oxford – the Mathew brothers, David (then Coadjutor to Cardinal Hinsley at Westminster, whom he hoped to succeed) and Gervase, a Blackfriar, besides my Benedictine and Jesuit pupils. We talked of D'Arcy's book and of Newman at the Birmingham Oratory (in fact, the book came largely out of Newman's *Grammar of Assent*). Webb weighed in with some Oratory stories, all conflicting in their evidence: one Father holding that the clue to Newman was music, another that he couldn't get a tune right. Then the voice: 'He was a great loss to your side.'

We went on to Arundell history, and the martyred Cuthbert Mayne. They told me that they had his skull, with the hole where the pike was driven in – Dorothy Arundell, a great relic-hunter, had secured it. 'You can imagine it is our greatest treasure. Would you like to see it?' They would have it fetched down from the reliquary to the sacristy for me to see it. I told them all I knew about Mayne – they were agog, I could hear them lean forward on the other side. It was their greatest hope, one said, to find some clue to the whereabouts of his body; there was a story, the other said, of treasure buried in their garden: if I came across any clues, would I let them know? 'Willingly', I said, 'but it is so unlikely'. 'Oh, but it is the unexpected that happens so often.'

What a world they lived in, of the unexpected and the providential and the incredible. Webb was telling them a wild tale of some British spy, whom the Bolsheviks had inoculated with twenty different diseases: a young man in years now crippled and aged. 'How dreadful', they said, with innocent horror; 'how can they do such things?' [Much progress in drug-inoculation has been made in Germany as well as Russia since the thirties!]

We went back to Newman and Manning, Webb telling a story of Father William Nevill and Manning's trying to worm out of him what Newman meant by his last letter to him. (These cardinals detested each other.) Nevill had destroyed numbers of Newman's letters under pledge, I gathered. A voice, surprisingly politic, said that it was a good thing Nevill had said nothing: he knew too much!

I conceded that the Reformation was very much a Cambridge affair, while Oxford had produced the leading Catholics, Cardinals Pole and Allen, Parsons and Mayne, 'Oh, and the Blessed Edmund Campion', a voice supplied. 'Perhaps it was Our Blessed Lady', and there followed a story of how a workman was instructed to demolish a window at the Reformation; but, a Catholic at heart, he was determined that Our Blessed Lady who had been there so long should not be left out. 'They say that right at the top, out of harm's way, in a little light there she is: did I know that window?' They were disappointed that I didn't – of all the stained glass windows I have seen!

They were so sweet and charming, and quite happy, the young farmer at the barton told me. When he came back from the war, from the Balkans, the old Reverend Mother had asked him in to tell her what things were like, for she had been in Greece forty years before. At her jubilee she was permitted to see people without the veil. She invited four or five of the people around to come in and talk to her. She told him that all the years had gone by as nothing, life had been like a dream.

7

The Crash of 1931

As an historian, I have always regarded 1931 as the disastrous turning point in Europe after the First German War, when all our post-war hopes of a better world were frustrated and the way taken that led to the Second War. It need not have been so – Churchill always thought that. All that was necessary was to stop Germany from re-arming, keep our allies and friends firm, so that, when the German abscess burst, it came internally instead of involving all Europe. In place of that, the nerveless government of the 'Old Men' – MacDonald, Baldwin, Chamberlain – by a process of muddle and humbug, with the connivance of the business world, especially the City under the lead of Montagu Norman (friend of Schacht, who made Hitler financially possible), made every concession to Hitler's Germany. They defended his remilitarising the Rhineland;* they sat pretty while he got away with Austria and Czechoslovakia, they refused to bring Soviet Russia into the balance against him, the only thing that would stop him. At the last moment the guarantee to Poland meant that he would be resisted in flat contradiction to the whole previous course of Appeasement.

I am not writing the history of that disastrous decade, or I should have to introduce qualifications and complications confusing to the reader. An autobiography is just one man's reaction to his time, but here was the heart of the matter. With my window into the German heart and mind through Adam, I knew what to expect better than most of the people in high places, our political 'leaders' who kept their attention concentrated on bemusing the electorate. Baldwin was a past-master in that art; and when Neville Chamberlain took over the lead, he led straight, with arrogant ignorance, on a disaster-course.

Neville Chamberlain was not only wrong over appease-

* See my *All Souls and Appeasement*, p. 40.

ment – he really thought it possible to do a deal with Hitler – and wrong about the war: a pacifist at heart, he thought it would be won without fighting! As Chancellor of the Exchequer he was mainly responsible for holding back rearmament, in the interest of keeping taxation down for the benefit of his clients. He had been wrong, too, in enforcing *de*flation, when everything cried out for the expansion of the economy – Keynes's advice, at that time. Instead of that, we have had inflationary Keynesianism at the wrong time, after the war. *Every* wrong turning has been taken: it is the end of historic Britain, the only Britain I care tuppence about. (Canning: 'Britain is either great, or it is nothing at all'.)

It was not difficult to see that there was no hope of appeasing Hitler's Germany, short of giving her everything and giving in, the logical end of the process. But one could not have foreseen the unexampled evil of the extermination of the Jews, which should never be forgotten and can never be forgiven. Our leaders had no idea what they were dealing with. I knew Germany and had read *Mein Kampf*, in which Hitler made clear exactly what he intended, – no-one was more consistent in his aims: they were the long-term aims of the Kaiser's Germany in Europe. Halifax, as Foreign Secretary, had never read *Mein Kampf*, until lent a copy by the present Queen Mother. On his return from colloguing with Göring, Halifax's impression of him was, 'a cross between a gangster and head-gamekeeper at Chatsworth'; like the impression he gave us at All Souls of Molotov as 'a buttoned-up schoolmaster'. No idea that each of these miscreants was abler than himself: superciliousness on the part of English politicians was another factor in their ignorance of what they were dealing with. What a decline from the days of Chatham and Pitt, Castlereagh and Canning, Disraeli or even Gladstone! They were not worthy of their ancestors – only Churchill was. Strangely enough, Bevin, who had no ancestors to boast of, was worthy of his place in history, along with Churchill: he was even more right in his grasp of the situation in the thirties.

This holds good of the home front, domestic and economic policy too. Bevin had been a member of the Macmillan Committee which was influenced by Keynes's ideas, and Bevin subscribed to them. When the financial crisis of 1931 assailed the Labour government – a matter of a deficit of £75 or £80 millions – Bevin was in favour of applying Keynes's ideas: going off gold-parity, at the mistakenly high rate both Bank and Treasury had enforced in 1926 (against Churchill's better intuition), to revivify exports, coupled with a 10 per cent tariff on imports to correct the deficit on our balance of payments. This would have been, we know now, the right policy to pursue. We can hardly blame MacDonald and Snowden for not seeing this – very few people did at the time. What we can legitimately blame them for was in allowing themselves to be bounced into a 'National' government, taking action completely contrary to the interests of the working classes and the Labour Movement they represented.

This *was* a betrayal. Having lost control and resigned, they should have handed over responsibility to Baldwin and the Tories. The damage done by the formation of the 'National' government and the election that followed was beyond belief. It practically wiped out the Labour Party in Parliament, only 55 MPs returned in a House of 615, and all the responsible leaders out. It overthrew the proper functioning of Parliamentary government, for there was no effective Opposition to speak of. Even in 1935 only 155 Labour MPs got back. From 1931 to 1939 the 'National' government could have done anything it chose in the nation's interests. They could have *led* the country, as the danger from Germany revived. Instead of that, Baldwin's chief concern was to keep his party's immense majority; marvellous party-manager, as Churchill described him. He made great play about being anxious to school the Labour Movement into a sense of responsibility to make it fit to govern, which it certainly needed. What he in fact did in action – over both the Coal Strike and the General Strike in 1926 – as again over the 'National' Government in 1931 and the betrayal of Collective Security in 1935, following an Election in which he once more deftly put the Labour Party on the wrong foot, was exactly conceived to undermine the very sense of responsibility throughout the Labour Movement. We all felt that we could never trust these people again, and at a time when the danger from Germany was coming ever closer.

However much people may defend Baldwin today, he was a leading factor in this country's decline; for fifteen years its most powerful figure in political life. He was a master at humbugging the electorate, when they should have been faced with the growing danger and *led*. Humbug rotted the guts of our political life during the whole of that decade; Churchill was no humbug, that is why they kept him out. When the war they brought down on us in the worst circumstances was over, a school-mate of mine in my constituency said, 'We didn't know what you were talking about. We understand now.' It should have been plain enough. I remember speaking in the market-place of my home-town, and saying in despair, 'Every time you vote for Chamberlain and appeasement, it is a nail in the coffin of your own sons.'

Hitler was no humbug: he was a German liar, i.e. a liar by conviction and policy, as anybody could see. He says in *Mein Kampf* that in advertising your wares, a brand of soap or whatever, a salesman doesn't say 'but so-and-so's soap is very good too'. He says you have only to tell a lie big enough and you can put it across; e.g. that Germany was not responsible for the war of 1914 (as she was), and that she only lost it by the 'stab-in-the-back', when it was Ludendorff and the General Staff who insisted on an armistice, and then shifted the responsibility on to the Social Democrats. Nothing could exceed Hitler's contempt for ordinary people's understanding – and that I appreciate. Evil as he was, he was also a great man and the Germans gave him his chance. What he achieved in the psychological preparation of his odious people for another attempt all over again was simply wonderful. When I was in Germany in 1935 I saw displayed in the bookshops a book on Hitler as the spiritual well-spring of National Socialism. Well, he was: it rose and fell with him. In addition was the organising, disciplining, licking into shape those hordes of the masses; it all came from his inspiration, the mass-manipulation, the mass-advertising, the mesmerising of the morons.

All the hatred and frustration of Germans, their envy and *schadenfreude*, their lust to get on top quick, their brutality and cruelty, their total inability to see any point of view other than their own, their bullying habits, their diseased egomania – it all came to the top in Nazism and was incarnated in Hitler. No wonder they were all terrified of him. There was *nothing* he would not do. That I also understood. Goethe, who had no illusions about Germans, gives a clue: 'There is no man so dangerous as the disillusioned idealist.'

Such was the background to the decade we were entering upon, the decade of my initiation into and involvement in political activity. My first experience, the General Election of 1931, was sickening. It opened the floodgates to all that followed. In eighteen months there came the advent of Hitler – with the connivance of the German upper classes – to power.

Innocent as we were, we could not imagine the disaster to all our hopes being prepared for us that summer in London. Our leaders, MacDonald and Snowden, advised by the Treasury and the Bank of England (i.e. the pro-German Montagu Norman), had appointed a Committee to suggest ways of meeting the Budget deficit. The Chairman they appointed was a disaster to begin with – a conventional City man, Sir George May – who reported in favour of slashing unemployment benefit, when the number of unemployed was increasing with the worsening of the World Slump. Keynes described the May Report as 'the most foolish document I have ever had the misfortune to read.' No Labour Movement could be expected to let the unemployed take the sole brunt of the cuts. Keynes's advice was the correct one: to go off the gold standard (to have returned to it at the rate of $4.88 was the great mistake, ultimately responsible for the disastrous Coal Strike of 1926, General Strike and all); a 10 per cent tariff on imports; a moderate degree of inflation to expand the economy.

I was in favour of a tariff on luxury imports to correct the mounting adverse balance against us. Surely this was right? My obsession with cutting down non-productive expenditure, largely waste, in favour of productive expenditure corresponded to Keynes's categories of consumption as against investment. The economists to a man – apart from Keynes – were opposed to any departure from economic orthodoxy. 'The economic theory from which their opinions sprang might be a century old – but it was still going strong: nobody had changed it. It was still the theory of the text-books and the undergraduate lectures. This, then, was one of the reasons why the policy-makers turned a deaf ear to Keynes's advice. The politicians and the civil servants were acting in perfect accord with the dictates of the traditional, received theory of how the economy worked.'*

I was not an economist, and therefore not hide-bound by their orthodoxy: I desperately *wanted* a tariff on non-production, i.e. luxury, imports. The stand taken by the Trade Unionists, Arthur Henderson and Ernest Bevin, was the right one. To be fair, it was too much to expect MacDonald and Snowden to go against the obstinate stand of the Treasury and Bank of England, backed by the bankers abroad; in any case, they could not have got Keynes's (and Bevin's) policy across the majority of Tories and Liberals combined in Parliament. Having lost control they should have handed the 'poisoned chalice' to the proper alternatives, the Opposition. The unforgivable mistake they made was going in with them.

I can well understand their motives. MacDonald and Snowden had been traduced all through the 1914–1918 war for their pacifism. Snowden, during the Hague Conference in 1929 on German Reparations, had tasted the delights of being hailed as a patriot for his obstinate defence of British interests. MacDonald, for all his internationalism – which gave him the equipment to be a better Foreign Secretary than most – had a residual patriotism, which made him respond overnight to King George v's appeal to stay on. Baldwin and Chamberlain seconded this – naturally: it put the Labour Movement in a hopeless position. The consequences to it were grievous. For the middle and upper-classes it was a heaven-sent opportunity, and they enjoyed it, making the most of it for themselves until 1939.

They ganged up against the working class. They took advantage of our immaturity – I have a stronger word for it, for of course humans in the bulk never will be really mature – to panic them in the Election of 1931, as they had done with the Red Letter Scare in 1924. Though only an undergraduate in 1924 I had been astonished at the way people had allowed themselves to be fooled. In 1931 they were panicked over the Gold Standard, MacDonald himself waving a German paper-note of astronomical dimensions that was worthless. Thus half the working-class vote was bounced into rallying behind them. When Halifax appeared in his beloved Yorkshire the

* Michael Stewart, *Keynes and After,* pp. 75–6.

menfolk drew his carriage for him through the streets; so I heard from Dawson at All Souls, with outward composure, bitterness in my heart. For myself, fighting my first election, I was confronted everywhere by enormous posters:

VOTE FOR ROWSE And RUIN
VOTE FOR PETHERICK And PROSPERITY.

I appreciated the alliteration, but not the whispering campaign that went with it – that I was an atheist, etc.

For by this time the book which had given me so much trouble to write, *Politics and the Younger Generation*, had come out: it could not have been at a worse time. The harmless utterances any progressive young man at the time would subscribe to – on sex, marriage, divorce, religion – were taken out of context, high-lighted day after day in *The Western Morning News*, and circulated throughout the constituency. Nancy Astor told me years after how keen they were to meet the young candidate who was in favour of free love. All is fair, perhaps, in love and war. But cunning as they were in taking every advantage of our innocence, they were not intelligent enough to realise that, beneath the surface of this young Left-ist, was someone who had a more informed care for the country's great past and what its interests demanded than they had.

All this hardened my heart. Oh, they had a marvellous time at our – and my – expense in those years: I wonder if they enjoy it so much looking back over it from the perspective of today?

As for the working classes, all I was asking, as a Labour candidate, was that they should realise their own interest and vote for that. Half the fools didn't: they were taken in and voted for the upper classes and *their* interest. That was all it came to. In the end the message seems to have got home: they vote for themselves mostly today: too late for me, no longer interested in a second-rate country bent on becoming a third-rate one. There is, of course, a permanent working-class majority in a modern industrial nation: this, when realised politically, translated into party, makes for permanent Labour government. *That* argument of my Politics book was at any rate a cogent one. This development was not hard to foresee: it was held up, in Britain, by the scares and fakes of the Elections of 1924, 1931, 1935, and then by the war. Not until 1945 was my forecast corroborated – the beginning of permanent social democracy in Britain, under whatever nominal Party – again, too late for me. In 1945, partly as the result of my efforts as candidate for a decade, Penryn and Falmouth went Labour. I was no longer interested in party politics: the country had had too narrow a shave; in a nuclear world, civilisation itself was at stake. And what could an enfeebled second-rate country do about it? Our future depended on the USA. The decisions would be made by America, Soviet Russia, and in time to come China.

In a way, I was before my time, caught betwixt and between. In the long run a working-class majority was inevitable: in the meantime was the hard grind of opening their eyes to where their interest lay.

It was vacation, and I was at home.

While I read through the final proofs of my book, the wretched kids outside in the avenue are singing 'God save the King'. Mother, on the rain that shows no sign of stopping: 'Oh dear life! We're living in Noah's time, I should think.' If the weather were too dry, the land was 'all dried up like a ram's horn' – something Biblical about that. At last there was peace in the avenue, the children gone to bed, or at least shut up:

> Night and strange shapes in the moongarden moving.

While waiting for Webb in the churchyard at St Mawgan I stopped by the grave of nine men and the boy Jemmy, 'who were drifted on shore in a boat, frozen to death, at Tregurrian beach in this parish, on Sunday 13 December 1846.'

Of what little consequence are our lives after all!

On one of my usual rounds I was at Charlestown, on an evening before rain: 'a sort of still lavender over the lakewater of the bay. A smokeless chimney stack outlined above the trees gives an impression of greater stillness; the houses outlined so distinctly, yet with such tenderness of colour.' I was in the Field of the Dead again – the enclosed prehistoric camp of Castle Gotha – about which I had written a poem:* it was being harvested: 'a harvester whistles to his horse. At the

---

* 'The Field' in *Poems of a Decade, 1931–1941*.

corner of the field people stop a moment and say, "Hark! hear the bells ringing." These say, oh, cherish your day, hold fast to it, linger a moment; for the day shall come when you shall be harvested,

> Shall be as the stubble that the harvest yields
> And that the harvesters leave behind them in the fields.'

Why did I not write up all the poems that came into my head, the lines that formed as I went about my solitary walks? Partly, I think, because writing poetry was not my first objective, as it was with Auden, Day Lewis and other contemporaries; I did not think of myself as first and foremost a poet – I had other interests, history, scholarship, politics. Day Lewis, for example, had no other idea but to be a poet, and so he wrote far too much verse – as they all did. Everybody prefers him, and the others, in selection. Eliot told me that I ought to work at my poetry. But this was contrary to my conception – that poetry came when one was moved to it: one did not work at it as one did with history. As against the loss in recognition of one's poetry – what is that worth in a society like this? – there has been a certain gain: a friend tells me that the smaller body of my verse contains more poetry than theirs. Certainly much of the verse of my contemporaries, Auden, Day Lewis, Spender is mere rhetoric; still more is really prose, cut up into lengths, as with so much journalist verse published today in the literary journals. I exempt from these strictures the work of true poets, MacNeice and Betjeman, Philip Larkin, Charles Causley, Sylvia Plath or Elizabeth Jennings.

Now, in pursuit of Tudor Cornwall, I was on my way to Godolphin.

At Nancegollan, a duck pond at the cross-roads – what could be nicer? – the ducks, wise birds, in the shadow of the hedge. In the field behind a turkey in superb array. Scented air, ferns, ragwort, heather in the hedges and – though inland, with rooks cawing – a flavour of the sea. A magpie gleams in a field at Lower Pengwedna; next farm, Retallon; next, Treliggo; then Trenear, old stone house among blown beaches. The soft air of West Cornwall brings out detail intimately – much honeysuckle down the road to Godolphin – even to the little lizard lying still on a spray in the hedge.

In a church approaching Godolphin I noted a memorial to an heroic only son: Francis Jack Chown of Townsend. 'He was killed in a fight with four enemy aeroplanes at the Battle of Menin Road, 20 September 1917, and was buried beside the wreckage of his machine in front of Château Wood, near Hooge.' He was twenty-seven; agnostic or no, I devoted my thought – my form of prayer – to him, as to many such fellows all over the country, in church as well as out of church. At All Souls, MacGregor the economist, had been blown up on the Menin Road and survived, though people said he was not the man he had been: he was always a little *décousu*. To him a horrid thing happened on moving house, – like John Stuart Mill's servant girl burning the manuscript of Carlyle's *French Revolution*. MacGregor had put a lot of work into what was to have been his *magnum opus* on Monopoly, and he would have been first in the field. A maid put it out on the rubbish heap for the dustmen to carry away. In my home a housekeeper similarly burned an album of old family photographs going back to the nineties and my father's days in South Africa. Such is the intelligence of ordinary people (what price democracy?)

I was studying the country of the Godolphins:

flattish on the side of Crowan (the parish of the St Aubyns); on the other, the ridge of Godolphin Hill falling away to the fold in the wider country that escapes you until you are close upon it. The valley right down to Breage and Looe Pool and Porthleven was streamed over and over for tin through the ages. Here is the background to Godolphin's grandeur, the material foundation that gave rise to it: the mineral wealth of Godolphin Hill, which made their fortunes and built this house.

I caught a glimpse of it at the end of its drive, the grey-green colonnade which made me think of St John's at Oxford. When I first penetrated the house it was ruinously in the hand of farm-people; the King's Room – in which Charles II had slept when, as Prince of Wales, he was escaping abroad at the end of the Civil War – used to store potatoes and farm implements. My friend Sydney Schofield, son of a good American painter, has devoted his life to rehabilitating that nostalgic house, full of memories, aided by his wife, sister of Peter Lanyon, our leading Cornish painter. How hard they have worked for it, in the discouraging circumstances of today, when only the elect work! (Why shouldn't working people work? What else are they *for*? I am reminded of Lenin's reply to a Spanish comrade who thought that there was not enough liberty in the New Jerusalem. 'Liberty?', said Lenin; 'what for?')

Shortly after, I paid a visit to the National Portrait Gallery to look up the well-known portrait of Queen Anne's Lord Treasurer, Godolphin, with his white staff of office: very dark Cornish face, intelligent black eyes, smallish, pursy mouth; a pompous look, at once complacent and querulous, eyebrows raised at the foolery of the world. (He thought people in politics mighty unreasonable, and inclined to be mad.) For years I have wanted to write a family history of the Godolphins to set beside that of the Churchills; alas, I shall not live to write it now.

In September I was invited to speak at a conference of Young Socialists at Bentveld, near Haarlem, in Holland, at which Karl Marx's grandson, Jean Longuet, was to be chief speaker. He was a big fellow with a large squarish head like Grandfather, though not a patch on him for what was inside it. Indeed he was much in contrast, for his was a euphoric personality, good-humoured and friendly. He was the son of *'lieber Mohr's'* favourite daughter, Jenny Marx: I am glad to have come so near the Prophet. A Cornish acquaintance, John Spargo of the American Socialist Party, knew Marx's daughters; he much admired Eleanor Marx-Aveling, who committed suicide on being deserted by the horrid Aveling.

On my way through London I took the opportunity to study not only Godolphin but his traducer Swift. One way and another I have been engaged with Swift all my life. In his portrait I noticed 'the contrast between the forceful head, with dark heavy chin and jowl, and the small, not to say delicate, hands. The head of a statesman, full of determination and power, no lack of confidence: the well-formed hands those of a writer, dexterous and sensitive, which nobody could think the face was. Rather the face of a bully, or a highwayman such as Swift claimed the Irish bishops were.'

Now I was 'going down the Thames, past the folded fishing smacks, past the lighters and the buoys, past the fringed shores fading, the little towns with church-towers; land; past a dockyard full of the noise of shipping, past low hills that confine the estuary, the last woods, the long horse-shoe of innumerable lights, the coasts at length opening out to receive the sea.'

Alas, it was a rough crossing.

The portraits in the National Portrait Gallery floated up and down before my eyes: Elizabeth with a fan; Swift in the blue satin coat he was so proud of. Up and down, up and down they went, then, worse, rolling sideways. Water was trickling from somewhere into my berth. I dared not explore for fear of being sick – I have always been a queasy sailor. Oh God, heave and lurch and roll! Like so many Cornish folk brought up by the sea, I can't swim: 'the hungry sea' my grandmother used to call it, living on top of it at Crinnis. Another series of plunges, the whole ship groaning and creaking, something rattling loose in the hold, and that ghastly trickle of water. Then somebody tapping, loud hammer-blows, stopping a leak: the water must be coming in!

I try to send myself to sleep by counting up the prime numbers as far as I can get. (A specific I regularly follow on airflights when bumpy over mountains, going over Colorado or Montana or the coast of California, or upheaved by the tail-end of a hurricane.) A few minutes' uneasy suspension of one's faculties, and one is brought up to surface by a heavy thud, a wave slapping flat against the side of the ship. The tapping begins again: there must be some plates ripped open – then the sickening swish of the wash and backwash. I resolve not to take these ghastly journeys by sea

– a resolve I regularly made in bad crossings, and as regularly broke; until in later life I took to the air.

Rotterdam: in those days this meant to me Erasmus. Today, it means the sudden swoop of German planes in 1940 to eviscerate the city. After all the friendliness the Dutch had shown the Germans in their First War, and helped them to evade the blockade! I do not think the Dutch will soon forget it – any more than the Poles and Russians, the Danes and Norwegians, or even the Italians – the sufferings they underwent at the hands of the *Herrenvolk*, of all European peoples the least fitted to rule over others.

Little of the Youth Conference remains in my mind, except Jean Longuet's jovial cameraderie, and at Sandvoort the odd effect of the houses appearing above the stunted trees. Nothing of politics in the Book of Life, almost entirely given up to pictures I was in pursuit of – the real object of my excursion.

The museum at Haarlem was full of its native Franz Hals, who did not appeal to me: too uproarious, too obvious, on too easy terms with life. I was more interested by a fine bronze bust of Cromwell, and portraits of William III with those marvellously intelligent eyes. I made a dash to Amsterdam, where I was at first fascinated by the chimes from the large Town Hall, formerly a royal palace. They rang out at every quarter, just across from my hotel, and at the hour played, I fancy, the famous marching song of the House of Nassau. How they brought back the historic resistance to Spain, out of which Holland came, most creative and fruitful of Europe's smaller countries! I was so taken with them, as always by bells, attentive every quarter of an hour, that they ended by getting on my nerves.

The Ryksmuseum is one of the grandest galleries of Europe, where one can see Dutch painting at its fullest: I must content myself with a few things that spoke specially to me. A Lamentation over the body of Christ, from the workshop of Hugo van der Goes, reminded me of the lovely fragment of the original at Christ Church. Naturally Rembrandt was the heart of the shrine, with a crowd to gape at *The Night Watchers* as before the Sistine *Madonna* at Dresden. What a picture! – golden light striking across the dusk, lighting up faces and catching the uniform of the Lieutenant. I followed the animation of the scene: the foreground figures gesturing, the older man giving orders, the younger attentive; the shadow of the elder's hand falling across the other's yellow costume. The captain has a red sash across shoulder, casque in one hand, demonstrates with the other. From a group a long lance is thrust across the background, highly dramatic and providing the axis; someone else holds up a flag. The stir and activity, the vitality in so elaborate and co-ordinated a composition! Painted in 1642: the apogee of Holland's golden age, here given romantic, yet quite realist, representation.

Another Rembrandt expressed another side to that age – Holland's pre-eminence in medicine. Here was an anatomy lesson: a dead man's stomach opened, feet in foreground outlined in sepia. At the head a surgeon holds a knife, a student a bowl, collar undone at neck. I could not get the horrid scene out of my mind, and passed on to the conversation piece of the

meeting of Governors of some charity, everybody looking
pleased at having their likeness taken – as with similar collective portraits by Franz Hals and others: a feature of Dutch civic
life, so close and cooperative. I made an exception for the cool
and charming Hals of himself and wife in an arbour, which I
had last seen in the splendid Dutch Exhibition in London.

Enough: one could go on for ever at such a feast.
Now I was at The Hague,

sitting in autumn sun in the square before the little Victorian palace
on which the light falls white – more like a town house of an old
family than a royal palace: a bourgeois monarchy. Midday rush of
people down the narrow street, the place alive with bicycles like a
plague of gnats. Bicycle bells the characteristic noise of The Hague.
A plain façade with a balcony and bust in central window; only a
flagstaff with crown shining at top to tell that this is the residence of
the last of the house of Orange-Nassau. The leaves fall one by one all
round me: At the corner of the Kneuterdijk was the house of Olden-
barneveldt, now the Ministry of Finance: happy the country that can
conduct its finances from a private house of modest size. Next door,
a small Orange palace [then Princess Juliana's, I think] at the function
of the Lange Voorhout, with pleasant lines of trees by the Vijver, the
open sheet of water happily at the heart of this town.

Best of all was the classic Mauritshuis, a small Renaissance
palace of the connoisseur Prince, with wainscoted rooms, like
Madame de Sévigné's Hotel de Carnavalet in Paris. Prince
Maurice had a charming view out over the Vijver from his
back windows – his place now devoted to memorials of the
most remarkable ruling house in Europe during the later six-
teenth and seventeenth centuries. Here was our Dutch
William, half a Stuart, small sensuous lips and fine features
when young; then the enormous nose of the Blommendaal
bust of him as King of England, eyebrows arched, a royal
haughtiness of expression: his career made, his place in history,
become the great man he was.

The new discovery for me was Cornelius Troost,
1697–1750: a kind of Hogarth, satirist of manners, only the
paint lighter, airy colours, grey, grey-blue, blue. A series
portrayed eighteenth century life and manners, a couple on the
popular theme of the betrayed husband coming home and

surprising his wife. A woman at her front door coyly puts up a hand at the suggestion she has invited, coming out in the dark with candle in hand. The man in black, in phallic steeple-hat, leers with expectancy in the candlelight: she obviously intends to let him in. 'What a contrast is this pleasurable room to Rembrandt's *Anatomy Lesson*, gruesome as that was.' Something was to be said for Holland in decline.

I sat in the afternoon sun 'drinking tea on the Buitenhof, opposite the prison where the De Witt brothers were caught by the mob and torn to pieces' – the savagery of the seventeenth century having more in common with the twentieth than the intervening eighteenth and nineteenth centuries, before the emancipation of the people. Now:

evening descends over Rotterdam. When I came, a rainbow lit it up; now the water is evening-green. Long barges go down towards the coast, tugs flit in and out the traffic, sun falls on the upper decks of the Holland-Amerika liner with yellow funnels. A bridge spans the whole harbour, a honeycomb of steel, grey and monumental, main artery of the city. The wharves are a forest: cranes, funnels, masts; tugs are ranged abreast, from small to bigger. Over the stones of the quay horses' hooves rattle with the wains.

Arrival at Gravesend: 'the Pool in soft fog, two or three liners along the route; a Wren church-tower on the bank. We pass a charity institution with an unbelievable statue of Victoria, Queen and Empress. The station squalid, but not unpleasant in early autumn softness. *England.*'

No less characteristic were the bill-posters of that cinema-dominated time. 'Marion Davies in *Daughter of Luxury*. Poor little rich girl – she was love-starved.' In real life, not so: she was much loved by the newspaper millionaire, Randolph Hearst, and presided at San Simeon in California, built to look like the transept of Toledo Cathedral. So David Cecil told me, who was invited there. In all my years in California I never penetrated the fastness – now a tourist feature, like everything else. But I overheard a couple of well-informed ladies in the Los Angeles Art Gallery commenting on pictures presented by the film star. 'Well, there's Marion Davies. She was poor, and now she's rich and, look! she can paint a bit too.' I observed that a portrait of a mistress of Charles II had *not* been presented with the others by the mistress of the newspaper-king. Oh no:

that had been presented by the Hearst Newspapers Incorporated.

Back in my rooms at Oxford:

coming in at the door, I thought I heard, beneath the bells, the voice of a dead man! Sitting in the blue chair, I read a young poet while the bells burst in at the window. In the garden – the tapestry-time of the year! – the women servants at the Lodgings gather the red fruit from the crab-apple; the cat on all fours sniffs the fallen leaves. It is too much, to be home again! The bells of Oxford ring out while the chimes of Amsterdam are still sounding in my ears.

I continued my watch on life as it passed me by, wherever I was. Here was a well-dressed woman taking a party into Addison's Walk at Magdalen – a favourite solitary promenade of mine – speaking in Mayfair cockney with a lisp: 'Thith ith where Addithon uthed to go and muthe; and (with a giggle) – you know – think of thingth.' I certainly made full use of it to muse and think of things.

How agreeable life was at Oxford in those days, to be young, with the friends of one's youth around one! In transcribing that note from the Book of Life – *his* term for it – I suddenly come upon the handwriting of my dead friend, Richard Pares. David Cecil is one of the few still alive, and there are several notes of things he told me. Hatfield has many letters in Elizabeth I's hand, 'the early ones written in an exquisite and careful Italian hand. The last is a note ordering Essex to the Tower – a hardly legible scrawl across the page, witness to what anxieties, what storms of state she had encountered, the ravages of time.'

A long note follows on 'The Last Days of Elizabeth', which shows how much we talked of her: hers was the dominating figure at Hatfield – as appears in David's book about it. We were less well informed then: his theory was that she was really a Catholic, and at the end found the want of the only religion which could offer her consolation. Not so, I thought. My view was that she had sacrificed everything in life, especially love, to politics.

Those who live by politics shall get its reward: her political success was astonishing. Against expectations she had established her country's independence, secured Protestantism in Europe and defeated Spain; but she had had to sacrifice her heart's desire in the course of it. She had had to deny satisfaction: her attitude towards other people's joys reveals this in every instance.

Much more follows to the same effect, with the idea of an essay on the subject. Why then did I not write it? With me everything was belated and postponed; perhaps it may be regarded as preparation for the historian I was to become. I detect an element of identification – sacrificing one's nature for politics!

Another time David was telling me of his youthful adoration of Shelley; and how, when he saw at the Bodleian the guitar that was his when he wrote:

> Ariel to Miranda: take
> This slave of Music, for the sake
> Of him who is the slave of thee –

he had been overcome with tears. Other pieces of Hatfield lore turn up. Here was a bishop coming away in the train, in the Prime Minister's time: 'I said his sermons were admired by competent critics: I did not say that I admired them. I said we all knew him to be a convinced Christian: I did not feel called upon to say that he was a quarrelsome one.' This sounds to me like Bishop Gore, a cousin of David's mother. Another story related to Arthur Balfour, another cousin, who had all the coolness of the Cecils. A colonial bishop, seated on a sofa with him when Prime Minister, thought himself getting on so well that he laid a hand on Balfour's shoulder. Balfour looked at the offending object, detached it, and coldly laid it down.

Oman told me a story of T. E. Lawrence which is not in the *Seven Pillars* – he had probably forgotten it: it came from a friend with him at the time. They were advancing up the Jordan Valley in the last stages of the campaign towards Damascus. His men camped in the valley; above on the hillside was a little palace, half in ruins, a hunting lodge of the Caliphs of Damascus. What was left was intact enough for Lawrence and his friend to sleep in. They put up there: a brilliant moonlight night, valley clear as day, sharp shadows of the rocks: stone floors, high rooms, gaping windows. All night long Lawrence was unable to sleep; in a dreadful nervous condition – he said afterwards that he was impregnated with the terrible memories the place held, the ghastly things that had happened there. Not sleeping, he believed himself to have sensed all that was in the memory of the house. (No doubt he was psychic.) The explanation may have been the excited expectation of the next day, when he was to fall on the Turkish rear and attempt to cut them off. But this was the form Lawrence's experience of that night took in the high moonlit rooms alone with his friend. Myself, I prefer T. E.'s account of it.

At home folklore accumulated, figures from the past re-appeared.

Returning from Carn Grey the other night I thought I met a ghost. It was old Frankie Dewings. People told me that he had committed suicide, yet there he was: unmistakable, that quick, short-stepped, hobbling gait, the face with the immobility of a mummy; leathery skin, two strong corner teeth in the lower jaw like tusks. In the lively eyes, like an adder's, mobile, questing, a suggestion of cunning. He was dressed in his best suit of black, with a doggy blue tie and bowler hat jauntily back on his head. He had always worn it like that. I remember him from childhood. He was then on the roads, with horse and cart, selling china, which he got from my old Uncle Rowe and not always paid for. He alternated bouts of work and pleasure. For weeks and months he would work hard and make money. Then off to Plymouth for a week-end, a week, sometimes for a fortnight – so long as the money lasted: on booze and women.

Uncle Rowe – 'Uncle' we called him without qualification, for he was well-to-do and expected to leave us the house we lived in – which he didn't – was very respectable and puritanically inclined, took a moral line against these aberrations. Frankie would break down and cry, and beg Uncle for more china on trust. Uncle almost always ended by giving in, for he made a good profit out of it – Frankie combed those upland hamlets in the clay district – and profit was more important than puritanism. He always asserted that Frankie would come to a bad end, which is by no means certain. Indeed Frankie finds it difficult to come to an end at all. He is now eighty-six, still healthy and active, while Uncle died miserably at seventy more than ten years ago. Frankie has had the laugh of him (Uncle used to call the old reprobate 'Monkey Brand'): it is not always the good who last in this world.

Frankie recognised me at once, longing to talk politics. I remember how terrified I was of him as a child, running helter skelter out of the village street when he came driving through, with that sinister gleam in his wicked eye, cracking his whip, with 'I'll have you!' Tonight I was fascinated by the problem whether he had tried to hang himself or to cut his throat. I couldn't see under the dropped chin, and the skin was folded like parchment – a mark might be in any one of those folds.

'Well, I'm not in your division now; I'm living in Redruth. If I was, I should, mind, vote for you. They turned me out and I'm living with my daughter. But, mind, I've got two homes here to come to.' This must have been at the time of the attempt at suicide.

'What you think of this present situation? Mind, I'm watching it, to see what they'll do. Can you conscientiously tell me that Mr MacDonald, Mr Snowden ['ow' as in snout], Mr Lloyd George and Mr Baldwin are all of one opinion?'

'No,' I indicated as required.

'Mr Snowden said no tariffs. But Mr Baldwin said – I read in the papers – their remedy was to tax the people's food. I don't believe that's any good to us.'

'No,' I said.

'But, mind, I doan't think they'll have a majority to put it through Parliament when Parliament meet.'

'No.'

'What I've got against 'em – Labour – when you send 'em to Parliament, they doan't get up and say what they ought to say. They sit there, saying nothing.'

It was uncanny: the quick reptilian eyes watching me closely, out of the mummy face; the animal jaws mushing the s's, lips dry and colourless.

'I'm in my eighty-sixth. I've only my old-age pension, and I do try to get along on that. But I've got me health.' Naughty old boy, in spite of his goings-on at Plymouth. And Uncle was so virtuous!

It was clear that Frankie couldn't die. To have been born in 1846: when Victoria had been only eight years on the throne; when Carlyle was writing; the year after Newman's conversion; the year Pio Nono was elected; of Cobden, Peel and Free Trade; of the Brontës and the Chartists. Hereabout the towns were then mere villages, but the villages full of activity, mines in full swing, the men coming and going, tanned and hairy-chested, tools on shoulder, the chuck-chuck of the stamps, whistles of the steam pumps. Here at Tregonissey the village was still full of the horses of the posting-station – watered and housed at Kellow's farm at the town-end. Uncle, when a lad, having to ride all through the night to the posting-station at Liskeard, starting at every moon-shadow on the moors.

That summer David Cecil made the transition to London,

not so difficult for him, since the family had a home in Arlington Street and he knew Mayfair well – still a focus of aristocratic life as in the eighteenth century – as it might be their village. He moved from the Jacobean beauty of Wadham to the eighteenth-century elegance of a house in Edwardes Square, and was gradually lost to my view; until his return to Oxford in different circumstances, married and with a young family to engage his attention, as a professor. Spring time was over.

In preparation for my own move to London, whither my All Souls research called me immediately, whatever prospects politics might offer, I gave up my teaching for Merton and took a temporary lectureship at the London School of Economics. This was something new, little as I liked the place. I had only to lecture to evening classes on a part-time basis; that left all my week-days free for historical research at the Public Record Office, the British Museum and the Institute of Historical Research.

The transition was sponsored by kind Lance Beales at the LSE; he was good enough to allow me to share his room there during those evening hours. Richard Pares helped to induct me into London life, where I had never lived and where I always felt rather alien: a countryman by birth and upbringing, I never took to it. Another difference from the Left Intellectuals: they lived a gregarious life, in and out of each other's parties, committee rooms, and beds. Richard and I kept to ourselves, each of us having a room in seedy No. 1 Brunswick Square, later demolished by a direct hit from the Germans. The neighbourhood was down-at-heel, though Brunswick and Mecklenburg Squares (where Tawney lived, with Eileen Power across the way) were still intact. They bordered the grounds of the Foundling Hospital, the fine eighteenth-century building unforgivably demolished shortly before by the Governors; including the Hall and Chapel together with the organ upon which Handel had performed.

Richard and I worked far too hard: he set a gruelling pace, and I was determined to keep up. We left our dingy quarters after breakfast and walked to Chancery Lane, where we incarcerated ourselves in the Record Office all day till 5 pm, with hardly a break at lunch time for a snack or a bar of chocolate. This was very bad for a duodenal ulcer, little did I know. At five we rushed up along the pavements to tea at the Institute, where we worked till 8 pm or so, when we went out and, exhausted, had a large meal. This was worse. Day after day, month after month, for five or six years; for me, intermissions were filled with the amenities of politics. Two or three evenings a week I toddled along to the LSE to an argumentative tea in the upstairs Senior Common Room, with the bombinating voices of the economists dogmatising Free Enterprise disagreeably to my ears, or the loud staccato of friendly Harold Laski, the deep insinuating tones of Mrs Mair, who ruled Sir William Beveridge, the dry cackle-and-snuffle of 'Sir Willem' himself, as she called him.

It was all very unlike All Souls. For one thing, there were the women; for another, the place reeked with malice. Everybody detested Mrs Mair, the power behind the throne. I did not. She was snobbish about All Souls, and good to me; and I thought her a humanising influence in that hideous building full of corridors of cement and lavatory tiles. She had contrived a large Common Room at the top of the building and furnished it well – for which they should have been grateful. I was – and the teas were excellent. However, she too had her animosities. An unforgivable one was for Eileen Power, whom everybody loved. Rather beautiful, with an appealing charm, chic, and a scholar, a distinguished woman, she was beyond competition. She had an Achilles' heel, however, in a disreputable old lag of a parent – and Mrs Mair told me the story few knew.

Mrs Mair was herself a handsome woman, dark, square face and low brow, rather like my dominating old grandmother. Mrs Mair was very dominating, with a will of iron: she always got her way, which made all the other women detest her. She was a man's woman, with an attractive, deliberately cultivated, Scotch accent. Feminine enough: I once got an invitation to dinner in the form, 'I've got such a duck of a wee hat' – the notes had got mixed up. When one went to her house to dinner, Mr Mair presided at his end of the table, rather silent in her presence – they were barely on speaking terms. After the ladies had left, he cheered up and chatted; on the way up to the drawing-room he disappeared into his sanctum. Upstairs 'Sir Willem' had arrived and took over. At the end of the evening she made him a deep curtsy, and we broke up.

After Mair's death they married. Everybody thought they were on marital terms before. With my head full of Elizabeth I, I did not. In later years at Oxford, when I knew them well, he was obviously besotted with her, the old goose. They were remote Scotch cousins. One day she told me that her own egoism had killed the life in Mair (he had accomplished little with his life). Few who knew this dominating woman would have suspected that she had the candid self-awareness to admit that. But she had candour. I remember the pure Doric vowels with which she said to me, 'Oh Leslie, I do so want to be a pee-eress!' It wasn't long before she was one.

Anyway I much preferred her to Beveridge, whom I did not like (another inflexion in common with Bevin: she told me that it was Bevin in power after 1945 who kept Beveridge out). He was a man of asbestos; she was the only human thing about him. Full of repressed activity running over into physical jerks and tics, restless and astringent with his look of a stringy old gander, and that staccato cackle, he hadn't time to talk to anyone. In all the years I knew him I never had a conversation with him. Of course he was a very able man, whose pre-war work in setting up Unemployment Exchanges made history; and I was duly impressed by his big book on Unemployment. The Beveridge Plan after the war, swaddling people in insurance from the cradle to the grave, did not elicit my enthusiasm: too easy to give away money, especially other people's. For so inhuman a man, he was extremely vain; his head was quite turned by the vast *réclame* that came to him as the nation's old Sugar Daddy. Bevin wasn't having any; good for Bevin.

There were nicer people on the staff – Beveridge's brother-in-law for one: R. H. Tawney, 'Harry Tawney' to Mrs Mair. Tawney's wife was Beveridge's sister; she lived much in retirement as an 'invalid'. Her invalidism was notional: she was an eccentric, no good whatever as wife or housekeeper to poor Tawney. Their half-house in Mecklenburg Square was kept in indescribable dirt and confusion. I penetrated only once into Tawney's downstairs study: not only piles of books and papers, nowhere to sit down, but littered with odds and ends, parcels, pipes, tobacco, bits of stale food, dirty cups and plates, kettle, teapot – it was evident that Tawney had to look after himself.

Next summer I was bidden down to the Tawneys' 'Rose Cottage', near Stroud, to be met by Tawney, immensely dilapidated and untidy – he had a way of stuffing his awful pipe, lighted or not, into his pockets, out at elbows, large battered straw hat. 'Doesn't he look like a duke,' said Mrs Tawney proudly. I had no acquaintance with dukes to make a comparison, but this working-class aesthete was put off by middle-class dirt and sluttishness.

I felt that Tawney didn't much approve of me: I was not his type, nor was I a disciple. I think that, with his inverted snobbery and his Balliol high-mindedness, he disapproved of All Souls and what it stood for. He would think it worldly – which it was – and I was not gone on ethics, as he was. Throughout the Labour Movement, the WEA and the LSE, there was a cult of his nobility – one could almost see the halo round his head steaming with righteousness when he was speaking. Though I did not subscribe to the cult – which cannot have been good for him – I respected him and appreciated his work. But it was riddled from top to bottom by his populist bias: the people were always right, government always wrong. I did not share this illusion; I did not even respect it, for it was not true. Government always has the harder job. Any fool can criticise, but can the critic do the job, run the institution, operate the machine, or even keep the house clean and tidy?

Tawney must have sensed this latent criticism, and after all I had a moral advantage over him in belonging to the working-class. He was never the least bit encouraging to my work (unlike Eliot, Trevelyan, Neale); come to that, he didn't warmly commend anybody else's work, though he encouraged research. He did once express approval of *Tudor Cornwall* – '*that* was a good book'; I inferred as against *A Cornish Childhood*, which was a more original one, nearer the coal-face. This is not the place to discuss his own work, almost wholly distorted by his *parti-pris*, original and suggestive as it was. My point can be objectively established, apart from my own *parti-pris*, by considering his last and best book, *Business and*

Politics in the Reign of James I. Naturally, this was much less influential than his biased books, *Religion and the Rise of Capitalism, Equality*, etc. He undertook his last research book with a prejudice against the eminent capitalist, Lord Treasurer, Lionel Cranfield. But he found that Cranfield had operated much more in the nation's interest than the lesser fry around him and, as an honest man, Tawney admitted it. Similarly, he would never re-publish his *Agrarian Revolution in the 16th Century*, because he knew it was inadequate (any more than I would re-publish *Politics and the Younger Generation*). In short, Tawney was a good and noble man; but one didn't want to be assured of that every time his name was mentioned.

Harold Laski, whom I saw much more of, was not in the same class, but he was more fun. And he had good qualities: he had courage, was more warm-hearted than Tawney, and livelier. Indeed he was as lively as a buzzing bee: the noise he made was worse than his sting. Again, he was more generous than Tawney, with a happier background. He was widely, and rapidly, read; superficial and something of a sciolist, he was not in the same class as Cole, with whom there was a certain rivalry. Laski was the more popular speaker and better journalist. Again this is not the place to go into his work: I never valued it much, it is now wholly superseded and forgotten, as it deserved to be – written too in ghastly jargon, full of the current clichés, 'magistral', 'seminal', 'in the last analysis', etc. I watched these tumbling out, rather horrified; the man himself I liked: he was friendly and helpful and kind.

Later, after the war, he attacked me as 'an apostate' from my class. Well, wasn't he an apostate from his own well-to-do Manchester-Jewish middle-class? By then, I was more than an apostate: I was *through* with it all, we had had such a narrow escape from destruction. I have never looked upon the shadow-boxing of party-politics with any favour again, under the appalling cloud of dangers today, nuclear and racist; Communism, Soviet Russian expansion, nuclear submarines in all waters; Africa, blacks, Moslems on the move; Uganda, South Africa; at home, Northern Ireland, murder and devastation. The trifling concerns of petty party-politics move me no more.

Before the war, in the thirties, there was urgent need to take a political line, before it was too late. Britain still enjoyed a certain primacy, even leadership, in Europe and was in a position to influence the course of affairs. That was when we should have done so, exerted every nerve; under those Old Men of the Sea every opportunity was lost. Now, this country is no longer in a position to influence affairs: they depend upon Washington and Moscow. As I have said, 'the past of this country is vastly more interesting than its future is likely to be.' The historian has prevailed over the would-be politician.

However, that was not the situation in the thirties, and politics were, as 1931 advanced, impinging ever more closely: in my personal contacts, in Oxford, at home, and now in London. I made brief acquaintance with Robert Marjolin, who was to have a soaring career in France, launching the European Community, etc. In my Engagements book appears his neat boyish signature and invitation to Paris. He was to attach himself to the star of General de Gaulle, becoming his Minister of Supply in the USA, and later put in charge of France's exterior economic relations. An economist by profession, he was a practical one, no idealogue. I note that he wasted no time in Spain, any more than I did, unlike so many contemporaries – Malraux, Orwell, Auden – who acquired much publicity by their useless cavorting around and behind those 'fronts'.

That autumn Middleton Murry came to visit me along with his financial (and intellectual) backer, Sir Richard Rees. I have already mentioned my attempt on Murry's easy virtue: I wanted to recruit him to the Labour Party, but after dithering for a bit he plumped for the ILP, so like an ass of an intellectual. I find a long letter from him, in his minute hand, full of the intellectualising on which we wasted so much time. 'The vital paradox of Marxism is that, though it is a doctrine of interest, it is an appeal to disinterestedness. The acid test of your true Marxist is his disinterestedness, that finds its supreme satisfaction in identifying itself without reserve with the interests of others. That disinterestedness is breathed out of your letter', etc. Highmindedness did not speak to or for me; all that I asked for was that the working-class should have the sense to see where and what their interest was. (Now they pursue it all too selfishly and short-sightedly, wrecking their own show.)

The practical point of the letter was that their periodical *The Adelphi* was changing course. It had been started to carry off Katherine Mansfield's unpublished work; a new phase was indicated and the main intellectual movement of the thirties was with the Left. 'For a month or two we shall be hampered by the necessity of unloading various mss accumulated before the definite change had been decided on; but by March next we ought to be in full swing. And you would be giving invaluable help by suggesting really relevant books for review, and getting into relation with any potential contributors.' *The Adelphi* had already published two or three prose-poems of mine (I fancied a short volume of them); but, when Murry declared for the ILP, that finished him for me: not a serious political outlook. I did not take up his invitation to cooperate; I was already actively cooperating with Eliot and *The Criterion*. Anything Murry touched was too acutely personal and got mixed up with his soul-searchings. Not my line.

All Souls continued to produce more rewarding contacts: André Siegfried, for instance, with whom I became friendly. He was Curtis' recruit as an Associate Member; of a rich industrialist-political family in Normandy, he was very Northern French: bright china-blue eyes, sharp features, harsh, rasping voice. His father had been a Senator in the Third Republic; the son was mesmerised by politics, but academically, as observer and analyst. He had made a reputation as an authority on the Anglo-Saxon world, the British Empire and the United States, with various books: he was really a publicist. Oddly enough, he had an inflexible mind for so fluctuating a subject: he had not the historian Halévy's understanding of the English mind, still less the novelist Maurois' tactile sense. I was amused by Siegfried's confession of being utterly incapable of understanding how a Socialist leader like Lansbury could be an Anglo-Catholic. To his *raide* mind – his whole personality was rather *raide* – the two were incompatible, in France inconceivable. Not very good for an authority on the English. On my side, I confessed to a nostalgic regret for the monarchy in France: I said that something had gone out of French life with the end of the historic monarchy in 1792 and that France had suffered from the fracture ever since. Then, he concluded sharply, you do not like the Third Republic. Of course, I didn't: who could? I saw completely eye to eye with de Gaulle on that, as on other things.

In October came the day of reckoning, the beastly General Election – and, to add to the strain, I was examining for the Fellowship Election at All Souls and had to rush up and down by train to Cornwall. On one occasion, I was in such a hurry that I found I had not enough money to buy a ticket, and had to raise a quid from a fellow All Souls man, Simon. (Or was that in the 1935 Election? More likely.) In College no-one loved poor Simon (I didn't dislike him); Douglas Cole professed a perfect detestation. Once those two met on the railway station at Oxford. Simon, intending to be kind, insisted on joining Cole in his compartment and, with his usual lack of tact, assumed that it would be Third Class. When the ticket-collector came round, they both showed up First Class tickets. I do not know that this story of Cole's wholly redounds to his credit.

To brace myself for the fray I find another set of Political Maxims in the Book of Life. During my undergraduate years I was an exceedingly nervous speaker – all the more vexing because I felt that, once I had conquered my nerves, I should make a good speaker, as I was already a lecturer. Public speaking and lecturing, however, are two distinct activities, with different techniques. Not until the General Election of 1929, when I had been thrown into the water and had to swim – speaking on soap-boxes around my home constituency – did I learn how to speak, as opposed to lecturing. Now I was steeling myself with such resolutions as the following:

It is a mistake to evacuate a position when challenged, without putting up some resistance: it makes your opponents think you are weaker than you are. If concessions must be made, make them one by one, and as slowly as possible: this will weary the attackers, and at the end you may find that you have preserved the essential position. When on the defensive, it is better to advance, so that in retreat you still retain the essential position. When in difficulties, do not force a decision: it could only be unfavourable, your opponents would gain something without even having to struggle for it. If you prolong the decision, chance may bring you a stroke of good luck, when your position could hardly be worse anyway. On the offensive, keep the agitation going, do not relax or give way: each relapse discourages your supporters. Though necessary to give an impression of confidence, for yourself never let this emotional pressure confuse your mind as to what is really possible. [As against the hopeless emotionalism of the Miners' leaders, Bob Smillie and A. J. Cook. The Miners had had an able, cool head in Frank Hodges: the fools lost him – like the dotty socialists in Spain preferring a rhetorical Caballero to a sensible Prieto, who knew exactly what was necessary and possible. Hodges became a successful business man; serves the Miners right for their folly.] Above all, keep a clear line of retreat open. [That, Bob Smillie and A. J. Cook never did: they lost the Miners everything.] Never lead your forces to attack an objective where there is no alternative to fall back upon. [How much one is struck by Stalin's habit of keeping options open, until the decision was forced upon him.] Never antagonise a supporter: always attack your opponents!

This counsel of perfection was different from Stalin's, who devoted a lot of energy to killing his comrades and supporters. Whether stiffening myself in this naïf way did any good or not, in October the Election was upon us, in the worst of all possible circumstances. Our most experienced and revered leaders had not only deserted us but were leading our opponents; what a heyday these last had before them, what hay they were to make while the sun shone! MacDonald flourished a 100,000 Mark note that was worthless – this was what would happen to the pound if we went off the Gold Standard. Snowden said that, if we went off the Gold Standard, there would be 10 million unemployed; evidently he had no idea of economics, let alone understood Keynes: going off the Gold Standard would mean cheapening exports and increasing employment. With them went the most popular of Trade Unionists, Jimmy Thomas: popular also with George v, who found his company no intellectual strain. ('Your Majesty, I've got an 'orrible 'eadache.' 'Take a couple of aspirates, Mr Thomas.' Improbable, for George v would hardly know what an aspirate was.)

They were followed by a small group of rag-tag-and-bobtail who constituted the 'National' Labour Party. Harold Nicolson clambered on to the National Labour bandwagon, with his usual ungainliness; afterwards, wobbling after Oswald Mosley with no idea where he was going. Then, with the Labour victory of 1945, he scrambled on to the bandwagon again, explaining that this was a conversion heart and soul, but at Sissinghurst fell into his moat, a very unsocialist thing to do. A more distasteful figure was Clifford Allen, who had won an aureole for his sufferings as a pacifist. Enjoying invalidism, a fund was raised for his support, which he invested to such good purpose that he was henceforth not a member of the Independent Labour Party but, better, independent financially. This holier-than-thou type was created a Labour peer. At Oxford, my neighbour at Queen's, Godfrey Elton, who had married a rich wife, had been the tutor of Ramsay Mac-Donald's son, Malcolm (pronounced by Ramsay 'Mawlcom'). Elton threw in his lot with the MacDonalds and received his reward, elevation to the peerage. Namier, contrasting this with his eighteenth century: 'In my time peers made their tutors under-secretaries; today under-secretaries [Malcolm was an under-secretary] make their tutors peers.' The peerage has declined in value with inflation, like everything else.

Oddly enough, I have little recollection of that first hectic Election. I tend to forget what I dislike. It began with an imbroglio between my opponents. Penryn and Falmouth had been a Liberal seat; since the Liberals had ganged up with the Tories to do Labour in – as they nearly did, in Parliament anyway – the arrangement arrived at in London was to send down E. D. Simon – a rich Manchester Liberal, as a carpet-bagger – to be the 'National' candidate. The local Tories would not give way for him: they had been 'nursing' the constituency with a local candidate of a leading St Austell family, my home-town. So there were two 'National' candidates. Later, E. D. Simon imputed to me the end of his political career, but it was not for me to stand down: I was the candidate of the Labour Opposition. Simon was not my type: I preferred a straight Tory any day. When France fell in 1940 and invasion was thought imminent, this eminent Liberal proposed to Arthur Salter, then in charge of shipping, that a ship might be made available for a joint getaway to America. But this was only a momentary aberration, a moment of panic – as with my friend André Maurois in New York.

What got under my skin were the rumours that flew round: the poor fools could not concentrate on the issue, their attention was taken by everything infantile and irrelevant. The 1931 Election was a turning point for me: it opened my eyes to the fallibility of human nature; it completed my education; I have never recovered from the revelation. It is true that the leaders on both sides had no idea what the Gold Standard meant – though this was supposed to be the issue – but they knew well enough how to panic the electorate, as they had done with the Red Letter in 1924, and were to defraud them again with the Election of 1935. Amery, a Tory Cabinet Minister, admitted as much to me.

Douglas Jay told me of an old lady's indignation – 'See what they've done! They've been and taken away the Gold Standard!' She saw it as something waving, probably over Buckingham Palace. Dick Crossman said that in Birmingham a fellow told him that, as he was a Trade Unionist, he had to vote Unionist. In hole-and-cornery Cornwall minds were even smaller. What they were interested in was whether I was an atheist or no; what was what about my family background; whether I ate my meals with my family (I mostly did not: I preferred a book for company). They said that my education had been paid for by my opponents; the meanness of that, after I had worked my guts out to win all those scholarships to Oxford! I never forgave them for it; but I learned the hard way what people are in the mass. Individuals may, or may not, be all right: the mass is always crapulous. This is what Swift thought, and Shakespeare for that matter: no one has ever known human nature better. (What price democracy? Lenin and Stalin and Hitler all regarded the masses who worshipped them with contempt, and such too are the obvious Communist assumptions.)

This corroboration was not a good recipe for going through an election, with duodenal ulcer. I do remember one comic episode, out in the clay area, at St Stephens, where I had once lifted up my voice in church as a solo-boy. For the Labour candidate the Rector's sister laid a trap. She hid herself behind a barrier of biscuit-tins and, when my meeting was going swimmingly, asked, with detonating effect, 'Mr Rowse, do you believe in God?' I regret to say that, for once, I compromised my convictions and subscribed to the Larger Hope. The Book of Life reminds me of 'a moment's wait at lunch-time in the office of Prideaux, the solicitor at Truro, consulting him about the reward of £10 offered for information spreading the rumour that I am an atheist. At first I thought I had no chance whatever of getting in.'

But they were taking no chances with me. As I have said, my book had now come out at the worst possible time for its circulation, the best possible for use as a handle against me. From my youth upwards I always held the conviction that circumstances would always be against me: nothing would ever be given me or come my way; anything I won would have to be won by the sweat of my brow and working my guts out. And so it has turned out. It does not make me in love with my fellow men; but then, a nice nature when I was young, I do not regard them as my fellows. Day after day the juiciest extracts from my book were headlined in the Plymouth paper, *The Western Morning News*. I did not know what I could do about it. Innocently, I got on the phone and warned them about offending against my copyright; a voice came back, 'Oh, I think the Editor has taken care of that.'

They had a heyday, they had a fine old time. Things were not so well for them eight years later when the chickens came home to roost in 1939; or when Plymouth lay in ruins around them. I have never forgotten or forgiven them.

Hardly a note of all this nonsense – I really should have left them to their nonsense – appears in the Book of Life. Just, 'I came down despondent and rather annoyed at work in London being interrupted, but with occasional gleams that I might get in. Since the actual contest I don't believe it possible. Friends in higher places, like F. R. Pascoe, have never thought from the beginning that there was a chance, and they must know.' F.R. indeed raised a slight coolness in my heart for dear Q., by telling me that Q. did not approve of my putting up for my home constituency. After all, I reflected, my opponents were friends of his. But he had had a similar nasty experience when he was active politically as a Liberal in the elections of 1902 and 1906; however, he was on the winning side, and had his reward.

A note registers my surprise at 'the woman in the granite village at Election time, who took me in to *see* her old husband dying.' Here was a blessed intermission:

sitting in the dark in the upper room at Clark's Restaurant at Truro, where I used to come to tea occasionally as a schoolboy. To think of them I used to come with: Steer, lithe and tall, a staunch back, a left-footer; and the two Clarks, Reg and John; John my particular friend, already dead, who used to walk about with me on the field while the match was on – hawthorn hedges and November nip in the air up in that exposed field behind the College. Then tea here afterwards, everybody warm and excited, steaming cups, and all the laughter and chatter ... Now alone: I have the room to myself, empty and deserted, all bare. I have slunk in for a moment's peace from all the fuss and fume of politics. Feeling better than yesterday: the backwash about my 'atheism' has hit me and has been wearing me down. Just here from a meeting in Victoria Square where even Joe [a Trade Union agent] noticed that I was done up, and sent me away. I came here for the sake of old memories, to the friendly room just across from the Cathedral. I am here, and there is nobody else.

In the event, the rumours that so seared me had little effect, and I did rather well. At a time when Labour majorities were turned upside down and the Party emerged with 55 seats, we lost only 1000 votes in Penryn and Falmouth. In the high water mark of the 1929 Election Labour had 11,000 votes; I had kept it steady at 10,000 – here was the rock bottom to build on. The Tory got in with 16,000 – only to lose his seat and his political career, such as it was, in 1945. The Liberal got 14,000. The problem in Penryn and Falmouth was to get the Liberal to the bottom, as I duly did in the Election of 1935, in spite of the confusion of the issue, and Baldwin's disingenuous assurance of support for Collective Security and the League. In fact, our Labour people considered that I had done so well in 1935, when I was second, with 13,000 votes, that I must go on. *That* was the mistake.

Justice compels me to admit that, altogether, Cornish folk did not do so badly. They did not panic, as the rest of the country did. One of the most eminent men in Britain, Gilbert Murray, wrote the morning after the Election: 'I, in common with millions of my countrymen, voted for the National Government – and regard the result with the deepest dismay.' If that is what a noble and great man did, simpletons may perhaps be excused.

At the declaration of the poll the candidates appeared on the balcony above the mob in front of the City Hall. Truro was a

Tory town, with few Labour voters; but I got a warm reception – sportsmanship, good will to the defeated, etc. (I don't like being defeated, and I am not a sporting type.) When Oswald Mosley came out on the plank after *his* defeat, he turned and said, with justified contempt: 'These are the people who have prevented anything from being *done* in this country.' This was just as I thought.

My dear friend Claude Berry wrote to me words of encouragement: 'When you came out smiling, as if you had scored a victory...' He was there in the crowd.

It was easy enough to smile. Little did anybody there know what was in my heart.

Epilogue

Readers, observers of this pilgrimage, may wonder at how things turned out with me – we know how they turned out with Mosley – and where I stand today. If they have followed this book, especially its undertones, they ought to find no difficulty – though people have always complained that they find it difficult to understand me. In fact, I think there is a singular consistency, and I am essentially unchanged from the boy of *A Cornish Childhood*. But they may wonder at the stages by which I have arrived at where I stand today. If I live to write a successor to this volume – I have never intended to go beyond 1940 with the story, for all the material I have accumulated – it may become clearer.

The progressive disillusionment with the thirties that brought on the catastrophe, and very nearly the end of this country, is already clear enough. And I have suggested that the escape was so close that party-politics ceased to have any point for me. In 1940 the best men of all parties came together to save the country from the consequences that the spineless Old Men had brought down upon it. The outstanding figures of that rescue operation were Churchill and Bevin, both men who had my whole-hearted admiration (as had De Gaulle, who saved France).

So there is nothing odd about my stance, or eccentric about my course: I was in agreement with them, and I detest minority-mindedness; the state of mind typified by a Bertrand Russell, for example.

I have already emphasised that the dangers of the post-war world, a nuclear and racist world, are hardly less than those of pre-war Europe. Then, the upper classes endangered their country by pursuing their class-interests against the interests of the country. Today, when the working classes have won their proper place in the country's well-being, they are now wrecking what is their own show, nobody else's, regardless of the country's well-being or of its long-term interests.

Perhaps only a historian can see the process as it is happening under his eyes – as I certainly saw and understood what was happening in the thirties.

I confine myself to that, and at that only the threshold of it, in this volume. But it has a moral for people to reflect upon, put by a philosophic intellect of the eighteenth century: 'Things and actions are what they are and the consequences of them will be what they will be: why then should we desire to be deceived?'

This is the historian's gospel: above all, no illusions; a very little of liberal high-mindedness and of the twilit world of ethics will be enough; far better, realism – no illusions – and for the rest, poetry.

Index